AMPHIBIOUS OPERATIONS

The Projection of Sea Power Ashore

BRASSEY'S SEA POWER: Naval Vessels,
Weapons Systems and Technology Series:
Volume 4

Brassey's Sea Power:
Naval Vessels, Weapons Systems and Technology Series

General Editor: PROFESSOR G. TILL, Royal Naval College, Greenwich and
Department of War Studies, King's College, London

This series, consisting of twelve volumes, aims to explore the impact of modern technology on the size, shape and role of contemporary navies. Using case studies from around the world it explains the principles of naval operations and the functions of naval vessels, aircraft and weapons systems. Each volume is written by an acknowledged expert in a clear, easy-to-understand style and is well illustrated with photographs and diagrams. The series will be invaluable for naval officers under training and also will be of great interest to young professionals and naval enthusiasts.

Volume 1 — Modern Sea Power: An Introduction
  DR GEOFFREY TILL

Volume 2 — Ships, Submarines and the Sea
  DR P. J. GATES AND N. M. LYNN

Volume 3 — Surface Warships: An Introduction to Design Principles
  DR P. J. GATES

Volume 4 — Amphibious Operations: The Projection of Sea Power Ashore
  COLONEL M. H. H. EVANS

Volume 5 — Naval Electronic Warfare
  DR D. G. KIELY

Volume 6 — Naval Surface Weapons
  DR D. G. KIELY

Volume 8 — Naval Command and Control
  CAPTAIN W. T. T. PAKENHAM, RN

Volume 9 — Merchant Shipping
  ALAN PEARSALL

Volume 10 — Technology and the Law of the Sea
  MARTIN KAY

Other series published by Brassey's

Brassey's Land Warfare: Battlefield Weapons Systems and Technology Series, 12 Volume Set
General Editor: COLONEL R. G. LEE, OBE

Brassey's Air Power: Aircraft, Weapons Systems and Technology Series, 12 Volume Set
General Editor: AIR VICE MARSHAL R. A. MASON, CB, CBE, MA, RAF

For full details of titles in the three series, please contact your local Brassey's/Pergamon Office

FRONTISPIECE LPD HMS *Fearless* (*MOD (Navy). Crown copyright*)

AMPHIBIOUS OPERATIONS

The Projection of Sea Power Ashore

MICHAEL EVANS

Foreword by
Major General J. H. A. Thompson CB, OBE

BRASSEY'S
(a member of the Maxwell Pergamon Publishing Corporation plc)
LONDON · OXFORD · WASHINGTON · NEW YORK · BEIJING
FRANKFURT · SÃO PAULO · SYDNEY · TOKYO · TORONTO

UK (Editorial)	Brassey's (UK) Ltd., 50 Fetter Lane, London EC4A 1AA, England
(Orders, all except North America)	Brassey's (UK) Ltd., Headington Hill Hall, Oxford OX3 0BW, England
USA (Editorial)	Brassey's (US) Inc., 8000 Westpark Drive, Fourth Floor, McLean, Virginia 22102, USA
(Orders, North America)	Brassey's (US) Inc., Front and Brown Streets, Riverside, New Jersey 08075, USA Tel. (toll free): 800 257 5755
PEOPLE'S REPUBLIC OF CHINA	Pergamon Press, Room 4037, Qianmen Hotel, Beijing, People's Republic of China
FEDERAL REPUBLIC OF GERMANY	Pergamon Press GmbH, Hammerweg 6, D-6242 Kronberg, Federal Republic of Germany
BRAZIL	Pergamon Editora Ltda, Rua Eça de Queiros, 346, CEP 04011, Paraiso, São Paulo, Brazil
AUSTRALIA	Brassey's Australia Pty Ltd., PO Box 544, Potts Point, NSW 2011, Australia
JAPAN	Pergamon Press, 5th Floor, Matsuoka Central Building, 1-7-1 Nishishinjuku, Shinjuku-ku, Tokyo 160, Japan
CANADA	Pergamon Press Canada Ltd., Suite No. 271, 253 College Street, Toronto, Ontario, Canada M5T 1R5

Copyright © 1990 Brassey's (UK)

All Rights Reserved. No part of this publication may be reproduced, stored in a retrieval system or transmitted in any form or by any means: electronic, electrostatic, magnetic tape, mechanical, photocopying, recording or otherwise, without permission in writing from the publishers.

First edition 1990

Library of Congress Cataloging in Publication Data
Evans, Michael (Michael H. H.)
Amphibious operations: the projection of sea power ashore/Michael Evans; foreword by J. H. A. Thompson.—1st ed.
p. cm.—(Brassey's sea power; v. 4)
Includes bibliographical references.
1. Amphibious warfare. 2. Sea control. I. Title.
II. Series.
U261.E93   1990
355.4'6—dc20   90—1656

British Library Cataloguing in Publication Data
Evans, Michael
Amphibious operations: the projection of sea power ashore.—(Brassey's sea power: naval vessels, weapons systems and technology series; v. 4).
1. Amphibious operations
I. Title
359.4

ISBN 0–08–034737–1 Hardcover
ISBN 0–08–034736–3 Flexicover

Printed in Great Britain by B.P.C.C. Wheatons Ltd., Exeter

Contents

Acknowledgements   viii
List of Figures, Tables and Maps   ix
List of Plates   xi
List of Abbreviations   xv
Foreword by Major General J. H. A. Thompson, CB, OBE   xix

PART I AMPHIBIOUS WARFARE IN MARITIME STRATEGY

1. **The Assault**   3
    Prologue   3
    Two Definitions   9

2. **Historical Perspectives**   13
    The Amphibious Power of Britain   13
    The British Way in Warfare   15
        The Lessons of Gallipoli   16
    The Development of a Doctrine   22
    The Second World War   24

3. **Towards a Modern Capability**   35
    Global Reach 1945–71   35
    Years of Survival   41
    Modern Amphibious Forces   47

4. **A Maritime Strategy for Modern Amphibious Warfare**   57
    The Forward Maritime Strategy   59
    Amphibious Warfare in the Forward Maritime Strategy   62
        Amphibious Operations in Norway: Second World War   71

5. **Limited Global Operations**   79
    British Perceptions   82
    US Perceptions   82
    Soviet Perceptions   85
    The Uncertain Future   86

PART II THE CONDUCT OF AMPHIBIOUS OPERATIONS

6. Broad Principles and Command — 91
- Main Principles — 91
- Command — 95
    - *Command at Narvik 1940* — 96
- Modern Solutions — 98
- The Staffs — 102

7. Planning — 104
- Initial Planning — 104
- Planning Ship to Shore Movement — 108
- Landing Craft and Helicopter Control — 110
- Soviet Methods — 112
    - *Amphibious Operations in Grenada 1983* — 116

8. Means of Delivery — 119
- Landing Craft — 120
- Amphibians — 124
    - *Walcheren—November 1944* — 126
- Air Cushion Vehicles (ACV) — 128
- Assault Support Helicopters and Tilt Rotors — 130
- Soviet Naval Infantry Airborne Forces — 133

9. Amphibious Ships — 135
- Planning Criteria — 135
- Specialist Ships — 137
- A Force Mix — 143
- Non-Specialist Amphibious Ships — 149

10. The Landing Force and its Fire Support — 153
- Amphibious Infantry — 153
- Layered Defence — 154
- Fire Support-Control and Co-ordination — 159
- Naval Gunfire Support — 159
- Close Air Support — 164
- Attack Helicopters — 166
- Artillery — 167

11. Logistics — 169
- Planning — 170
- The Logistic Support Structure — 173
- Logistic Units and Control — 175

12. The Setting—Maritime Operations — 177
- Defence Against Amphibious Forces — 177
- The Passage — 178

	Air Operations in Norway 1940	180
	Advanced Force Operations	181
	Reconnaissance	181
	The Defence of the AOA	184
	Maritime Operations Close to the Shore	184
13.	**Land the Landing Force**	**189**
	Operational Planning	189
	The Threat	189
	Concepts of Operations	190
	Timings	195
	Orders for the Operation	195
	Command and Control of the Landing	196
	Landing the Headquarters	197
	Termination	198
14.	**Fighting the Land Battle**	**199**
	Maneuver Warfare	199
	Directive Control	204
	Lessons from Dieppe 1942	205
	Conclusion	**206**
	References	**208**
	Bibliography	**213**
	Index	**215**

Acknowledgements

I could not have undertaken this book without the advice and help that I have received from the many officers both here and in the United States who have given me so much of their time. I would like to thank them all, and only regret that they are too many to mention by name.

I owe a particular debt to those who have read and commented upon the drafts, including Lieutenant Colonel Donald Bittner USMCR on historical aspects, Captain Simon Moore RN on strategic and maritime issues, Lieutenant Colonel Robert Tucker RM of the Joint Warfare Staff on planning procedures, Lieutenant Colonel Ewan Southby-Tailyour OBE, RM on amphibious ships, Major Alistair Harvey RA on Naval Gunfire Support, Lieutenant Colonel Gerry Wells-Cole RM on logistics, and Brigadier Andrew Whitehead DSO on command. Overriding all, however, must be the contribution of Major Ian McNeill RM who read the whole book in draft. The trenchant and constructive comments of all these long suffering readers have been invaluable. I must, none the less, take full responsibility for any errors or misconceptions, and give the usual disclaimer that the contents of this book represent a personal view and are in no respect intended as a reflectance of Ministry of Defence policy.

For photographs, I can thank another host, including Douglas Mayhew and Major Neil Johnstone of ATTURM, Bridget Spiers of the Royal Marines Museum, Anthony Watts of *Navy International*, Colonel John Greenwood USMC (Ret.) of the *Marine Corps Gazette* among many others. For permission to publish the official photographs, kindly provided by the Ministry of Defence, I have to thank the Controller of Her Majesty's Stationery Office. The splendid illustrations were mainly the work of Corporal Patrick Bentley who interpreted my rough and inept sketches with remarkable insight.

I am deeply grateful to James Ladd for his initial work on the project, to Major General Julian Thompson for his authoritative Foreword, to Geoffrey Till, who edits the whole series, for his inspiration and guidance, to Eric Grove for keeping me abreast of the pace of change in NATO and to Jenny Shaw and her excellent team at Brassey's for their great help in many ways. Finally, many, many thanks to my wife Sue and my family for their tolerance over the past year.

List of Figures, Tables and Maps

Chapter 1
1.1	Map	Central Pacific Campaign in the Second World War	4
1.2	Map	Assault on Saipan, 14 June 1944	6

Chapter 2
2.1	Map	The Landings at Gallipoli, 1915	17
2.2	Map	The German Landings in Norway, April 1940	18
2.1	Fig.	USMC Battalion Landing, Second World War	29
2.3	Map	Soviet Sea Desant During Second World War	32
2.4	Map	British Assault at Termoli, October 1943	33

Chapter 3
3.1	Map	Assault at Inchon, 15 September 1950	36
3.2	Map	Assault at Suez, 5 and 6 November 1956	38
3.1	Table	Organisation of a Marine Expeditionary Brigade USMC	48
3.2	Table	US Amphibious Shipping	50
3.3	Table	UK/NL Amphibious Force Organisation	51
3.4	Table	Some Allied Amphibious Shipping	53
3.5	Table	Outline Organisation of a Soviet Naval Infantry Brigade	54
3.6	Table	Warsaw Pact Amphibious Shipping	54

Chapter 4
4.1	Map	Soviet Air Control Options over Norway	61
4.2	Map	Soviet Attack Options in North Norway	64
4.3	Map	Narvik Campaign, 1940	71
4.4	Map	Soviet Campaign at Murmánsk, 1944	74

Chapter 5
5.1 and 2	Figs.	Spectrum of Conflict Graphs	83

Chapter 6
6.1	Fig.	Sea and Air Control	93
6.1	Map	Assault at San Carlos, Falkland Islands, 21 May 1982	98

Chapter 7
7.1	Fig.	Outline Organisation of an Amphibious Landing	109

x   List of Figures, Tables and Maps

| 7.2 | Fig. | Main Stages of a Soviet Amphibious Assault | 113 |
| 7.1 | Map | Amphibious Operations in Grenada, 25 October 1983 | 116 |

Chapter 8

8.1	Fig.	Planning for Movement of FH 70 in LCU	119
8.1	Table	Landing Craft Characteristics	120
8.1	Map	Assault on Walcheren, 1 November 1944	127
8.2	Table	ACV Characteristics	128
8.3	Table	Assault Support Helicopter Characteristics	131

Chapter 9

| 9.1 | Table | Amphibious Shipping Characteristics | 138 |

Chapter 10

10.1	Fig.	Layered Defence	154
10.2	Fig.	81-mm Mortar Bomb MERLIN	158
10.3	Fig.	A Soviet View of NATO Control of NGS	160
10.1	Table	USMC Aircraft	166

Chapter 11

| 11.1 | Fig. | Outline of the Logistics System in the UK/NL Amphibious Force | 173 |

Chapter 12

| 12.1 | Fig. | The Complexity of Modern Naval Warfare | 178 |

Chapter 13

| 13.1 | Fig. | The Over the Horizon Concept | 191 |
| 13.2 | Fig. | Opposed Landing by a Soviet Naval Infantry Battalion | 193 |

List of Plates

Frontispiece
    HMS *Fearless*

Chapter 1
1.1	The Battle of the Philippine Sea	5
1.2	Landing craft approach Saipan	7
1.3	Aircraft covering the Saipan landing	8
1.4	US Marines on the beach at Saipan	9
1.5	45 Commando RM on the march in the Falklands	11
1.6	LCAC	12

Chapter 2
2.1	RM landing at Gallipoli	19
2.2	Troopship off Norway, 1940	20
2.3	1932 landing craft trials	21
2.4	Japanese aircraft shot down during Battle of the Philippine Sea	25
2.5	The Maracaibo oiler, forerunner of the LST	27
2.6	The *Panjandrum* on trial	27
2.7	USS *Pennsylvania* at Guam	30
2.8	Landing craft (Infantry)	34

Chapter 3
3.1	LSTs beached at Inchon	37
3.2	HMS *Theseus* at Suez	39
3.3	HMS *Bulwark* operating Wessex helicopters	40
3.4	Volvo BV 202 oversnow vehicles in Norway	43
3.5	USMC F/A 18 *Hornet*	49
3.6	The Italian amphibious ship *San Giorgio*	52
3.7	Soviet Naval Infantry landing	55

Chapter 4
4.1	USS *New Jersey* firing *Tomahawk*	58
4.2	USS *Nimitz*	60
4.3	Norwegian terrain	63
4.4	*Sea King IV*	66
4.5	A British LCU in a Norwegian fjord	67
4.6	HMS *Antelope* sinking at San Carlos	68
4.7	HMS *Fearless* camouflaged	70

4.8	French troops ashore after the Bjerkvik landing, 1940	72
4.9	Soviet landing in 1942	73
4.10	USS *Ticonderoga*	76

Chapter 5
5.1	HMS *Beaver* illuminated on Global 86	80
5.2	A Maritime Prepositioning Ship	81
5.3	A USMC Light Armoured Vehicle (LAV) being loaded on to a *Galaxy* aircraft	81
5.4	The Soviet LPD *Ivan Rogov*	85
5.5	Royal Marines arrive at a landing site in Oman	87

Chapter 6
6.1	A wet landing	92
6.2	USS *Nassau* firing *Sea Sparrow*	94
6.3	SS *Canberra* during the Falkland Islands War	99
6.4	The CVS HMS *Illustrious* in the helicopter carrier role	101
6.5	USS *Mount Whitney*	102

Chapter 7
7.1	AWACS early warning aircraft	105
7.2	The Ro-Ro ferry *Mercandia*	106
7.3	The Amphibious Task Force forms up	107
7.4	40 Commando cross decking before the San Carlos landings	109
7.5	Beach Armoured Recovery Vehicle (BARV) recovering a LCU . . .	
7.6	. . . and a LCVP Mk IV	111
7.7	The Soviet hovercraft *Aist*	114
7.8	US Marines emplaning for Op *Urgent Fury* off Grenada	117

Chapter 8
8.1	Waterproofing the cab of a Rover 90	121
8.2	A vehicle mechanic waterproofing an engine	122
8.3	The proof; a deep wade from LCU	122
8.4	A Rigid Raiding Craft	124
8.5	The USMC Assault Amphibian Vehicle–7A1	125
8.6	LCT(G) firing rockets	126
8.7	A Soviet Wing-in-Ground-Effect (WIG) vehicle	129
8.8	The SAH 2200 hovercraft	130
8.9	The *Osprey* tilt rotor aircraft	132
8.10	Parachutists of the Soviet Naval Infantry	133

Chapter 9
9.1	The RFA *Reliant* fitted with *Arapaho*	136
9.2	Artist's impression of the USS *Wasp* (LHD)	140
9.3	AAV-7A1s being despatched from a LST	142
9.4	Outline design of the Dutch Amphibious Transport Ship	144

9.5	Artist's impression of the British helicopter carrier (ASS)	144
9.6	LSD-42 *Germantown*	145
9.7	LKA-116 *St Louis*	146
9.8	LST unloading	147
9.9	British LSL and RSP	148
9.10	Soviet *Ropucha* class LST	149
9.11	The semi-submersible STUFT *Este Submerger*	151

Chapter 10

10.1	The M1A1 *Abrams* tank	155
10.2	The USMC Light Armoured Vehicle (LAV)	155
10.3	Soviet PT-76 amphibious tanks landing	156
10.4	Engineers laying minefield	156
10.5	TOW2 mounted on USMC *Hummer*	157
10.6	The *Merlin* anti-armour mortar bomb	157
10.7	The *Milan* ATGW	158
10.8	Mk 8 gun on HMS *Glasgow*	161
10.9	The Soviet ship *Sovremennyy*	163
10.10	The *Sprite* RPV	163
10.11	*Harrier* GR-5	165
10.12	*Sea Cobra* firing *Sidewinder*	167

Chapter 11

11.1	BV202s in the vehicle deck of a LPD	171
11.2	A British Army LCL beached	172
11.3	*Fiat Allis* laying trackway	174
11.4	Stores in the Beach Support Area	175
11.5	Helicopter Casevac to HMS *Herald*	176

Chapter 12

12.1	*Sea Harrier* operating from a CVS	179
12.2	A SBS team operating with a submarine	182
12.3	Mountain Leaders	183
12.4	*Sea Wolf* firing	185
12.5	*Rapier* firing during Arctic trials	185
12.6	Periscope view of HMS *Brilliant*	186
12.7	USN *Super Stallion* minesweeping	187

Chapter 13

13.1	The USMC concept of the Advanced AAV	192
13.2	The Soviet *Pomornik* ACV	194
13.3	The headquarters of the UK/NL Landing Force in the Arctic	198

Chapter 14

14.1	105mm Light Guns of the UK/NL Landing Force	200
14.2	*Super Stallion* lifting the 155mm M-198	201

14.3	*Sea Cobra* and CH-46 on deck	202
14.4	The British *Lynx/TOW*	203
14.5	The RNLMC 120-mm mortar	203
14.6	Ski power!	206

List of Abbreviations

AAV	Amphibious Assault Vehicles
ACE	Allied Command Europe
ACV	Air Cushion Vehicle (hovercraft)
AD	Air Defence
ADP	Automatic Data Processing
AFOE	Assault Follow-On Echelon
ANGLICO	Air/Naval Gunfire Liaison Company
AOA	Amphibious Objective Area
AOR	Assault Operations Room (in amphibious ship)
APC	Armoured Personnel Carrier
ARG	Amphibious Readiness Group (USN), i.e. ARG/MEU (qv.)
ASS	Aviation Support Ship (new British LPH)
ASW	Anti-Submarine Warfare
ATF	Amphibious Task Force
ATP	Allied Tactical Publication (NATO)
ATGW	Anti-tank Guided Weapon
ATS	Amphibious Transport Ship (NL)
ATTURM	Amphibious Trials and Training Unit Royal Marines
BALTAP	Baltic Approaches (NATO area)
BARV	Beach Armoured Recovery Vehicle (UK)
BMA	Brigade Maintenance Area (UK) (similar to the USMC Combat Support Service Area)
BMD	Soviet armoured personnel carrier
BR	British, i.e. 1 (BR) Corps
BSA	Beach Support Area
CAS	Close Air Support
CATF	Commander Amphibious Task Force (a Naval Officer)
CCATF	Commander of the Combined Amphibious Force
CHOSC	Commando Helicopter Operations and Support Cell
CINCNORTH	Commander-in-Chief Northern European Command (NATO)
CIWS	Close-in Weapon System (air defence for ships)
CLF	Commander Landing Force (usually a Marine officer)
COHQ	Combined Operations Headquarters (UK: Second World War)

List of Abbreviations

COMAW	Commodore Amphibious Warfare (RN)
COS	Chief of Staff
CR	Central Region of Western Europe
CVBG	Aircraft carrier battle group
CVS	Light aircraft carrier
C3I	Command, Control and Intelligence
DCOS	Deputy Chief of Staff (pre-Second World War, UK sub-committee of Chiefs of Staff Committee)
DD	Duplex Drive (swimming Sherman tanks, 1944)
EW	Electronic Warfare
FEBA	Forward Edge of the Battle Area
FIE	Fly-In Echelon
FMF	Fleet Marine Force (USMC)
FOB	Forward Operating Base
FSCC	Fire Support Coordination Cell
HMS	Her Majesty's Ship
HQ	Headquarters
ISTDC	Inter Service Training and Development Centre (UK: pre-Second World War)
JFC	Joint Force Commander (UK)
LASH	Lighter Aboard Ship (large container/lighter carrier)
LCA	Landing Craft Assault
LCAC	Landing Craft Air Cushion (USN) (a hovercraft)
LCC	Command Ship (USN)
LCL	Landing Craft Logistic (RCT)
LCU	Landing Craft Utility
LCVP	Landing Craft Vehicle and Personnel
LFM	Landing Force Manual (USMC)
LHA, LHD	Multi-purpose assault ship (USN)
LKA	Amphibious cargo ship (USN)
LPD	Landing Platform Dock (assault ship)
LPH	Landing Platform Helicopter (helicopter carrier)
LSD	Landing Ship Dock (support ship)
LSL	Landing Ship Logistic (UK LST type ship)
LSM	Tank landing ship (USSR)
LST	Landing Ship Tank (assault/support ship)
LVT	Landing Vehicle Tracked (now called AAV)
LZ	Landing Zone (for helicopters)

MAB, MAF, MAU	Marine Amphibious Brigade, etc., now called MEB, etc. (USMC)
MAGTF	Marine Air/Ground Task Force (USMC)
MAOT	Mobile Air Operations Team (helicopter controllers)
MCMV	Mine Counter Measures Vessel
MEB	Marine Expeditionary Brigade (USMC)
MEF	Marine Expeditionary Force (USMC)
MEU	Marine Expeditionary Unit (USMC)
MLRS	Multiple Launch Rocket System
MOD	Ministry of Defence (UK)
MPS	Maritime Prepositioning Ship (US)
NATO	North Atlantic Treaty Organisation
NBCD	Nuclear Biological and Chemical Defence
NCO	Non-Commissioned Officer
NGFO	Naval Gunfire Forward Officer
NGS	Naval Gunfire Support
OOA	Out-of- (NATO) Area
OODA	Observation–Orientation–Decision–Action (US concept)
OTH	Over The Horizon (evolving concept for US amphibious operations)
PANGS	Planning Aid for Naval Gunfire Support
RAF	Royal Air Force
RCL	Ramped Craft Lighter
RCT	Royal Corps of Transport
RM	Royal Marines
RN	Royal Navy
RNLMC	Royal Netherlands Marine Corps
RPV	Remotely Piloted Vehicle
RSP	Ramped Support Pontoon
SACC	Supporting Arms Co-ordination Cell
SACEUR	Supreme Allied Commander Europe
SACLANT	Supreme Allied Commander Atlantic
SADA	Search and Destroy Armour
SAS	Special Air Service (UK Army)
SBS	Special Boat Service (RM)
SEAL	Sea Air Land (USN Special Forces)
SLEP	Service Life Extension Programme
SLOCs	Sea Lines of Communications
STUFT	Ship Taken Up From Trade (or merchant ship)
TACC	Tactical Air Control Cell
TOW	Long range ATGW system

UK/NL	United Kingdom/Netherlands, e.g. UK/NL Amphibious Force and UK/NL Landing Force
USMC	United States Marine Corps
USS	United States Ship
WIG	Wing-in-Ground-Effect

Foreword

By Major General J. H. A. Thompson, CB, OBE

Under the letter 'A' in an article headed, 'The Weasel Art of Defence from A to Z', in *The Times* of 16 October 1981, reflecting bitterness in the Ministry of Defence following a Defence Review, appeared the following:

> 'AMPHIBIOUS: an out-of-date concept of operations, requiring no particular expertise, which is temporarily undertaken by the Royal Marines.'

Although written tongue-in-cheek, there was at the time, a substantial body of opinion among politicians, servicemen, officials, and members of the public, who would have agreed with the sentiments expressed above. They were proved wrong in all respects some seven months later. But perhaps one of the biggest howlers in the quote is the implication that amphibious operations are the exclusive preserve of the Royal Marines, or indeed any other marines. Amphibious operations, as Michael Evans has made crystal clear in this excellent book, are an integral part of maritime strategy. As such they demand the wholehearted support and co-operation of sailors and airmen (dark and light blue), the Merchant Navy, and often considerable numbers of soldiers. Amphibious operations are not a ploy invented by marines to ensure their continued existence. They exist because the amphibious art requires a proportion of specialist practitioners, but it is not exclusively a marine preserve.

Michael Evans has three main themes in this book. The first is the value of an amphibious force-in-being, with specialised shipping and a balanced landing force. He has vividly demonstrated the penalties that await those who become involved in amphibious operations, without any of these assets. Sometimes the involvement has been reaction to an opponent's move, as in Norway in 1940, and therefore with minimum warning. On other occasions, as at Gallipoli in 1915, there was time for planning, but insufficient time to build a balanced amphibious force from scratch; let alone arrive at a doctrine.

The word doctrine, with its connotation of tablets of stone, issued by some higher power to a chosen few, can convey the wrong message; rigidity, exclusivity, and mystery. It must be seen as a collection of well understood procedures and guidelines, a bag of 'snap-on tools' carried by all those who would embark on an amphibious operation. These procedures must be frequently practised in peace-time, so that all practitioners and planners, at whatever level, and whatever the colour of their uniforms, understand how best to use them; including the ability to recognise when to depart from one, or more, of the precepts. Or, to continue with the bag of tools analogy, which tools to pick for the job, and making the right selection requires commanders, and specially staffs, who are thoroughly versed in the amphibious art. It would be hard to find a better example of this than the staffs of 3 Commando Brigade and Commodore Amphibious Warfare in the Falklands War. Without their comprehensive expertise, it is doubtful that the knitting together of the plan with such a paucity of assets, and variety of ships, could have been achieved in the time available. Michael Howard's condemnation of amphibious operations, quoted in the book, although made in a different context, is in itself a case, perhaps unconsciously, for an amphibious force-in-being; specialised troops, staffs, ships, equipment, and doctrine.

Michael Evans's second theme, which flows from his first, is the need for sound and flexible command and control to overcome the uncertainties and friction of amphibious warfare. Only by exercising in peacetime, with the right equipment and shipping, will those who have to practise it in war be able to slip quickly and easily into the driving seats of an amphibious operation; seats, plural, because it is a matter of dual control, with all that that implies. Also important, is the chain of command above the amphibious task force commander and the landing force commander. Lessons learnt in the Falklands War have led to a Joint Force Commander being incorporated in United Kingdom plans for Out of Area operations.

Finally, there is the realisation that amphibious operations within the framework of the Forward Maritime Strategy, provide a key, in some circumstances the only key, to unlock stalemate, and return to manœuvre warfare on land. Maritime operations are not an end in themselves. As Michael Evans points out, Admiral Gorshkov saw this very clearly:

> 'Since the goals of war were achieved mostly by taking over the territory of an enemy, successful operations of fleet against shore brought better results than operations of fleet against fleet.'

By including Soviet amphibious operations and concepts, the Author has produced incontrovertible evidence that they regard the projection of power from the sea as an indispensible club in the bag of options that they could deploy. Unlike a former British Secretary of State for Defence, they are certainly not deterred at the prospect of operating in the age of the stand-off missile, nor do they regard keeping a modern force of amphibious ships as sentimentality.

This is a long-awaited book, and fills a gap that has existed for too long in works in this country on maritime strategy and operational art. Perhaps this gap has been the result of the, at times, myopic view of a nation that, in the Grand Fleet, once possessed the largest navy the world had ever seen, but lacked the means to project its power more than a few thousand yards above the high water mark.

JULIAN THOMPSON

Part I

Amphibious Warfare in Maritime Strategy

1
The Assault

PROLOGUE

Amphibious warfare came of age during the Second World War, and a brief description of one of the many landings of the Central Pacific campaign, at Saipan on 15 June 1944, gives a flavour of the amphibious battle.

The war in the Pacific opened on 7 December 1941 with the Japanese attack on Pearl Harbor. Between August 1942 and March 1944 the US Pacific Fleet, with its amphibious forces, had halted the subsequent advance at Guadalcanal, and had itself advanced on the most direct route to Japan through the Central Pacific islands, seizing Tarawa and the Marshall Islands as they went. The next stage was the attack against the Marianas, to break into the inner line of island fortifications constructed by the Japanese, and to secure further advanced air bases for the bombing of their homeland. The first objective was Saipan. For this campaign the Pacific Fleet was divided into three major forces; the Joint Expeditionary Force which included two US Marine Corps (USMC) divisions and one from the US Army, the Fast Carrier Force, and a land based air force. The amphibious forces were split into two groups, the Southern forces destined for Tinian and Guam, and the Northern forces for Saipan.

Sea and air control for the Saipan operation were ensured by three major engagements spread over the vast Pacific region. First, the main Japanese submarine strength was seriously crippled by the escort carriers of the Southern Attack Force in the Solomons in May. Then the Japanese mal-deployed half their naval land based aircraft to New Guinea, where they were destroyed by General MacArthur's airforces.

Finally, four days after the start of the assault on Saipan in June, American submarines and aircraft from the Fast Carrier Force defeated the main Japanese fleet in the Battle of the Philippine Sea—'The Marianas Turkey Shoot'—sinking three carriers and leaving only 35 out of its 430 carrier aircraft operational, a blow from which Japanese naval aviation never recovered.

In mid-May, the landing forces had been embarked in their shipping in the Hawaii area, where they conducted rehearsals of all the phases of the ship-to-shore movement, plus a full-scale simulated landing with naval gunfire support and air bombardment. En route for Saipan, the shipping paused at Eniwetok for the beach assault units to cross deck from transport ships to the tank landing ships carrying the amphibian tractors. By 11 June, the amphibious shipping was beginning to close upon the objective.

4   Amphibious Operations

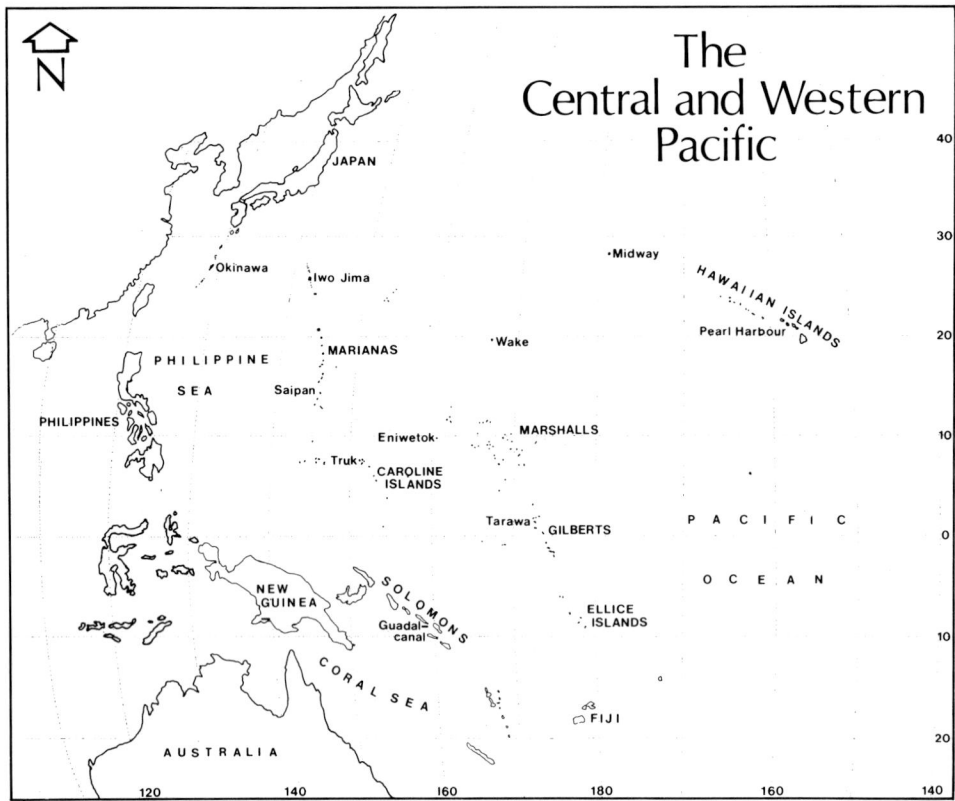

MAP 1.1   The Central Pacific Campaign

Saipan was defended by at least 21,000 Japanese troops and the defences were being rapidly improved, despite being pounded by American land-based aircraft since March. The main Japanese defences were on the Eastern side, so the Americans planned to assault on the Western shore where the beaches straddling Afnetna Point were just wide enough to permit the landing of eight battalion landing teams abreast. The concept of operations was to neutralise the enemy defences with a lengthy and heavy bombardment, and to capitalise upon this by landing the assault troops in amphibian tractors which would thrust inland some 1500 yards.

The intense preliminary bombardment began on 11 June with strikes by carrier based aircraft. Two days later, seven fast battleships gave covering fire while the underwater demolition teams cleared obstacles on the approaches to the beach and minesweepers cleared shipping lanes. On the day before the landing, the old battleships of the Joint Expeditionary Force, plus cruisers and destroyers, combed the island with harassing and counter battery fire. In fine weather, the naval gunfire support began at 0530 hrs on 14 June for the landing by two USMC divisions scheduled at 0830 hrs. Let an American tell the story of the first day of the battle:

'Soon after daylight, the troop laden tank landing ships began to disgorge their

PLATE 1.1 The Battle of the Philippine Sea—'The Marianas Turkey Shoot'—ensured sea and air control for the amphibious landings at Saipan, Tinian and Guam in 1944. A large Japanese carrier of the Shokaku class burns from bombs dropped by US carrier-based aircraft, and is still manœuvring as further near misses land off her bow and stern. (*US Navy*)

amphibian tractors, and the movement towards the line-of-departure began. Unavoidable delays in getting the amphibian tractors into the water necessitated postponing the landing ten minutes, but with this single exception the disembarkation of troops proceeded as planned. As the tractors crossed the line-of-departure, they were preceded by infantry landing craft converted to gunboats whose job was to give the landing beaches a last minute shower of 40-millimetre, 20-millimetre, and $4\frac{1}{2}$-inch rocket fire'.

Artillery and mortar fire from the shore peppered the water as the troops approached the edge of the abutting reef. It was not dense enough to retard the ship-to-shore movement seriously, and the first 8000 men were ashore. The tactical plan, however, broke down early. In most sectors, tractor drivers would not or could not proceed to the beachhead line as ordered, but instead disembarked the troops near the water's edge causing untold confusion and congestion. The Second Marine Division was landed through unavoidable error some 900 yards north of the assigned beaches and hence had to fight in two directions, south as well as east. Contact between the two divisions was consequently lost, creating a dangerous gap which was not to be closed for four days. Resistance was fierce, and casualties were unexpectedly heavy.

Yet, in spite of these obstacles, by the end of the day the marines had established a front of about five miles with an average depth of 1500 yards.

6   Amphibious Operations

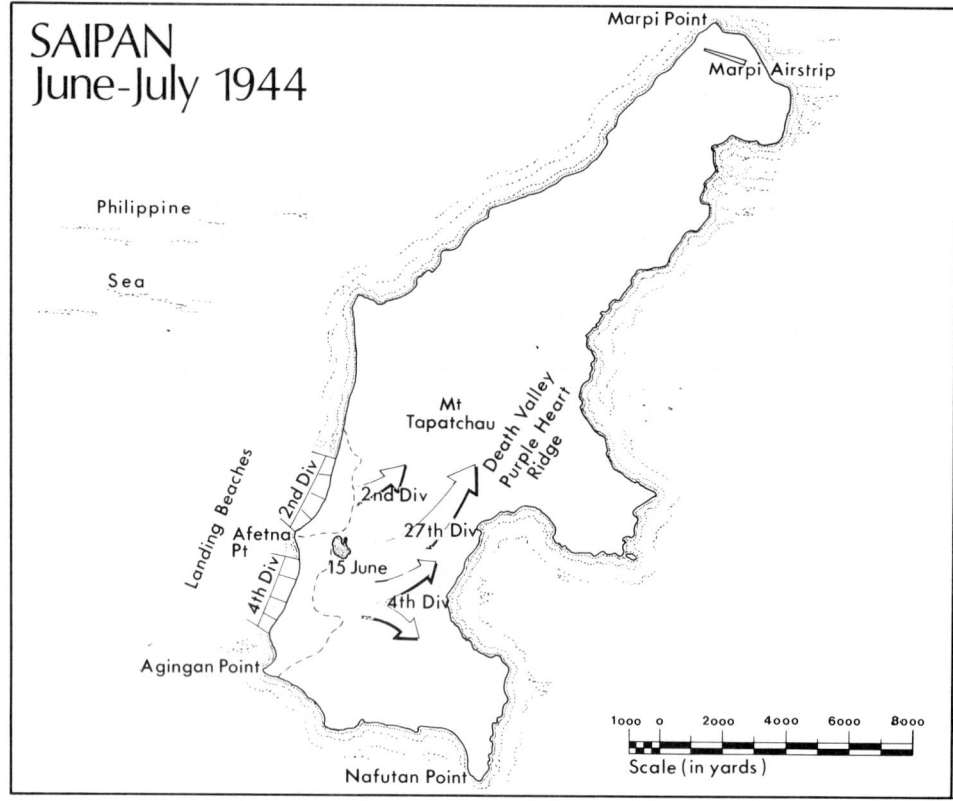

MAP 1.2   The Assault at Saipan, June 1944

Artillery regiments of both divisions had landed a large portion of their weapons and personnel, and the most hazardous phase of the amphibious assault had been successfully executed. But the enemy still held both Agingan Point and Afetna Point, and the danger of infiltration and counterattack was great.

That danger was realised in the early morning hours of June 16 when well organised counterthrusts were carried out at various points in the zones of both divisions. These were repulsed, but only with severe losses to the marines. Not until afternoon of the second day of the operation were the American lines well enough reorganised to allow the launching of an offensive drive toward the line selected for protecting the beachhead.'[1]

Although the standard landing procedures, or doctrine, had generally worked well, it was a most difficult battle and there had been mistakes in two important aspects. Most unusually for the Pacific Campaign, the bombardment had been inadequate for the task in hand and had left many of the Japanese batteries intact, so the defenders were able to inflict some 4000 casualties on the USMC in the initial stages. Compare the mere two days intense preparation at Saipan with the thirteen

PLATE 1.2 Loaded landing craft approach the shore of Saipan on D-Day, with LCMs carrying tanks in the foreground. (*US Navy*)

days against similar defences at Guam, which was taken relatively easily a month later. Secondly, the plan made insufficient allowance for the difficult terrain facing the amphibious tractors inshore from the beach, so they had little real hope of penetrating to the planned disembarkation point. Admittedly, this was the first time that the amphibious tractors had been used in this way, and the lightly armoured amphibians were unable to provide the shock effect and mobility needed for the task in hand.

The USMC commander was forced to modify his plan, ordering 2nd Division to move southward to close the gap at Afetna Point, while 4th Division pressed remorselessly inland, by-passing pockets of resistance until it had reached the East coast and cut the enemy defences in two. The reserve army division was completely ashore by 20 June, by which time the first line of enemy resistance had been defeated and the force could swing northwards against the second line. The fighting continued to be heavy for several days and resistance was not finally overcome until 9 July.

Time and technology have moved on since Saipan, but this battle illustrates many of the central naval, air and ground elements of an amphibious operation. Some might question why Saipan has been chosen rather than, say, the next landing at Tinian. Certainly, Tinian would illustrate the use of deception and how the command decisions on the choice of beaches might be addressed, and the operation there went more smoothly, especially the fire support. Yet the fact that some

8   Amphibious Operations

PLATE 1.3   Aircraft provide cover over landing craft during the Saipan landings. (*US Navy*)

important phases of the plan at Saipan went awry serves to emphasise that factors such as: the difficulties in obtaining adequate intelligence; the enemy's advantage of fighting on known, well prepared, ground; and (although not on this occasion) the weather and the sea, make these operations as hazardous and unpredictable as any. In this case, the Americans displayed that ability to overcome such adversity by the combination of strong command, good staff work, quick thinking, aggressive tactics, determination and hard fighting, all based on a sound plan, which must be the hallmark of any successful amphibious and, indeed, any military operation.

PLATE 1.4 US Marines of the first wave disembarked from their amphibious tractors on the beach at Saipan. (*US Navy*)

TWO DEFINITIONS

This book sets out to describe the part amphibious warfare plays within the overall maritime strategy today, and to explain the tactics, procedures, technology and techniques, with a glance at the possible impact of new technology. It will be essentially a British view but, as we have seen already, it must draw heavily upon American experience and, to a lesser extent, upon that of the Soviets. It is in two parts. Part I covers the development of amphibious warfare during this century, seeking to draw out some of the main influences upon modern concepts, and giving a view of the role of amphibious warfare in maritime strategy. Part II concentrates upon the conduct of operations today.

But first, what do we understand by amphibious warfare? Compare these two definitions—the first British and the second American:

> ▶ An amphibious operation can be described as the delivery of a force of all arms, tactically grouped for combat ashore; landed independently of ports and airfields, and in a hostile or potentially hostile situation.[2]
> ▶ An amphibious operation is an attack launched from the sea by naval and landing forces embarked in ships or craft involving a landing on a hostile shore. It normally requires extensive air participation and is characterised by closely integrated efforts of forces trained, organised, and equipped for different combatant functions.[3]

There is much that is common to both, in that they refer to tactical operations by joint forces and they exclude a range of administrative landings of men and equipment; an amphibious operation is not merely the transport of men and material by sea. As the commander of the V Amphibious Corps at Saipan, Lt. Gen. Holland M (Howlin' Mad) Smith USMC, wrote in 1946:

> 'It was only when the naval phase of our operations—the sea-borne approach and the ship-to-shore or shore-to-shore movements—was visualised, not as a ferry ride, but as a tactical movement, culminating in an assault, that successful landing operations were possible.'[4]

The main difference, however, concerns this focus of an amphibious operation, the assault, which is at once the culmination of the maritime phase and the start of the land campaign. Although most amphibious forces use the term assault to describe the landing, it has degrees of emphasis in its interpretation which are central to an understanding of the conduct of this form of warfare.

The first definition, although very similar to the official NATO version, might be viewed as an essentially British perception, and it envisages *an operation mounted against little or no resistance on the beachhead*, and depends upon the use of good intelligence, imaginative deception measures, and strategic manœuvring to ensure a virtually unopposed landing. This does not imply that the landing force must be unprepared to fight, for it must be able to suppress unexpected resistance in the beachhead, stand ready to meet any immediate enemy counter stroke, and force inland to its objective.

Several of the landings in Europe and many of those by General MacArthur's forces in the Southwest Pacific theatre during the Second World War were of this nature, as was the landing at San Carlos in the Falkland Islands campaign. With comparatively limited technology at their disposal, British commanders have to rely upon cunning rather than brute force to get ashore, as Major General Thompson (then the Brigadier commanding the landing force) concluded:

> 'An assault in the vicinity of Port Stanley would probably run into well prepared defensive positions, wire, mines and beaches covered with gunfire both direct and indirect. The Amphibious and Landing Force Task Groups simply did not possess the firepower and, more important, the armoured amphibious vehicles and close support, direct fire assault guns in ships or amphibians to contemplate such a plan. Any beach selected had therefore to be out of the range of the guns defending Port Stanley, and if possible be far enough away so that any Argentine reaction, even by heliborne forces, would arrive after the beachhead had been built upon sufficiently to hold and beat off such a counter attack.'[5]

The second is an American definition and is chiefly the legacy of their campaign in the Central Pacific in the Second World War, where they mounted operations which, as we have seen, were characterised by the very determined resistance at the water's edge. These demanded *the employment of strong assault forces to fight their way ashore*, and the concepts that were derived from their campaign against the Japanese still dominate US amphibious thinking.

It is not that the Americans rule out the possibility of avoiding the main enemy strength, for General Vandergrift USMC, who commanded the landing force at Guadacanal in 1942, wrote that

> 'A comparison of the several landings leads to the inescapable conclusion that landings should not be attempted in the face of organised resistance if, by any combination of march or manoeuvre, it is possible to land unopposed and undetected at a point within striking distance of the objective.'[6]

The Americans maintain, however, that *a commander should never assume that he will achieve an unopposed landing*, and thus should always plan to meet opposition on the beachhead. Therefore their definition of an amphibious operation is worded more directly, and they equip their forces accordingly with armoured amphibians which spearhead relatively heavy ground forces, backed by integral fixed wing aircraft and helicopters, and still formidable naval gunfire support. In the past the USMC has shown a doctrinal reluctance to plan landings against an undefended shore, but there are now signs of impending change, as the introduction of the

PLATE 1.5 A classic photograph of the Falklands War: 45 Commando RM on the long march, or *yomp*, from San Carlos to Bluff Cove Peak. (*RM Museum. Crown copyright*)

12   Amphibious Operations

PLATE 1.6   The LCAC is the first element in the evolving US concept of over-the-horizon assault, and a total programme of 90 craft is planned. It can carry an M1 *Abrams* tank, has a range of 200 miles and a speed of 40 knots. Here it is seen landing from the dock landing ship USS *Pensacola* (LSD-38). (*US Navy*)

Landing Craft Air Cushion (*LCAC*) and the MV 22 *Osprey* tilt rotor aircraft, together with other technological and conceptual advances, mean that an increasing emphasis is being given to speed and tactical surprise. Thus the US amphibious forces are developing new over-the-horizon techniques for landing and for fighting ashore, encapsulated in the concept of *Maneuver Warfare*, with a greater stress upon the attacking the enemy where he is weak.

No similarly worded Soviet definition is available, but their fundamental concept of the assault would be close to that of the Americans, since they expect to have to fight their way ashore. There are, however, significant differences in the equipment and approach between the two, mainly because the United States give their amphibious forces a strategic as well as a tactical role, whereas the Soviets tend to concentrate upon tactical employment. A most important principle of the Soviet offensive is that forces have to be inserted to the rear of the enemy to disrupt the defence, and this operation is called a *desant*. It could be conducted by helicopters, airborne forces, tanks or, along the coastline, by amphibious forces. These *desants* would be launched relatively close to the forward line of battle in the expectation that the main ground forces would link up soon after the landing.

2
Historical Perspectives

'The chief utility in history for the analysis of present and future lies in its ability, not to point out lessons, but to isolate things that need looking at. . . . History provides insights and questions, not answers.'[1]

Geoffrey Till

The employment of amphibious forces today and the methods they use have their roots in the ideas evolved since Gallipoli and the experiences of a wide range of operations. In this chapter we will look at some central themes from recent history which have had an influence upon the development of modern concepts and perceptions, from early difficulties in applying amphibious warfare to continental campaigns, through the myths surrounding the concept of 'the British Way in Warfare', to the emergence of an amphibious doctrine and its employment in the Second World War.

THE AMPHIBIOUS POWER OF BRITAIN

It has been said that the turning point of the debate, during the 1974 Defence Review, about the retention of an amphibious capability was a chance meeting on Hungerford Bridge between an influential and hitherto sceptical senior civil servant and the Royal Marines Chief-of-Staff. The telling words in the conversation were reported to have been: 'Can you imagine the British nation being unable to land forces on a foreign shore as and when she chooses, without depending upon the use of friendly ports?'

Those words reflect a traditional perception that there is an inherent 'amphibious power of Britain',[2] reminiscent of Francis Bacon's resounding 'He that commands the sea is at great liberty and may take as much or as little of the war as he will'[3] or the declaration, by the writer of *Conjunct Expeditions* in 1759, that 'The fleet and the Army acting in concert seem to be the natural bulwark of these Kingdoms.'[4] Indeed, in those days when the Royal Navy commanded the seas, continental commitments had often been met, not by sending armies across the Channel, but by the judicious financial and material support of alliances, together with the use of economic blockades. Meanwhile, that 'amphibious power' had offered her the opportunity to seize the enemy's worldwide possessions as a bargaining counter in the subsequent peace negotiations. For much of the eighteenth century and for all the nineteenth century, our command of the sea was such that Britain was able to launch imperial expeditions unhindered and untroubled by the need to obey any but the most basic of operational procedures.

Undoubtedly this strategy was appropriate for its time but, at the beginning of this century, the growing prospect of war in Europe presented an increasing dilemma which was recognised by the naval historian Sir Julian Corbett in his book *Some Principles of Maritime Strategy*.[5] Corbett emphasised the importance of harmonising land and sea warfare, with the importance of maritime power being its influence on military operations. Although this influence could be applied outside Europe within the traditional strategy, opportunities to do so effectively might not arise, and he recognised the importance of, and the difficulties inherent in, making naval supremacy tell in a continental war—where the best that might be achieved was a limited intervention in an unlimited war. He drew examples from that period after Trafalgar when a number of abortive expeditions, Copenhagen (1807), Dardanelles (1807) and Walcheren (1809), proved the strategic value of an amphibious capability, which could threaten a wide area of the littoral and commit disproportionately large enemy forces to coastal defence, although these had not achieved significant military objectives.

Before the First World War, limited interventions were considered in the debates about the relative merits of a continental or a maritime strategy; the Admiralty considered operations against Borkum and the Frisian coast and proposed that a British expeditionary force would best be employed in an amphibious operation at some point on the flanks or the rear of the advancing German Army. They suggested first Antwerp and later the Pomeranian coast some 90 miles from Berlin as the objective. The latter had been considered in the previous century when Bismarck is said to have retorted that, if the British were to land their army on the German coast, he would send the local policeman to arrest them! Aware of the dangers of exposing the Channel coast of the Low Countries to German invasion and of the practical difficulties in reaching Pomerania in the teeth of the German High Seas Fleet, the Committee of Imperial Defence discouraged all such adventures. Even so, the Admiralty, with Churchill as First Lord, continued to search for a suitable maritime target, and sent a small force of Royal Marines to Antwerp in 1914. They eventually settled upon Gallipoli.

The means to embark on amphibious operations were sadly lacking; some experts understood the main and eternal principles, but the Army and the Royal Navy lived in watertight compartments, very rarely exercised together, and 'no combined plan of operation for . . . any given contingency had ever been worked out'.[6] Therefore little consideration had been given to the application of technological advances to combined operations against the shore, especially in naval gunnery. Admiral Fisher contemplated the establishment of a flotilla of suitable craft for landings, but few were built. There was no support for a proposal in 1905 that the Royal Marines should form a force in readiness, trained to disembark rapidly on a hostile shore.[7] Amphibious warfare was by no means the only undernourished and ill-considered sphere of operations in 1914, but the resulting débâcle at Gallipoli in 1915 was to have long-lasting repercussions.

THE BRITISH WAY IN WARFARE

The chief reaction to Gallipoli in the inter-war years was a widely held conviction that such amphibious operations were no longer feasible. Technology favoured the defender; the enemy could respond quickly by redeploying troops by train and, increasingly, armoured forces by road. In Britain, the Air Staff opposed the concept as they considered that, with the advent of the aeroplane, open craft could not reach the shore, and in any event power projection was best achieved by bombing. The Admiralty did not demur, since mines and submarines added to the hazards facing amphibious landings, and declared that it was 'contemplating war as an affair on the high seas'.[8] In 1938 the Deputy Chiefs of Staff (DCOS) sub-Committee confirmed these views in the policy statement that 'the provision of material for training in combined operations in peacetime should be based on the assumption that a combined landing on a large scale against opposition was not a likely operation in the early stages of war'.[9]

Surprisingly, however, there was also still a strong and influential body of opinion which maintained that Britain could retain her ancient strategy, and such a course was advocated in Liddell Hart's book, *A British Way in Warfare* in 1932. Convinced that there must be a more effective and less costly method than the major battles of attrition seen on the Western Front during the First World War, he sought to evolve a limited form of warfare and, foreseeing that aircraft and armour would give new mobility on the battlefield, developed his strategy of the indirect approach. This line of reasoning led naturally to his concept of an overall strategy for Britain, which would limit our military commitment in Europe and enable us to revert to the historic practice: the material support of allies, economic blockade and amphibious expeditions.

Liddell Hart's polemic forebore to explain how this—particularly, the amphibious element—might be translated into action. The Government, beset with economic problems, made no better provision when it espoused a form of the British Way in Warfare as the most cost effective option. From 1935 to 1939 it pursued a strategy of 'limited liability' to avoid allocating strong forces to the Continent; it concentrated instead on Home and Imperial Defence, albeit with significant reservations, and adopted that trusted concept of strangling its European enemies by an economic blockade. Although the sheer size and immediacy of the German threat finally led Britain to commit forces to France, one of the first offensive plans designed to implement the blockade was the despatch of a joint expedition to halt the German iron ore trade through Narvik. The Germans struck first against Norway in April 1940 and the British amphibious response was, as one writer has succinctly put it:

> 'unhappy as a campaign could be: unplanned, unprepared, divergent instructions, non-tactical loading, inadequate equipment and intelligence—all the familiar trappings of a real hurrah's nest'.[10]

It was not as though the concept of combined operations had been totally ignored during this period. The Madden Committee in 1924 had proposed that the Royal Marines should form independent forces able to join the fleet on mobilisation and provide the landing force for expeditions, but once again such a concept was not

THE LESSONS OF GALLIPOLI

'. . . in no operation of war are happy-go-lucky methods more certain to result in failure than those of the amphibian type.'[11]

By early 1915 the stalemate on the Western Front had led Churchill to advocate a campaign to force the Dardanelles and capture Constantinople.[12]

The attempt on 18 March 1915, a purely naval operation commanded by Admiral de Robeck against the Turkish forts guarding the Narrows, was abandoned when the fleet sustained heavy losses. The initiative passed to the Army, and there was a delay as the 29th British Division, the Royal Naval Division and the Anzac Corps were assembled as the landing forces under General Hamilton. This gave the Turkish Army, commanded by a German, Marshal Liman von Sanders, time to prepare their defences to such good effect that the assault by some 40,000 troops on 25 April only secured a precarious lodgement ashore. Despite heavy reinforcement, and another landing at Suvla Bay on 6 August, the Allies never broke out of the beachhead and both sides suffered vast casualties in the slogging trench warfare before the Allies withdrew in January 1916.

The subsequent analysis of the failings of this campaign played a significant part in the development of modern amphibious doctrine, and it still merits study. In this instance, however, we will weigh its conduct against governing factors for the success of amphibious operations which might be assumed to have been known in those times; surprise, forethought, co-operation between the commanders, a clear objective, and good planning.

▶ **Surprise.** *Between the naval attempt to force the Narrows in March and the assault in April little was done to disguise the intentions of the forces assembling in the Mediterranean. All the mail to the troops, for example, was addressed to the 'Constantinople Field Force'. Hence, strategic surprise was lost, although on the day of the landings some tactical surprise was gained by making a feint towards Bulair. This lesson was learnt at the time, but planning for the second assault at Suvla Bay on the night was conducted in such secrecy that the subordinate commanders were largely unaware of their commander's intentions, and the operation has been described as 'a shot in the dark'.*[13]

▶ **Forethought.** *The British paid dearly for their lack of preparation for amphibious operations before the war. Insufficient forces were committed to the operation from the start and reinforcements were despatched piecemeal. None were trained for amphibious warfare, there were no landing craft and there were few rehearsals. Before the landings, Hamilton's army was 'scattered around the Mediterranean in spectacular confusion: battalions were split up, wagons were separated from their horses, guns from their ammunition, shells from their fuses,*[14] *and throughout the operation the logistic support continued to be inadequate.*

▶ **Co-operation between the Commanders.** *The system of joint command was sound in principle, and differed little from British concepts used early on during the Second World War, but its execution was faulty. The two commanders were not co-located during the important planning phase. When Hamilton did join de*

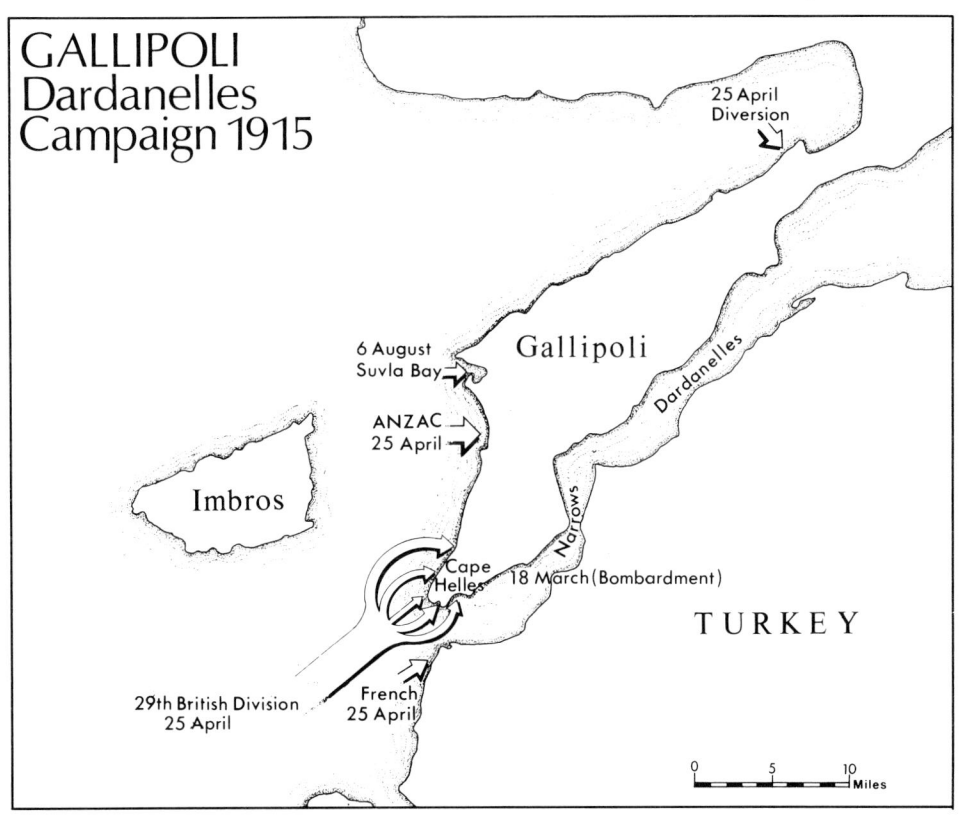

MAP 2.1 The Landings at Gallipoli

Robeck in HMS Queen Elizabeth *for the landings at first light on 25 April, he could not take his staff with him, and poor communications prevented him from exercising effective command. Subsequently, the commanders separated again and communications difficulties caused further disruption.*

▶ *A Clear Objective.* There was no joint aim for the operation. Hamilton believed that the Army was to assault in concert with further naval pressure in the Dardanelles, while de Robeck had decided not to attack until the Army was established ashore. Thus the two commanders had different concepts of operations from an early stage.

▶ *Planning.* Hamilton left London with sparse intelligence about the Turkish army and Gallipoli, although a considerable amount was available. Reconnaissance was poor and information about the beach defences obtained by naval aircraft was not passed to the Army staff. The plan for the first landing was reasonably sound, but inflexible; through poor communications, and misguided reticence, Hamilton missed the opportunity to redeploy unopposed forces from Y Beach to support the hard pressed landings on W and V Beaches during the initial landings.

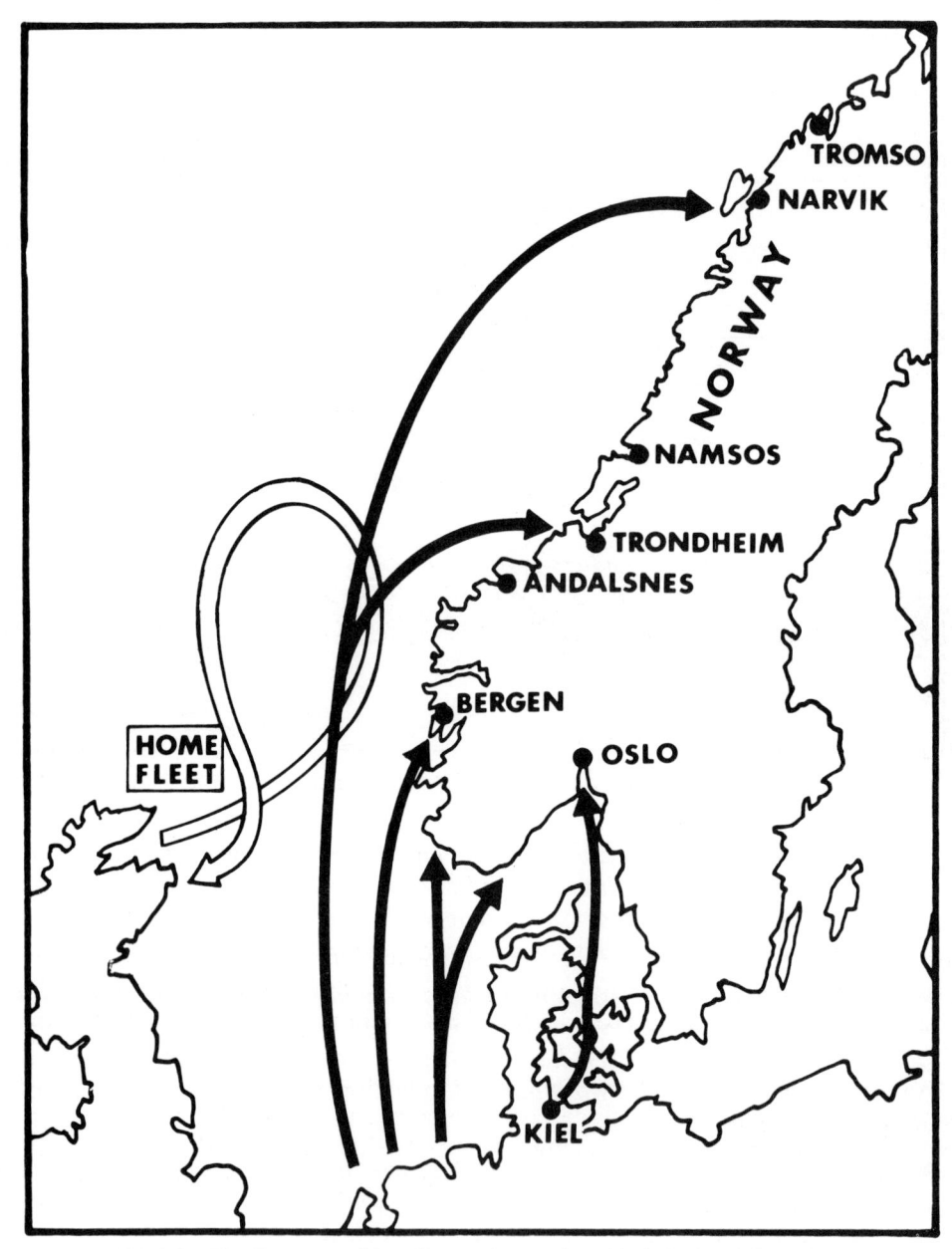

MAP 2.2 The Germans achieved strategic surprise with their six landings along the length of the Norwegian coast in April 1940. The British Home Fleet had deployed to counter an anticipated breakout into the Atlantic and the Germans met no opposition en route, and little immediately on landing

PLATE 2.1 Naval cutters landing men of the Plymouth Battalion, Royal Marines Light Infantry on Y Beach on 25 April, 1915. (*RM Museum. Crown copyright*)

pursued. More positively, there were a few brigade landing exercises and some of the basic groundwork was carried out; as a result of Staff College exercises and a study of the lessons of Gallipoli, the DCOS Sub Committee published *The Manual of Combined Operations* which laid down a sound doctrine. In 1938 the Inter Service Training and Development Centre (ISTDC) was formed, so the creation of the specialist amphibious equipment and techniques began. But these were all small and poorly funded undertakings, lacking both influence and an institutional bedrock of officer training, since the inhibiting legacy of the disaster at Gallipoli and the lack of support from resource-starved single Service departments prevented any significant progress. Given the confused policies and lack of real preparation in the previous decades, there can be little surprise that the British forces in Norway, and the staffs at sea and in London showed little willingness to seize amphibious opportunities, since there was no widespread knowledge of the art, sparse equipment and few trained and experienced officers and men. Even the existing doctrine was ignored.

PLATE 2.2 During the Norway campaign in 1940, neither side had any amphibious ships, and the British depended upon merchantmen and Royal Navy ships for transport. Here the troopship MA *Shoba* has been bombed during a German air attack near Harstad and the crew and Royal Marines are being pulled ashore in lifeboats. The effectiveness of air power in maritime operations was one of the major lessons of the campaign. (*RM Museum. Crown copyright*)

The Gallipoli and Norway campaigns marked the death knell for the traditional concept of the 'Amphibious Power of Britain', of those apparently halcyon days when 'virtually every writer on strategy . . . acknowledged that, in the broadest sense, Britain's strategy must be "amphibious". Then, having made this announcement, the theorists almost without exception ignored it. At least they ignored what is the most crucial area of such a strategy, the point where land and water actually meet'[15] . . . as did the military and naval establishment. The most thunderous condemnation of that tradition is by Sir Michael Howard:

> 'The amphibious diversion . . . the attack on the Dardanelles, a brilliant, almost flawless strategic concept, had met the fate of virtually every British amphibious operation since the Age of Elizabeth . . . all brilliant in conception, all lamentable in execution. The surprise and mobility which Liddell Hart had seen as the essence of British maritime strategy, so far from ensuring success, had resulted over the centuries in an almost unbroken record of expensive and humiliating failures from which Wolfe's seizure of Quebec stands out as one of the few exceptions.'[16]

The theme that pervades all the invective, advocacy and polemics of the maritime/continental strategy debate in those years was the obstinate reluctance of many of the protagonists to recognise that the two were not mutually exclusive. History had shown that, *in extremis*, Britain had to dispatch troops to protect the Low Countries, while retaining a strong basic naval defence. In other words, as

PLATE 2.3 Amphibious exercises were rare in the inter-war years, and the Royal Marines were limited to Mobile Naval Base Defence Organisation (MNBDO) tasks. Here a light tank is being landed during trials at Fort Cumberland, Eastney, Portsmouth in 1932. (*RM Museum. Crown copyright*)

Brian Bond has explained, the 'maritime strategy' was complementary to or an extension of Continental strategy: they were not alternatives . . . the problem was always to harmonize land and sea operations as part of a coherent strategic plan.[17]

In the absence of a strategic solution, and for associated financial, single Service or doctrinaire reasons, the problems of projecting maritime power, especially in continental campaigns, had not yet been solved. One of the Army commanders in Norway recommended that:

> 'the least that can be done now is to ensure that this undesirable situation does not occur again, and that provision is made for a force headquarters and certain formations and units . . . which can be held as a reserve . . . able to act swiftly and decisively at any point overseas . . . with an allotment of landing craft and ships fitted to carry them'.[18]

Thus the irony of that conversation on Hungerford Bridge in 1974 is that, until 1940, Britain very rarely had a peacetime force in being that gave her the capability to land forces on a foreign shore, and she certainly did not have the technology to enable amphibious forces to cross the beach quickly and in strength. The dominant lesson of Gallipoli and Norway (as well as France in both 1914 and 1940), was that the early engagements of a conflict expose any weaknesses in peacetime capabilities and preparations. But we also learned that it is not realistic to endeavour to employ an amphibious capability without due forethought about the doctrine, the supporting training institutions, the equipment and the practice which are essential if we are to overcome the *friction* that is inherent in these complex operations.

THE DEVELOPMENT OF A DOCTRINE

The USMC took a more positive view of the outcome of Gallipoli, possibly because they, unlike the British Armed Forces, were not scarred by the disaster. Thus, unhindered by prejudice in the inter-war years, and driven by the imperatives of institutional survival, they could use its lessons as part of a platform for establishing a new primary role as amphibious forces after being employed as colonial infantry in the early years of the century, as line infantry in the First World War, and as ships' guards and base defenders throughout their history. Their approach was epitomised by the concluding words of a lecture on Gallipoli at Quantico in 1923: 'It is the business of us all, each in his proper sphere, to see that the Marine Corps never has such a story to tell.'[19] The protagonists of a new concept pursued their objective with unremitting zeal, overcoming some opposition within the Marine Corps. We can identify three main elements in their development of an amphibious doctrine and the capability to implement it.

Strategy. Soon after the First World War, the United States recognised the growing threat from Japan and began contingency planning for a campaign in the Pacific. As a result, the US Navy examined the options with such thoroughness during wargames at the Naval War College that, in 1945, Admiral Nimitz commented that every eventuality had been foreseen except the Kamikaze attacks. The Marine Corps saw the importance of securing Pacific island as advanced bases and in 1921 the Commandant, Major General John A. Lejeune, commissioned a study by Major Earl H. Ellis which resulted in the first detailed plans for amphibious operations in this theatre.[20] Lejeune used these to proselytize for a clear mission to be assigned to the Expeditionary Force, and by 1929 it had been accepted as official policy that 'the special role of the Marine Corps within the military establishment was to provide a small well trained amphibious assault force to seize and occupy overseas bases for fleet operations'.[21]

Doctrine. To provide the intellectual background for this special role, it was decided in 1933 that the courses at the Marine Corps Schools should no longer be based upon US Army curricula but directed to the specific needs of the Corps. The new syllabus included a research project on Gallipoli which in itself was not exceptional, thorough as it was, but its importance lay in its association with a parallel study of 'The Advanced Base Problem' and together, in simple terms, these added up to an analysis of how the Corps should undertake its new mission. The outcome was the production in 1934 by a committee of students and instructors of *The Tentative Manual of Landing Operations* which covered command relationships, naval gunfire, air support, ship to shore movement, securing the beachhead and logistics. This work was further refined to emerge as *Landing Operations*

Doctrine, US Navy 1937 and was sufficiently well founded to serve as the basis for all US amphibious operations throughout the Second World War, with relatively little amendment.

Organisation, Training and Equipment. In parallel with the doctrinal work, the USMC decided to create, from the old Expeditionary Force, the Fleet Marine Force as a combined arms formation which included infantry, artillery, air defence, aircraft and support units. Financial restraints and the demands of providing Marine detachments for an expanding fleet prevented the force from being built up to full strength in the 1930s, but at least there was sufficient to enable amphibious operations to be tested on a series of fleet landing exercises from 1935. From these arose a demand for specialist equipment, such as flat bottomed landing craft with bow doors, improved troop transport ships, modern attack aircraft and an amphibian tank. From 1940 the size of the Corps was expanded and the exercises and equipment procurement took on a new urgency, so by the time that the Fleet Marine Force and the US Navy were summoned to their first joint operation at Guadalcanal in 1942 they were, if not fully prepared, sufficiently well practised to conduct the unopposed landing there.

British Doctrine

Both the British and the Americans have a deep rooted suspicion of the word *doctrine* with its somewhat undemocratic undertones, and at best regard it as guidance for wise men. The British were the more uneasy about the term, but their amphibious past emphasised the foolhardiness of attempting to coalesce in a happy-go-lucky manner the flexibility of naval tactics and procedures with the more rigid military approach for land operations, when facing the natural hazards in reaching and crossing the beach. Their *Manual of Combined Operations 1938* was developed further by the Inter Service Training and Development Centre, and one view of the ISTDC approach was given by Bernard Fergusson:

> 'By the end of 1938, after an interruption for Munich, when they were temporarily disbanded,[22] the Brains Trust for the ISTDC had hammered out a broad policy for landings, and defended it at Staff College discussions. With variations won by experience, it was broadly the policy that was used in the North African and Sicily landings. . . . The system provided for an approach under cover of darkness in fast ships carrying special craft: the craft being sent ashore while the ships lay out of sight of land: small-craft gave smoke and gun protection while the beachhead was seized: the landing of a reserve: the capture of a covering position far enough inland to secure the beach and anchorage from enemy fire; the bringing in of the ships carrying the main body; and finally the discharge of vehicles and stores by other craft specially designed to do so directly on to beaches. And in all this it was important to achieve tactical surprise. . . . The gospel having been declared sound, the ISTDC wasted little time on epistles.'[23]

The Landing Operations Doctrine, US Navy 1937, and the British manual were drawn up independently, were not identical, but there were many similarities between them since they were both combed from the ashes of Gallipoli, and could both be regarded as seminal works. There were inevitably some differences; when they first saw the British manual in 1941, the Americans commented that it paid too little attention to the air side of combined operations. This was hardly surprising since, as has been said, 'Between 1918 and 1939 the Royal Air Force forgot how to support the Army . . . and the Navy too.'[24] The USMC with the distinct advantage of integral air and ground forces had, on the other hand, done much pioneering work on land/air warfare, making strides matched only by the Germans. Overall, however, these early doctrines provided a framework which has served allied amphibious operations reliably until the present day.

The Soviet Navy

We have made no mention of the Soviets up to this point. They had conducted one of the few successful amphibious operations in the First World War, when the Army and the Black Sea fleet combined in 1916 to attack Trebizond in Turkish Anatolia. After the Revolution, however, 'they considered' as Admiral Gorshkov has told us 'as unrealistic the use of naval forces in a struggle against a shore defended by a strong enemy, so the fleet were not trained for it.'[25] They were more concerned with the defence of the homeland against amphibious forces, a bitter lesson of their struggle against the White Russians and their allies in 1919.

THE SECOND WORLD WAR

After the initial, often amphibious, triumphs of the Axis Powers in the early years of the war, the Allies were forced to adopt a strategy heavily dependent upon a massive amphibious strength. Both alliances exercised the full gamut of the genre, including assaults, raids, diversions and withdrawals, and Admiral Gorshkov has calculated that:

> 'The warring sides (leaving aside the Soviet fleet) staged over 500 landings, not counting minor diversionary reconnaissance raids. The Soviet fleet in the years of the Great Patriotic War mounted over 100 landings, varying in scale.'[26]

He reminds us that there were only two major failures to effect a landing, when in 1942 American aircraft, mainly carrier based, defeated the Japanese amphibious task groups approaching Port Moresby and Midway respectively. There were also comparatively few reverses once ashore and in these we should include the British efforts in Norway, Crete and Dieppe, as well as the stalemate at Anzio, but the overall record was good; why did this previously inconsistent form of warfare suddenly achieve such surprisingly good results?

The most significant factor in all the maritime theatres was the ability to achieve local sea and air superiority to give the amphibious and landing forces scope to conduct their business. In achieving this goal, some shibboleths were exposed, especially when it was discovered that air power, instead of inhibiting landing operations, was a positive and decisive factor in their success when land and carrier based aircraft were properly integrated into the plan. Allied air interdiction slowed the reinforcement of bridgeheads in Europe by the Germans and in the Central Pacific, US air and naval power eventually isolated the target islands. The submarine, for all its effectiveness against resupply shipping in the Atlantic and the Mediterranean during certain stages of the war, was never allowed to interfere significantly with landings, and equally mines did not deter these operations. Thus the fears of the pre-war staffs had been misplaced, although Sir Michael Howard was correct to say that 'Not until the massive industrial supremacy of the United States was cast into the balance, making possible an overwhelming local superiority

PLATE 2.4   Air superiority was essential when mounting large scale landings. A Japanese aircraft shot down as it attempted to attack USS *Kitkun Bay* during the Battle of the Phillipine Sea. (*US Navy*)

by land, sea and air, did amphibious operations come into their own as a major tool of strategy.'[27]

Notwithstanding all this, landings had failed under apparently favourable conditions in the past, so success must have depended upon other factors as well. Let us discuss each major theatre in turn.

Western Europe and Atlantic

In Western Europe, the Mediterranean and the Atlantic, the Allies started with a doctrine but very little else. After the ill-conceived Norway campaign in April 1940, the early operations were on a small scale, mainly designed to harass the Germans on the Atlantic coastline from Norway to France, such as the raids on the Lofotens in March 1941 and on St Nazaire in March 1942. The main objective, however, was to build up the ability to mount a major landing to establish a second front, and Churchill considered it essential that a large scale operation should take place to gain experience for the main invasion. The Dieppe landing by the 2nd Canadian Division and three British Commandos in August 1942 proved to be 'a costly but not unfruitful reconnaissance in force. Tactically it was a mine of experience.' [28] The scale of operations increased with Operation *Torch* in November 1942, the largely unopposed landing by the British and Americans in North Africa. The first major opposed assault was in Sicily in July 1943 and the subsequent campaign in Italy included a number of amphibious landings; such as Salerno, Taranto, Termoli and Anzio. But the main focus of effort continued to be the establishment of the Second Front, and Normandy in June 1944 was the grand climax of the overall campaign, when all the innovation and experience of the past few years was given its greatest test. The final landing in this theatre was at Walcheren on 1 November 1944. Taken overall, the most important influences included:

▶ *Combined Operations Headquarters (COHQ)*. At Churchill's instigation, the British set up for the first time a joint Services organisation to co-ordinate the preparations for future operations. This, the COHQ, under successively Bourne, Keyes and then Mountbatten, was viewed with a suspicion that reflected the bitter resistance in the inter-war years to the concept of a unified Ministry of Defence. None the less COHQ became 'the forcing house for new techniques and amphibious equipment (and) the power house for harnessing our maritime potential',[29] and this central direction proved essential for developing a coherent approach to maritime power projection.

▶ *Specialist Equipment*. Once the importance of specialist craft and equipment had been fully recognised, invention flourished on both sides of the Atlantic; after 1942 the Allies harnessed the strength of US industry to realise the myriad ideas for ships and craft for landing operations. After the abortive attempt to capture Dakar in 1940, there arose a need for an ocean going ship able to land tanks over the beach, so the British adapted the design of Maracaibo oilers, peculiar tankers with little draught, so that they could cross the sand bar at this port, to become one of the workhorses of the amphibious fleet, the Landing Ship Tank (LST). In America, the New Orleans boatbuilder Andrew Higgins designed several craft, including the widely used landing craft mechanised (LCM). In all there was a total of some 80 different types of landing ships and craft designed to meet a wide variety of specialist tasks, and this new capability proved to be a critical factor in the planning and timing for the main operations. Indeed, a shortage of craft due to industrial limitations influenced the timings of several operations.

▶ *Experience*. Invaluable lessons were learned from the early raids, which Churchill instigated to maintain an aggressive posture when the main effort was concentrated upon defending the British Isles, and from each of the major operations that followed; lessons which refined the basic conceptual work of the ISTDC. Norway and Crete confirmed the essential need for securing air superiority. The landings in Vichy controlled Madagascar in May 1942 revealed the need to

PLATE 2.5 A Maracaibo oiler, the forebear of the LSTs shown in Plate 3.1. (*RM Museum. Crown copyright*)

PLATE 2.6 Invention ran riot during the Second World War, and this *Panjandrum* was designed to clear mines and obstacles on beaches. It was propelled by ninerockets on each wheel, and here it has just completed its first 222 yard trial run. Its most famous moment, however, came during an episode in the TV series 'Dad's Army'. (*RM Museum*)

28   Amphibious Operations

strengthen the beach organisation. Dieppe showed the importance of a heavy bombardment by sea and air, including the use of close support from landing craft during the approach to the beach; requirements that had been identified in theory before the war but only experience could show how much was enough. The North Africa landings in November 1942 confirmed that a dedicated Headquarters ship was essential; the landing force commander, General Patton, had been 'borne away protesting from his battle because the ship in which he was sailing was needed for a naval one'.[30] And so on, in what were effectively rehearsals on an increasing scale leading inexorably to the grand finale at Normandy.

▶ *Warfare is Joint.* As experience grew, so the Armed Forces began to realise that warfare is joint. In peacetime the Services tend to bicker over scarce resources, but the history of failure to combine against a common national enemy in war defies belief. Early operations in North Africa and the Atlantic were rife with examples, but fortunately also with lessons that strong and farsighted commanders can bring harmony. It is axiomatic that the development of a mutual understanding is a prerequisite for combined operations. Fergusson gives a good example:

> 'In the old *mystique* of the Navy putting the Army ashore, it had always been held that the really tricky part was the actual landings. It was the Navy's part to say to the Army: 'We can put you ashore there, or there. You choose which, and we'll do it. After that, we can only hope that it will keep fine for you'. Gradually, as the members of each Service got to know each other's problems better, and the soldiers especially grew to learn . . . what were possible and what were impossible demands, the sea came almost to be regarded as just another obstacle, however temperamental, between the Army and its chosen battlefields. The fashion had been to say: "This is the best place to land: how shall we fight thereafter?" It now gave way to saying: "There are our objectives; this is the battle we want to fight; can we find landing places to fit?".'[31]

The Central Pacific

We have seen that the US amphibious forces started the war in a much better state than their British counterparts. They mounted the assault on Guadalcanal in August 1942 with some confidence . . . although not in copybook fashion, as it was one of the rare cases when the commanders risked landing without ensuring local maritime superiority . . . and stemmed the Japanese advance towards Australia in a lengthy battle of attrition. Once clear of the Solomon Islands, the Central Pacific campaign developed into that well known litany of USMC achievement, including Tarawa, The Marshalls, Saipan, discussed in the opening chapter, Tinian and Guam; then on to Pulau in September 1944 to secure the Eastern flank of MacArthur's advance into the Philippines. Iwo Jima in February 1945 was 'the supreme test' but Okinawa on 1 April was on a different scale to any previous operation in this theatre, with about half a million troops and over 1200 ships in direct support of the landing. As the campaign was fundamentally naval, with the USMC providing the core of the assault forces, the benefits of having an agreed and practised US Navy/USMC doctrine were felt from the outset. This is not to say that mistakes were not made, or that no lessons were learned, but 'the modifications wrought between 1942 and 1945 in the art of amphibious warfare did not seriously affect (the) underlying principles'.[32] These modifications included:

▶ *Specialist Equipment.* As with the European campaign, a chief element in the increasing capability of the amphibious forces was the rapid development of the

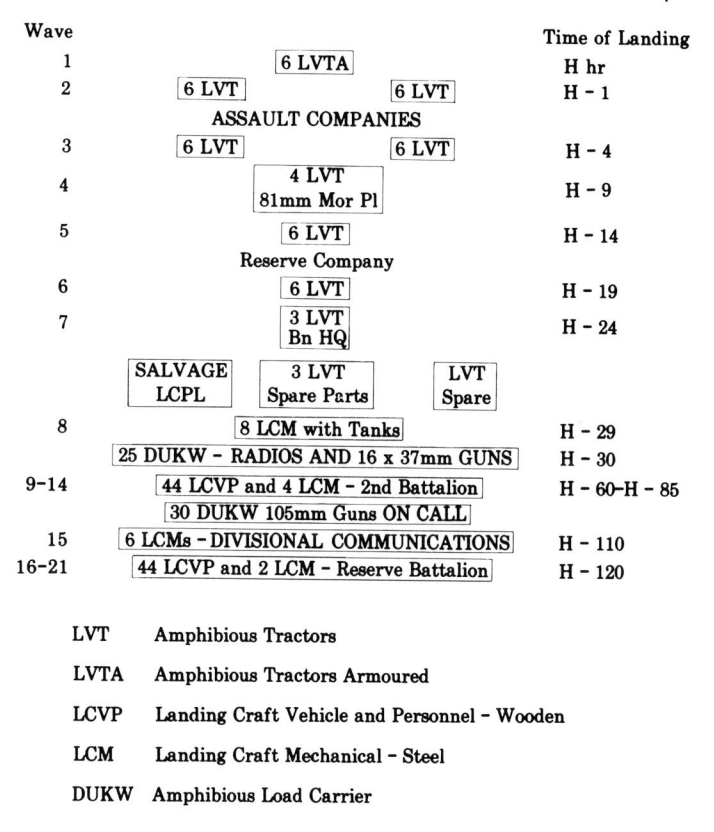

Wave				Time of Landing
1		6 LVTA		H hr
2	6 LVT		6 LVT	H - 1
		ASSAULT COMPANIES		
3	6 LVT		6 LVT	H - 4
4		4 LVT 81mm Mor Pl		H - 9
5		6 LVT		H - 14
		Reserve Company		
6		6 LVT		H - 19
7		3 LVT Bn HQ		H - 24
	SALVAGE LCPL	3 LVT Spare Parts	LVT Spare	
8		8 LCM with Tanks		H - 29
	25 DUKW - RADIOS AND 16 x 37mm GUNS			H - 30
9-14	44 LCVP and 4 LCM - 2nd Battalion			H - 60–H - 85
	30 DUKW 105mm Guns ON CALL			
15	6 LCMs - DIVISIONAL COMMUNICATIONS			H - 110
16-21	44 LCVP and 2 LCM - Reserve Battalion			H - 120

LVT   Amphibious Tractors

LVTA   Amphibious Tractors Armoured

LCVP   Landing Craft Vehicle and Personnel - Wooden

LCM   Landing Craft Mechanical - Steel

DUKW   Amphibious Load Carrier

FIG. 2.1   An example of the layout of a USMC battalion assault landing during the Central Pacific campaign

equipment, and there was a constant exchange of ideas between the two theatres. A good example is the amphibian tractor, which was designed specifically for the Pacific campaign. During the assault on Tarawa in November 1943, the landing craft failed to negotiate the reef and many troops were cut down as they waded ashore. Some tractors were available and they could have crossed the reef and swum ashore, but these few were then considered as logistic vehicles. The lesson was soon learned. On future operations, they were provided in much greater numbers, some armoured or even armed with guns, and were used extensively for both assault and logistic purposes; before long, they were produced to support the European landings as well. As a form of *quid pro quo*, the British-designed LST was employed to deliver these vehicles into the combat zone.

▶ *Naval Gunfire and Air Support.* In the early stages, the co-ordination of the naval gunfire and air support was found wanting, and at Tarawa there was a lack of flexibility once the planned timings started to go awry. Good progress in the development of naval gunfire support was possible thereafter since, on most occasions except Saipan, sea control was absolute and there was time for a leisurely destruction of the beach defences; at Okinawa this occupied seven days. In these conditions, the skill was honed to a fine pitch; Admiral Connelly initiated the

PLATE 2.7 USS *Pennsylvania* bombarding Guam in 1944; ships of this type have been re-activated to support the modern US amphibious forces. (*US Navy*)

technique of delivering pinpoint fire from only 2000 yards range and thus earned himself the nickname of 'Close in Connelly'. Progress in the art of controlling air support was not as rapid, partly because the Marine aircraft were deployed with MacArthur in the South West Pacific—not with the fleet, and the landing forces believed that the US Navy aircraft could not provide the intimate and flexible support they had come to practice with their own air wings. Escort carriers were provided to provide air support for landings but USMC pleas for an escort carrier for their own aircraft were not answered until too late in the war for the concept to be fully developed.

▶ *Surprise*. The Pacific Fleet's sea and air dominance, denying the Japanese the ability to move in significant reinforcements and permitting lengthy preparations, meant that tactical surprise was not essential in the island campaign, so the assaults were made in daylight. This was in sharp contrast to the stress placed by the commanders in the European theatre on ensuring both strategic and tactical surprise, with elaborate deception plans and feints, lest the enemy should discover the objective and react accordingly. Consequently, Pacific landings were by daylight and European ones usually at night, or at least at first light; Normandy was an exception since the massive size of the fleet and its landing force presented particular control problems for the navy.

South West Pacific

There was also a sharp contrast between the Central Pacific campaign and General MacArthur's advance along the New Guinea coast in 1943 and 1944. He was short of amphibious shipping and was fighting along a littoral which gave his enemy greater scope for manœuvre, so he could not be certain of Japanese deployments. He therefore sought to land relatively small forces against weak opposition and to use his reserves to reinforce success, withdrawing if the landings met with sterner resistance. Many of these operations were carried out in the face of enemy air and naval superiority.[33]

The Eastern Front

Gorshkov regretted the Soviet lack of an amphibious capability at the start of the war, and commented: 'when there emerged the problem of staging landings as a very widespread form of combat activity, carried out on the sea flanks of the Soviet-German land front jointly with the army . . . we had to pay a heavy price for the neglect of this form of combat preparation of the fleet and army'.[34] None the less, the Soviets showed a refreshingly pragmatic approach to amphibious operations which enabled them, by dint of improvisation and often hard experience, to develop a doctrine which still serves as the basis for their operations. There were indeed signs of initiative which belie their reputation for overcentralisation; one example of their tactical flexibility was at Novorossiisk in February 1943 when the Soviets had began to claw their way back from the Caucasus. The main assault failed to secure a bridgehead, but a concurrent diversionary landing looked more promising and the main effort was switched to reinforce its success.

▶ *Organisation and Equipment.* They quickly learned and applied the basic tenets of the art, placing their emphasis upon operational and tactical surprise, speed, heavy fire support, although that could be dispensed with to ensure surprise, and quick consolidation of the beachhead. Some early misunderstandings made them acutely conscious of the importance of sound co-ordination between the assaulting force and the shipping; this was mainly because they used line infantry in the assault, untrained for these skills and sometimes converted to their new role at only 24 hours notice. Soon the value of specialist troops was recognised and the Naval Infantry were formed to provide the spearhead for follow-on army units. The Soviet Navy made little or no special provision for landing equipment, merely adapting existing ships and craft, and this severely limited their scope.

▶ *Amphibious Desants.* The Soviets favoured the use of amphibious forces in the classic desant role by inserting them along the coastline in a flanking hook from the sea to disrupt the enemy's rear. This was always co-ordinated with a decisive land offensive and, as the war progressed, airborne landings were increasingly incorporated into the operations. It was considered that 'In a difficult situation such a deep

Soviet Desant During the Great Patriotic War

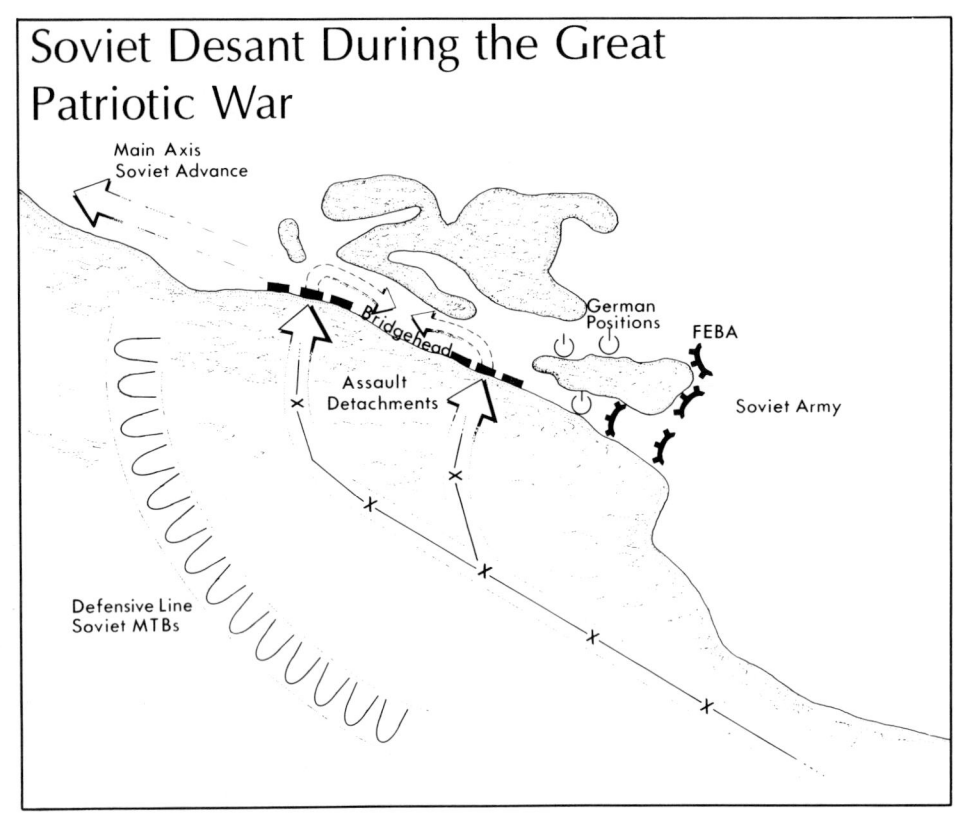

MAP 2.3 During the Soviet advances in the Great Patriotic War (Second World War), Soviet amphibious landings, or desants, were used to outflank major enemy defences. This example demonstrates vividly the very limited depth of the assault landing ahead of the main Soviet forces. (*Source: Donnelly et al. Soviet Amphibious Warfare. Crown copyright*)

envelopment was usually helpful, and it was sometimes the only way of achieving the aim of speeding up the advance of the main forces on land.'[35]

Scale of Operations

Most Soviet operations were on a small scale, rarely deploying as much as a division, aimed to achieve limited objectives at operational or tactical level, and thus usually planned at short notice. Whereas the major Western landings were strategic, the Soviets never aspired to this scale. Anzio and Walcheren were two rare examples of Western operational level landings and it is arguable that the Western forces did not exploit the lower level opportunities to the full.

The British formed the Commandos as lightly equipped raiding units which were based upon very high quality infantry, but had no supporting artillery, armour or logistic sustainability. They were designed to operate from a firm base against the enemy coast, or to spearhead a landing. They were also a valuable tactical level capability to destroy enemy positions which might otherwise cause the advancing

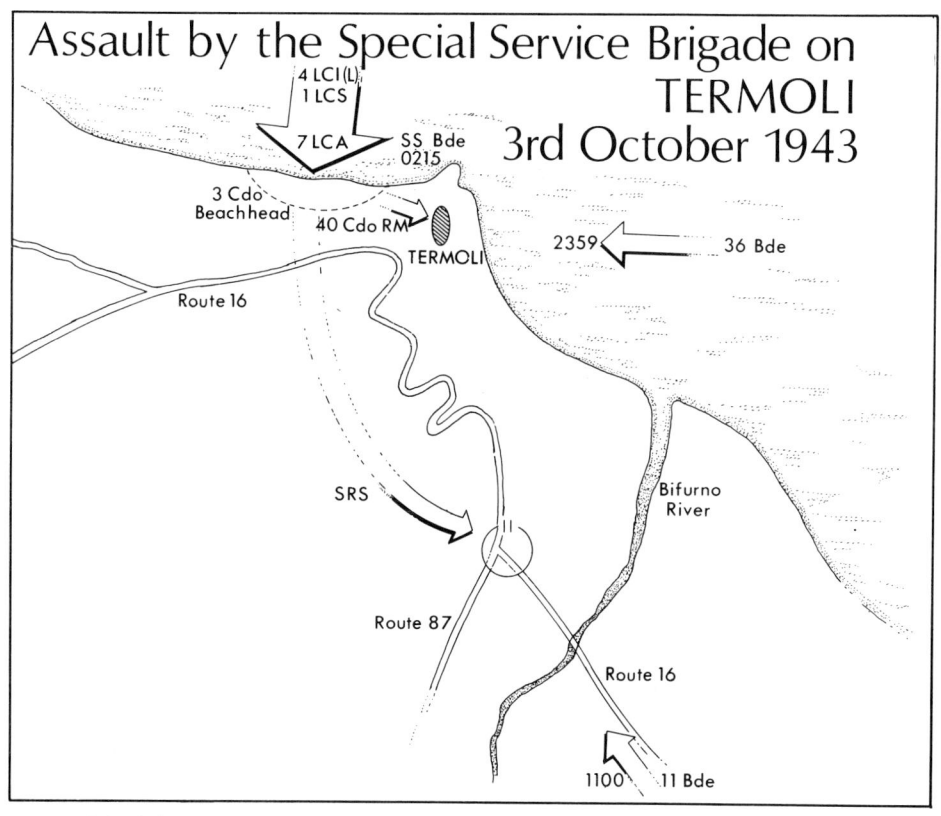

MAP 2.4 The assault on Termoli bore striking similarities to the desant landing by the Soviets shown in Map 2.3; a short range hook operation ahead of the advancing ground forces who joined up with the assault forces within 12 hours of the landing

army some embarrassment but, with their lack of firepower, it was important that they be landed no more than twelve, or at the most twenty-four, hours ahead of the main ground forces. In Italy, in October 1943, for example, the Special Service Brigade (3 (Army) Commando, 40 Commando RM and the Special Raiding Squadron of the SAS) carried out what might be regarded as a classic amphibious desant operation to seize and hold Termoli until Army formations arrived by road and sea during the following 24 hours. The operation outflanked the left of the intended German line on the Bifurno River, and kept the enemy on the retreat.

Despite this success, the Allies made only intermittent use of the short range tactical amphibious hook, and the advance through France and Belgium in particular lost some momentum through a reluctance to exploit the sea flank aggressively; Walcheren was the sole exception and then, with no amphibious reserve, the force had to be specially assembled. Chester Wilmot highlighted the limitations of the commanders' attitude in his book *The Struggle for Europe*:

> 'Immediately after the capture of Antwerp . . . an amphibious force could have been landed at the mouth of the Scheldt without great difficulty. . . . At SHAEF, however, no provision had been made for taking advantage of such an opportunity. All the planning had been based on the

PLATE 2.8 Troops landing from a LCI similar to those used during the Termoli operation. Then the LCIs towed LCAs to the line of departure and followed in as the second wave, only to ground some distance from the beach; a wet landing for the troops. (*RM Museum. Crown copyright*)

assumption that any ports or pockets of resistance on the Channel coast would be taken from landward and no amphibious reserve had been kept in mind to exploit the Allied command of the sea.'[36]

Conclusion

The USMC planners at Quantico and the British ISTDC had proved to be remarkably sound prophets about the potential for amphibious warfare, and about the operating techniques that would be required. Remarkable, because they flew in the face of the current conventional wisdom, and because there were a number of examples from the inter-war years of predictions on the application and effectiveness of new technology, such as strategic bombing, which had been found wanting in the test of war.

The experiences of the Second World War demonstrated that amphibious forces could be used to significant effect in a continental war. Skills, procedures and equipment had been honed to meet a magnificent climax at Normandy, yet the vast scale of those operations has subsequently tended to confuse rather than clarify the post-war debate; there has been a natural inclination to conclude that the huge investment in amphibious operations necessary for continental warfare could never be repeated. There has perhaps been a reluctance, a legacy of the inertia of Anzio, to appreciate that operational and tactical level landings could play as important a role as strategic ones, perhaps in a development of the South West Pacific and Soviet concepts. And then there was Hiroshima.

3
Towards a Modern Capability

GLOBAL REACH 1945–71

With the advent of nuclear warfare the concept of conducting vast amphibious landings such as those in Normandy and at Okinawa was swiftly consigned to history, leading the Chairman of the Joint Chiefs of Staff, General Bradley to make a frequently quoted prediction in 1949 that 'large scale amphibious operations will never occur again'.[1] Later writers have enjoyed the apparent debunking of Bradley when the landing of 1st Marine Division at Inchon less than a year later seemed to prove him wrong; but did it? The questions faced by all concerned with amphibious operations since the Second World War have been *Are They Important? . . . Are They Possible?*

The reduction of the amphibious fleets after the war was inevitable, especially as the new strategy of nuclear deterrence envisaged the need for only a relatively small army on the continent to guard against a surprise attack which would, if it came, be countered by the ability to deliver a massive retaliatory nuclear blow; the so-called *Tripwire Strategy*. Under these circumstances, there would be no time to amass the amphibious forces needed to regain a foothold in Europe, so their whole future came under question. In the mid-1950s, the Soviet Naval Infantry were disbanded by Mr Krushchev, ostensibly because he was influenced by the nuclear missile 'modernists' into a belief that amphibious forces could not survive in the modern nuclear battle. In Washington, the USMC survived a fierce attack from within the Pentagon only by mobilising the sympathy of congress who enacted a law to establish three Fleet Marine Forces in the United States Defence organisation, although this guaranteed no amphibious shipping. The British also placed amphibious operations low on their list of immediate post-war priorities and retained merely a small residual force based on the amphibious warfare squadron which could carry a unit from 3 Commando Brigade RM . . . but this did mean that, for the first time, the British had a small trained landing force in peace . . . and it provided an amphibious role for the Royal Marines Commandos. Both nations had global strategies which might call for these forces to intervene at short notice, and they were soon in action.

Inchon. The North Korean attack in July 1950 swiftly drove the South Korean and American forces into a desperate defence of their last bastion at the Pusan

36   Amphibious Operations

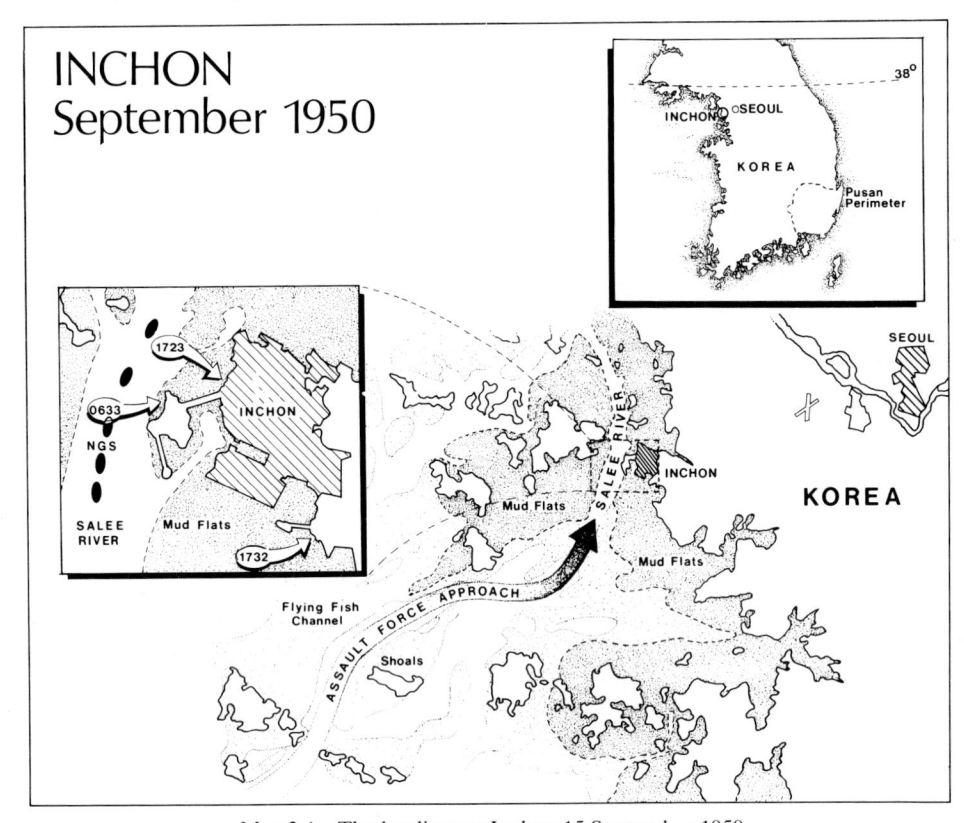

MAP 3.1   The landings at Inchon 15 September 1950

Perimeter. General MacArthur had the vision to grasp that a deep amphibious hook against Inchon would provide 'an anvil upon which his Eighth Army and the Republic of Korea forces would break the North Korean army'.[2] It was a strategic masterstroke, but one fraught with tactical risk, as the distance between the Pusan perimeter and the landing point was considerable, the approach to Inchon was up a narrow and tortuous channel which could be easily defended, and the hazards of landing were multiplied by the 33 foot rise and fall of the tides and the absence of proper beaches; there were only moles, breakwaters and seawalls. In many respects, it was the worst possible place for an amphibious assault, but the choice of such an unlikely objective also enhanced the chance of achieving surprise. The JCS and the USN had understandable misgivings about the wisdom of the concept, but MacArthur convinced them, and the sleeping American amphibious giant was awakened. Ships, craft and equipment unused since the Pacific campaign were called out of retirement and the USMC mobilised with such singlemindedness that the Fleet Marine Force on the Atlantic coast was reduced to a cadre to provide men for the Inchon operation. The planning process was fragmented and hectic, tending to be dominated by the marines who had remained the guardians of the doctrine. The landing was made on 15 September, 1950 by 1st Marine Division with X Corps US Army providing the bulk of the follow-up troops. Surprise was complete, and

PLATE 3.1 The fastest means to unload shipping; four LSTs beached at Inchon. (*US Navy*)

the operation completely successful; within 12 days Seoul was captured, thus cutting the lines of communications and forcing the North Korean army to withdraw from the Pusan Perimeter. Then the Eighth Army and its allies struck northwards to regain the 38th Parallel, enabling the United Nations to preserve the Republic of Korea.

Suez: Operation Musketeer. Gamal Abdel Nasser's decision to nationalise the Suez canal in July 1956 provoked a furious reaction from its erstwhile owners, Britain and France. The British Government could not, however, intervene at once, since the planners found 'a state of military unpreparedness that had never been appreciated until the need arose to mount an operation like *Musketeer*'.[3] The minute amphibious warfare squadron could provide the core of the force, together with the commando brigade, which had exercised for the role whenever commandos could be spared from counter insurgency operations in Cyprus. But more were needed, and the problems of assembling sufficient tanks, ships and aircraft to support the amphibious and airborne forces precluded a rapid response. Planning was complicated by the dispersion of the staffs and the ad hoc arrangements for co-operating with the French who had joined this venture. Overall, the mounting phase revealed that the expertise required for a combined operation had been dissipated in the years since the Normandy landings.

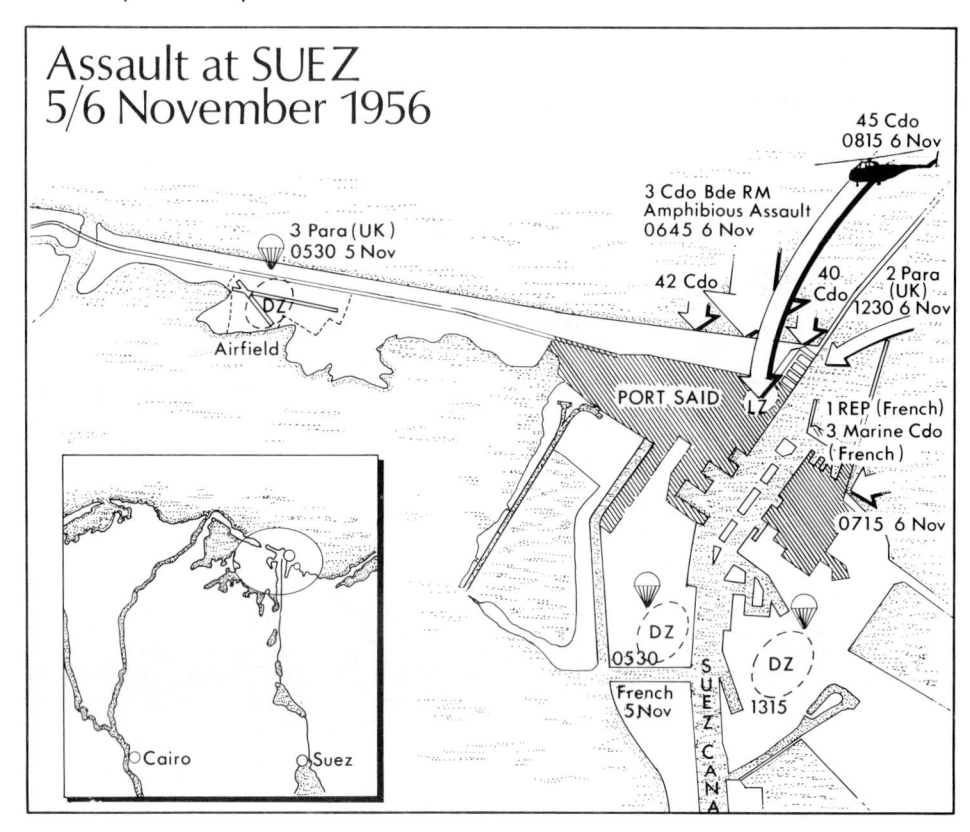

MAP 3.2 The Suez Landings 5 and 6 November 1956. This was a good example of the combination of airborne, heliborne and amphibious assaults

Yet the greatest stress arose from political indecision during the months before the operation. It reached a climax in the final weeks before the landing when there were desperate but unsuccessful diplomatic negotiations to secure American support. Israel, however, secretly agreed to lend positive military support to the venture; on 29 October she dropped paratroops on the Mitla Pass, and followed this up with an armoured thrust into the Sinai. This gave Britain and France the opportunity to issue an ultimatum that both Israel and Egypt should withdraw their forces from the area of the canal, which Egypt, not surprisingly, rejected.

It is worth mentioning two political decisions which seriously affected the military operation. First, only days before the force sailed from Malta, the lack of international support led the government to alter its initial plan for a landing at Alexandria, with a subsequent advance upon Cairo. It selected instead Port Said for the assault with the Canal Zone as the subsequent objective; in other words, the political aim had changed, from one of destroying Nasser to the more limited one of seizing and holding the canal. Secondly, Prime Minister Eden forbade the amphibious force to leave Malta until the ultimatum had been rejected on 31 October, instead of allowing it to poise at sea. So the military reaction was unnecessarily delayed. Moreover, it would have been unsound to deploy the small airborne force

PLATE 3.2 View of Suez during the assault, from HMS *Theseus*. An ad hoc helicopter force had been formed from the Royal Navy's first anti-submarine helicopter squadron and the Army–RAF Joint Helicopter Unit (JHU) in Malta only shortly beforehand. The landing by 45 Commando RM was the first vertical envelopment operation. (*RM Museum. Crown copyright*)

more than twenty-four hours ahead of the main amphibious landings (a lesson from Arnhem).

Thus, while the amphibious force sailed across the Mediterranean, the RAF conducted a four-day bombing campaign against the Egyptian airfields to ensure air superiority, and these ponderous tactics only served to increase international disapproval. Eventually, a combined force of some 1,100 paratroops was dropped outside Port Said on 5 November (see Map 3.2), with a further drop in the early afternoon, both meeting little resistance. On 6 November, the amphibious landings were conducted equally successfully and Port Said was surrendered later that afternoon; perhaps the most notable military event of the day being the execution of the first helicopter landing by 45 Commando Royal Marines and the improvised group of *Whirlwinds* and *Sycamores* operating from the Aircraft Carriers HMS *Theseus* and *Ocean*. Shortly afterwards, diplomatic pressure from the United States and the United Nations brought the operation to an early conclusion.

Both the Americans and the British had drawn upon the last remnants of their

PLATE 3.3 During the 1960s and 70s HMS *Bulwark* operated *Whirlwind* helicopters before they were replaced by the larger *Wessex*, seen here. The ship could carry a complete commando group, including its supporting light artillery and engineers and its transport. (*RM Museum. Crown copyright*)

wartime amphibious strengths to mount these operations. Without these practical illustrations of their effectiveness in limited conflicts, the amphibious capabilities of both nations might well have been allowed to wither on the vine. As it was, both were able to confirm that, if a peacetime global intervention capability was required . . . *amphibious operations were important and possible*. This was sufficient to justify a major re-equipment programme based on the concept of being able, as the British Government announced, 'to concentrate relatively small but hard hitting mobile forces wherever they are required'.[4] The increased mobility was to be provided by the helicopter carrier (LPH) in a concept of vertical envelopment by light helicopter-borne troops, backed up by heavier equipment landed over the beach in the conventional way. This was inaugurated with the conversion of the fleet carrier USS *Thetis Bay* by the Americans in 1956, although the concept was first used in earnest by the British at Suez, albeit in an embryonic fashion.

Throughout the 1960s the US Navy built an impressive array of LPHs, assault ships (LPD) and supporting specialist amphibious ships, all of whom we shall meet later. The British followed suit with the two LPDs and six LSLs to add to the two converted light fleet carriers, *Bulwark* and *Albion*, as LPHs. With 3 Commando Brigade RM they constituted at long last the nucleus of a strategic reaction force although there was still a call for something more substantial, as the improvisation needed to intervene in Kuwait in 1961 revealed. It caused Major General J. L. Moulton to write at the time:

> 'That vital role (of a strategic force) must be placed by joint forces in being—training, planning and finally operating together as one team, owing allegiance to one ideal. The great weakness of the 1962 White Paper is that no mention, no forecast, no awareness of the need, even, appears in it. How long are we to put our trust in improvisation?'[5]

The British went through several contortions of organisation in the 1960s to provide this standing force, although the units frequently became too embroiled in long term campaigns such as Aden and Borneo for them to maintain a consistently high level of immediate readiness for contingencies. The future of the amphibious force was constantly being questioned, and Field Marshal Carver recognised the pressures with his double-edged praise of its contribution to the Borneo campaign; . . . an invaluable force, keen to justify its existence.[6] American amphibious forces became even more enmeshed in Vietnam. Both the British and Americans managed to maintain their specialist amphibious skills on exercise and operations such as the Limbang operation in Brunei in 1962 and the USMC rescue of the SS *Mayaguez* in 1975. But the long standing issue of how these forces were to be employed in a general war, in a continental context, was never resolved. The withdrawals of the British from East of Suez, and of the Americans from Vietnam, forced upon them a re-appraisal of this question.

YEARS OF SURVIVAL

The United Kingdom

The modern British amphibious forces were designed in the 1950s and early 1960s to meet the needs of the last colonial wars. They constituted a capability to deploy by sea, and at short notice, a limited infantry force with basic supporting arms, such as artillery and engineers, which could land in a fighting posture and tackle light opposition. The shipping had to be capable of long sea voyages at a reasonable speed, since otherwise the force would not have been able to earn its keep, which it undoubtedly did until the withdrawal from East of Suez was completed in 1971. Then started a lengthy debate about how, or even whether, to employ these high quality troops, with their limited technology at the time, in the service of NATO with its more sophisticated demands.

The adoption of a strategy of flexible response in the late 1960s created a greater demand for conventional forces, and the bulk of the amphibious forces were initially committed to the Southern Flank of NATO, although 45 Commando Group was designated as the Mountain and Arctic Warfare unit in 1969 and earmarked for North Norway. Soon afterwards the Royal Marines began to forge closer links with another member of the old colonial club, The Royal Netherlands Marine Corps (RNLMC), and in 1973 the UK/NL Amphibious Force was inaugurated in a Memorandum of Understanding. This has proved to be an effective and remarkably harmonious example of NATO co-operation, in which The Netherlands have entrusted operational command on exercises and in war to the British. No two proud organisations could maintain such a relationship on standard NATO politesse, and it prospered once both sides realised the value of mixing straight talking with tact.

The increasing threat from the Soviet Navy in the North and economic constraints led to the dropping of the Southern Flank commitment in the 1974 Defence Review, at one stage of that review it was reported that the Royal Marines would be reduced to 45 Commando Group alone. In the event, it was decided that:

> An amphibious force, consisting of Royal Marines brigade headquarters plus three commandos (one mountain and arctic warfare trained) and army support units; one Wessex helicopter squadron; HMS *Hermes* in a secondary role as a commando ship: two assault ships (one in reserve) and afloat support.[7]

would be retained as a specialist reinforcement force. *Bulwark* and *Albion* were to be paid off and the plans to order two purpose built amphibious ships were abandoned. It was a fundamental decision which was used as the yardstick for planning until the mid 1980s; in particular, the determination not to build new LPHs made it unlikely that the remaining amphibious ships would be replaced when their useful life expired.

Initially only one commando was given a NATO role; the others were retained mainly for employment in Northern Ireland. Fortunately, other NATO nations stressed the importance of the UK/NL amphibious capability, and it was eventually decided to commit the whole amphibious force to SACLANT for employment in Norway, the Baltic Approaches (BALTAP) and the Atlantic Islands.

From 1974 on the fortunes of the Amphibious Force waxed and waned. Mountain and arctic warfare training was extended to most of the Commando Brigade, and specialist equipment was procured, such as Volvo 202 oversnow vehicles. *Bulwark* was recommissioned for a while, but *Hermes* was employed increasingly in an anti-submarine role and plans were made, then dropped, for the RFA *Tarbatness* to be converted for amphibious use. Throughout these years the UK/NL Amphibious Force had only a limited amphibious role; the shipping was essential to deploy the force to North Norway but, once ashore, the landing force was to be employed in similar fashion to any light infantry brigade holding ground in defence. Having delivered the force the amphibious ships were to return south and were unlikely to take any further part in the campaign.

Another searching review by Mr John Nott in 1981 asked more difficult questions and the *Hermes* was to be phased out. The saddest news was that

> 'It had already been decided that likely needs did not warrant replacement of the specialist amphibious ships *Intrepid* and *Fearless*; and these ships will be phased out earlier, in 1982 and 1984 respectively.'[8]

Very soon after this announcement, and weeks before the Falklands War, the LPDs were given a temporary reprieve. In this brief campaign they, and the whole amphibious force, proved their fighting worth. But it was not a major continental war and, although the climate improved in the succeeding years with the formation of 539 Assault Squadron of landing craft (of which more later) and the decision to

PLATE 3.4 The Volvo BV-202s were introduced into the UK/NL Landing Force during the 1970s. They have a good oversnow capability, are unarmoured, and are used as command vehicles and as general cargo carriers in the forward units. They are gradually being replaced by the larger BV-206s. (*Royal Marines. Crown copyright*)

provide a *Rapier* air defence battery, the future of the core of the force, the ships, lay in the balance for some time.

The United States of America

The USMC went through a similar period of uncertainty after Vietnam and prevalent views were reflected in a Brookings Institute study in 1974 *Where Does the Marine Corps Go From Here?* which was looked upon as the obituary for amphibious warfare. The USMC saw the amphibious fleet reduced from 162 ships in 1969 to 65 in 1979, and many of the remainder growing towards obsolescence without any plans for replacement, for these main reasons:

▶ The maritime strategy of the time offered little opportunity for amphibious forces in a general war. Considerable doubt was expressed whether they could carry out landing operations successfully in a high threat environment.

▶ The Central Front was viewed as the main and, indeed, only area of strategic priority. Any forces not designed for the main battle were regarded as of secondary importance and investment in amphibious shipping was of little value. Secretary of Defense James Schlesinger exerted great pressure on the USMC to move away from what was implied as the 'ponderousness' and 'overspecialisation' of amphibious operations towards a conventional role on the Central Front.[9] Indeed, during these years the USMC procured a substantial amount of heavy equipment more suited for the NATO role.

▶ Even the role for which the amphibious forces were ideally equipped, global power projection, was a minor concern in the aftermath of Vietnam.

Soviet Union

It is perhaps no surprise that the credit for the re-establishment of the Soviet Naval Infantry in 1963 has been accorded to Admiral Gorshkov who was the architect of the ambitious maritime strategy . . . and had distinguished himself in amphibious operations near Odessa in 1941. To provide shipping, the *Polnocny* LSM and *Alligator* LST classes were introduced and have served as the useful but somewhat limited core of the capability since then. Despite the substantial build up of the Soviet Navy in the 1960s and 70s, the amphibious forces did not expand significantly after their re-establishment, although they were used regularly on exercises and on foreign deployments. Indeed, it appears to have taken some time before the importantance of an amphibious capability was accepted, for the first public endorsement did not come until 1970 when Admiral Stalbo, a leading Soviet writer on maritime strategy, wrote:

> 'We would stress that the basic reasons which forced the warring sides to revert to amphibious landings (during the Second World War) have not only been maintained under modern conditions, but have been considerably enhanced. Because of this, amphibious landings have not lost their importance to the slightest degree.'[10]

This was an interesting declaration, since the Soviets had expressed, more openly than the Western powers, their concern about the survivability of the amphibious force in nuclear war. Gorshkov had recognised the importance of naval and landing operations in local wars, but he indicates that he might have once been among the doubters when he commented that this experience 'is not fully applicable to the waging of armed combat at sea with use of nuclear weapons or to encounters between equivalent naval forces'.[11] As Geoffrey Till has pointed out, the standard Soviet response to criticism that large scale amphibious operations are particularly vulnerable to nuclear attack has been:

▶ The dangers of nuclear attack can be mitigated by a number of palliatives, such as making the best possible use of . . . surprise, of deception and of dispersing forces amongst a large number of fast moving platforms.

▶ All military operations in a military environment, ashore as well as at sea, will likely be much more dispersed, fluid and decentralised than usual. The lack of operational density makes the enemy's rear areas particularly susceptible to assaults from the sea.

▶ Amphibious forces can use nuclear weapons too, and this might be a very good way of suppressing landward defences before the amphibious assault goes in.[12]

Clearly this argument was sufficient to quell Gorshkov's doubts since he concluded that the 'ancient task of sea landings "retains" . . . its importance even in present day conditions'.[11]

Recent Developments

The value of an amphibious capability had therefore been a subject of contentious debate in all the major maritime nations since 1945. The discussion ranged over such central issues as; the utility of the relatively lightweight forces and the survivability of the ships in general war; the importance of wars of intervention and the role of amphibious forces in them; and technological concerns such as solving the awkward equation between shipping capacity and the firepower and weight of the landing force. But the main factor was money.

For Britain, the fundamentals are dramatically simple, and were encapsulated in that question posed on Hungerford Bridge *'Can you imagine the British nation being unable to land forces on a foreign shore as and when she chooses, without depending upon the use of friendly ports?'* To which there is a body of opinion that would reply 'Yes, we must do without it if we can only afford to maintain sufficiently strong ground and air forces in the Central Region, which will be the main battleground'. Another body has been known to say 'yes' as well, but on the grounds that naval warfare is a matter for the high seas. The ultimate decision must reflect Defence priorities, especially financial ones. Indeed the commons Defence Committee, when discussing, in 1985, the need to replace the two assault ships, was concerned that the final decision would probably depend 'far more upon whether it would be financially inopportune than on whether the military case for the capability has been made out'.[13]

In December 1986 the Secretary of State announced in the House of Commons that the Government had decided to retain an amphibious capability in the longer term. He said that feasibility studies were to be set in hand to examine the replacement of *Fearless* and *Intrepid* by a new build, or by an extension of their present lives. In 1988 industry was invited to tender for building an Aviation Support Ship (ASS). At about the same time the Dutch Government announced that it was planning to build an amphibious ship as a major contribution to the UK/NL Amphibious Force.

These decisions reflected, perhaps unconsciously, an earlier commitment in 1982 by the Pentagon to uprate and modernise the United States amphibious capability. Why this apparently sudden change of heart on both sides of the Atlantic? Within the supportive atmosphere generated by the Reagan Administration and by the success of the Falkland Islands campaign, the main influences have been:

▶ The development of a coherent maritime strategy which incorporated amphibious warfare. Wishful thinking about a *British Way in Warfare* cuts little ice. The military case has to be convincing, since nations have only maintained a worthwhile amphibious capability when this is so; the Americans in the face of a latent threat in the Pacific in the 1930s, the Allies striving to regain a foothold in Europe, and both America and Britain exercising global reach in the 1950s and 60s. We will examine how amphibious warfare fits into current maritime strategy in the next chapter.

▶ A recognition of the importance of intervention operations after the events in Iran, Afghanistan and Nicaragua in 1979, the Falklands in 1982 and Grenada in 1983. As has been demonstrated, time after time, throughout this century, contingencies demand quick reactions. Both grand strategy and crisis management have demanded an ability to land forces at short notice, and the lack of the capability, or its inadequacy, has exposed politicians and generals to some embarrassment. The only way to avoid a continuation of what Sir Michael Howard has called 'an almost unbroken record of expensive and humiliating failures' has been shown to be the maintenance of a force in being, with a sensible doctrine, practised in the skills, and able to modernise as technology advances. The classic examples of triumph being seized from the jaws of obsolescence were Inchon and the Falklands.

▶ *Warfare is Joint.* The third factor is the willingness and ability of the Chiefs of Staff and Ministers to adopt a *Joint Service* approach to higher Defence policy. This is not a problem peculiar to Britain, although the British experience provides a good example. Over the years the ability of the Central Staffs in the MOD to override single Service vested interests and to take a joint view of Defence policy has varied considerably, depending upon personalities and other circumstances, especially the state of evolution of the organisation. This syndrome has been a major contributor to the fortunes of the amphibious capability. When there has been a strong joint influence, during Churchill's wartime administration, and when Mountbatten was Chief of Defence Staff in the late 1950s, the need for an amphibious capability has been recognised and fostered. The worst period was between the wars when the single Services squabbled unremittingly for scarce resources, and the amphibious capability reached a nadir. Ironically, the leading opponent of proposals to create a coherent central staff in those years was the influential Secretary of the Committee of Imperial Defence, Sir Maurice Hankey; an ex-Royal Marines officer. It is, however, perhaps no coincidence that the recent decisions to retain an amphibious capability have been taken in a MOD which had recently been substantially reorganised by Mr Michael Heseltine to strengthen the power of the Chief of the Defence Staff and the Central Staffs.

Finally, it would appear that the Soviet Navy embarked upon a programme to uprate the amphibious ships, hovercraft and the Naval Infantry in the late 1970s and early 80s. This was probably provoked by the approaching obsolescence of the ships laid down in the early 1960s, and might have been due to the influence of Admiral Gorshkov. His fall from grace and the adoption of a 'defensive doctrine' may well lead to a change in policy but, as yet, we do not know. The events in Eastern Europe during the last quarter of 1989 and since have had an inevitable affect upon the strategic situation. Coupled with the likely result of the arms control talks in Vienna the emphasis on the Central Front is almost bound to reduce. The role of amphibious forces, however, remains fundamentally unchanged. They must continue to be an essential ingredient of the defence forces of any modern state and of any alliance in what has now become a potentially unstable world, albeit that the nature of the threat to our security may be undergoing changes of which the final outcome is quite unpredictable as this book goes to press. One thing is certain, the need to be ready for the unexpected is greater than ever.

MODERN AMPHIBIOUS FORCES

We can now introduce the main amphibious forces, before looking at their potential employment. More details will be given in Part II.

United States of America

The USMC is about 196,000 men strong. Its main combat units are organised into two Fleet Marine Forces (FMFs). FMFLANT (Atlantic) is located on the East Coast and consists of one division, an air wing and a service support group. Its area of interest is Europe, the Caribbean and the Mediterranean. FMF Pacific consists of two divisions, two aircraft wings and two service support groups, based on the West Coast and in Okinawa which are dual tasked to Europe and the Far East.

The fighting organisation of the Marines is the Marine Air-Ground Task Force (MAGTF) which is tailored in size and structure for the particular situation. It is a combat organisation that fully integrates ground forces with air, naval gunfire, artillery and other supporting arms under the direction of a single commander. The composition and size of a MAGTF may vary, but each will always have four elements; the command element which provides a single headquarters for command and co-ordination of ground, air and combat support units. The ground elements, which may vary in size from a battalion to a division. The air combat element which includes air command and control, air defence units and service support units, together with as many fixed wing aircraft and helicopters as are needed for the mission and, finally, the service support element. This is tailored to provide supply, maintenance, transportation, medical and administration.

The smallest task force is the Marine Expeditionary Unit (MEU), built around an infantry battalion with helicopter and possibly AV-8 Harrier support. One MEU is usually deployed in its shipping, the Amphibious Readiness Group (ARG), in the Mediterranean and there are another two ARG/MEUs in the Pacific.

The next size up is a Marine Expeditionary Brigade (MEB), whose notional organisation is shown in Table 3.3.

The largest is a Marine Expeditionary Force (MEF) which could include 9 infantry battalions and a very large air wing of some 180 aircraft and 160 helicopters; its manpower could total 55,000. To put the strength of the force into perspective; the ground combat element does not have the firepower of a Soviet

TABLE 3.1

Outline Organisation of A Notional MEB

COMMAND ELEMENT
Commander, Brigadier General

GROUND COMBAT ELEMENT	AIR COMBAT ELEMENT	COMBAT SERVICE SUPPORT ELEMENT
Regiment (Reinforced)	**Marine Aircraft Group**	**Brigade Service Support Group**

2 to 5 Infantry Battalions
Artillery Battalion
Tank Company
Combat Engineer Company
Reconnaissance Company
AAV Company
TOW Platoon

Equipment	**Fixed Wing Aircraft**
24 81mm mortars	40 AV-8 V/STOL attack
	24 F-4 or F/A-18 fighter/attack
72 Dragon ATGW	10 A-6E all-weather/night attack
48 Tow ATGW	4 EA-6B Electronic Warfare
	4 RF-4B Photo-recce
138 .50 calibre machine guns	10 OV-10 observation
	6 KC-130 refuelling
24 155mm M198 (towed)	5 OA-4 tactical control
6 155mm SP (self-propelled)	**Helicopters**
6 Eight inch howitzers (self-propelled)	48 CH-46 medium lift assault
	16 CH-53 (A or D) heavy assault
17 M-60 tanks	16 CH-53E heavy lift assault
27 Light Armoured Vehicles (LAV)	12 AH-1 (W&T) attack
47 Assault Amphibian Vehicles (AAV)	12 UH-1N utility and C2
Amphibious Shipping	**Surface to Air**
Approx. 26 Ships	8 *Hawk* SAM launchers
	45 *Stinger* SAM teams
Manpower	**Sustainability**
Marines 15,000	30 days' worth of combat supplies
US Navy (medical, dental, etc.) 700	
US Navy Support Elements (SEAL, beach support) 1,250	
Total 16,950	

PLATE 3.5 Aircraft such as the F/A-18 *Hornet*, with a good air defence, fighter and attack capabilities, give the USMC MAGTFs a considerable fighting strength; here it is seen firing the *Sidewinder* air-to-air missile. It is, however, dependent upon fixed runways and the USMC would like, in the future, to have short take-off and landing (STOL) aircraft for all their close air support and interdiction. (*US Navy*)

Motor Rifle Division, but add in the firepower of the Air Wing and you have a very potent force.

At present there are some 65 amphibious ships in service. These are enough to lift only one MEF, including the air wing, although it is planned that by the mid-1990s there will be 76 ships able to lift about one MEF and a MEB, unless Defence cuts make inroads into this plan. The balance of the force would be deployed by merchant ships. . . . Ships Taken Up From Trade (STUFT), or by air to join up with its stockpiled or prepositioned equipment. Notwithstanding this apparent shortfall in shipping, the US amphibious fleet is still a most formidable force. There are, however, major long term concerns about the block obsolescence in the period 2000–2008 when 47 of the current ships come to the end of their 35-year service life.

A new element in the United States inventory is the Maritime Pre-positioning Ship (MPS) which is a converted civilian ship designed to carry a mix of heavy equipment, store and fuel. The first of these ships was introduced in 1984. There are three squadrons now in commission, deployed in the Eastern Atlantic, the Indian Ocean (based at the British island of Diego Garcia) and the Pacific. The 4 or 5 ships

TABLE 3.2

United States Navy: Amphibious Ships

Type	Class	Year	Number	Remarks
LPH	*Iwo Jima*	1961–70	7	First custom built helicopter ship. To be replaced by LHD in late 1990s
LHA	*Tarawa*	1976–80	5	
LHD	*Wasp*	1989–	1	Total programme planned as 10. 2 building
LPD	*Raleigh*	1962–3	2	Remain in service to 1997/8
LPD	*Austin*	1965–71	11	SLEP programme planned
LSD	*Anchorage*	1969–72	5	
LSD	*Thomaston*	1954–7	3	To be replaced by LSD-41. 5 more in reserve
LSD-41	*Whidbey Island*	1985–	6	2 building, total programme: 13 including 5 cargo carrying variants
LST	*Newport*	1969–72	18	2 more in reserve
LCC	*Blue Ridge*	1970–1	2	
LKA	*Charleston*	1968–70	5	Amphibious cargo ships

in each squadron carry sufficient to equip a fly-in MEB with its tanks, artillery and vehicles, and to maintain it in combat for 30 days.

United Kingdom and The Netherlands

The British amphibious forces are based upon 3 Commando Brigade Royal Marines and its associated amphibious shipping. For NATO operations this formation includes Dutch units, and is thus an excellent example of NATO interdependence. The parent organisations, the Royal Marines and the Royal Netherlands Marines Corps are about 7,500 and 3,000 men strong respectively. In the hope of avoiding some confusion about the naming of parts of this force, it is worth pointing out that it appears to have at least two titles:

> *The UK/NL Amphibious Force* (Table 3.3) is the title used for the shipping but, for obvious reasons, it includes the landing force when it is embarked, and it is commanded by the Commodore Amphibious Warfare (COMAW). The existing specialist shipping consists of the LPDs *Fearless* and *Intrepid*, plus the remaining four LSLs of the *Sir Lancelot* class and the new *Sir Galahad*. At present there is a considerable shortfall of shipping required for the landing force, as one LPD is usually not in commission, and there is little or nothing that can carry the helicopters. Therefore much reliance is placed upon STUFT.
>
> *The UK/NL Landing Force* refers, as its title suggests, to the fighting elements ashore. It is commanded by a Brigadier Royal Marines, and is about 7,000 strong including three Commandos Royal Marines and one Netherlands Amphibious Combat Group (all infantry battalion size). The artillery, engineers and part of the Logistic Regiment are provided by the Army, while the 24 support helicopters are manned by the Royal Navy and the 18 light helicopters by the Royal Marines. There are no armoured cars or tanks. Most of the force trains each winter in Norway in readiness for mountain and arctic operations.

TABLE 3.3

Outline Organisation of the UK/NL Amphibious Force

Shipping		*Commander:* Commodore		
Class	Type	Year	Number	Remarks
Fearless	LPD	1965–7	2	One in refit/reserve. Replacement being studied
Logistic Landing Ships	LSL	1964–8 1987	4 1	Crewed by Royal Fleet Auxiliary. After Falklands War, *Sir Tristram* rebuilt and *Sir Galahad* replaced

Landing Force

Commander: Brigadier

Headquarters and Signal Squadron

Infantry	Support Arms	Air/Air Defence
3 × Commando RM	Commando Regiment Royal Artillery (RA)	Air Squadron RM
Amphibious Combat Group (RNLMC)	Amphibious Observation Battery RA	2 × Naval Air Commando Squadrons RN
	120mm Mortar Battery RNLMC (1992)	*Rapier* Battery RA (1991)
	2 × Independent Commando Squadrons Royal Engineers (one TA)	Air Defence Troop
Reconnaissance	*Landing Craft*	*Logistics*
Special Boat Service Mountain and Arctic Warfare Cadre	Assault Squadron RM	Commando Logistics Regiment (includes RNLMC elements)

Equipment		
81mm Mortars MILAN ATGW DRAGON (RNLMC)	105mm Light Guns 120mm Mortars 4 × LCU 4 × LCVP 24 Rigid Raiding Craft	6 × *Lynx*/TOW 12 × *Gazelle* 24 × *Sea King* *Rapier* *Javelin* *Stinger* (RNLMC)

Manpower: Approx. 8–9,000   *Sustainability:* 30 days

The title 3 Commando Brigade Royal Marines is normally only used for British national operations . . . but then it can be called the UK Landing Force. No wonder the press never get any of the titles right! We will use the two main ones as far as pedantry will allow.

Other Western Forces

There are, of course, other Western nations with amphibious forces, although time and space precludes them from being central to this account. Most of them use

52 Amphibious Operations

PLATE 3.6 The Italian Navy's *San Giorgio* class are imaginative, cheap and versatile ships which could be used for amphibious, ASW support and disaster relief operations. The Italians have adapted the commercial *Lighter Aboard Ship* or LASH, concept for stowing their landing craft in the dock, by which one craft can be hoisted above another for passage. This saves space and cost, but the complexity of the stowage might present difficulties during fast moving amphibious operations. (*Jane's*)

Towards a Modern Capability 53

TABLE 3.4

Some Allied Amphibious Ships

Country	Type	Class	Year	Number	Remarks
France	*TCD 90	*Foudre*	1991	1	Building. Two more of class delayed to 1990s
France	BTS	*Bougainville*	1988	1	Pacific (rated as an auxiliary)
France	TCD	*Ouragan*	1965-8	2	Atlantic Fleet
Italy	LPD	*San Giorgio*	1987-8	2	Based at Brindisi
Spain	APA	*Castilla*	1958-61	2	Ex-US *Paul Revere* Class
	LST	*Velasco*	1952-3	3	Ex-US *Terreboune* Class

* TCD = LPD.

the same doctrine as the Americans, the British and the Dutch, agreed in one of those delphic NATO committees, and they regularly exercise with their allies. The Italians have a battalion-sized landing force called the San Marco Battalion Operational Group supported by two army battalions, the Serenissima, and two LPDs, including a new ship which we will look at later. Turkey has a brigade-sized force of naval infantry with their own amphibious shipping. Greece has the Hellenic Marine Regiment, Portugal the Corpo Fuzileros, and Spain the Infanteria Marina of 12,000 men.

The French have an amphibious potential with three ships, seven medium sized vessels and about 30 landing craft. They are building a new ship of the *Foudre* class which will be able to lift a mechanised regiment between them. The Rapid Reaction Force, which includes the 9th Marine Division, ostensibly provides the landing force, but it has been redesignated to a primary role on the Central Front, and the regular exercise with the amphibious ships in the Atlantic Fleet appear to be at battalion level. Some ships are used for servicing the French nuclear testing facility in the Pacific; there does not seem to be, at present, much more than a sea landing capability overall.

Warsaw Pact

The 16,000 men of the Soviet Naval Infantry and their amphibious shipping are divided among the four Fleets. Until about 1980, there was a brigade in the Far East and a regiment with the others. These have since been enlarged into a division of about 6,000 men with the Pacific Fleet, and brigades of some 3,000 men in each of the Baltic, Northern and Black Sea Fleets. In the north, 63rd Naval Infantry Brigade (ominously named 'Kirkenes') is reported[14] to be a Category A formation and thus at short notice for action. None the less it, like the others, might be expanded on mobilisation for war (say 9–11,000 for the division and 4,000 for the brigades). The balance of the manpower might be expected to be in reserve, in training or on the staffs.

The Naval Infantry Brigades are light by Soviet standards, although they are not issued with specially designed light equipment, unlike the equivalent airborne or heliborne formations. Even so, they pack quite a punch for their small numbers,

TABLE 3.5

Outline Organisation of a Soviet Naval Infantry Brigade

Headquarters
Signal Company

Infantry	**Support Arms**	**Air/Air Defence**
4 × Naval Infantry Battalions	Tank Battalion Multiple Rocket Launcher Battalion 122mm SP Howitzer Battalion Anti-Tank Battalion Engineer Company	Air Defence Battery

Reconnaissance		**Logistics**
Reconnaissance Company Chemical Defence Company		Supply Company Maintenance Company Medical Company

Equipment

About 90 BTR-60BP and BRDM 6 120mm mortars	A total of about 40 PT-76 amphibious tanks and T-54/55 or T-72 medium tanks 18 BM-14 17 tube/40mm or BM-21 40 tube 122mm multiple rockets 18 122mm SP howitzers 6 AT-3 or -5 SP anti-tank	4 ZSU-23-4 4 SA-7, -9 or -13

Manpower: approx. 3–4,000

TABLE 3.6

Estimated Numbers and Deployment of Soviet Amphibious Ships and Air Cushion Vehicles

Class	Type	Year	Total	Northern Fleet	Pacific Fleet	Baltic Fleet	Black Sea Fleet
Ivan Rogov	LPD	1976–83	2		2		
Alligator	LST	1966–77	14	2	5	2	5
Ropucha	LST	1975–89	24	6	9	7	2
Polnocny	LSM	1961–73	43	7	5	18	13
Aist	ACV	1970–	20				
Lebed	ACV	1975	18				
Tsaplya	ACV	1982	3				
Gus	ACV	1969–79	34				
Utenok	ACV	1980–1	2				
Pomornik	ACV	1986	3				
Approx. deployment ACVs			80	7	24	28	21
Poland							
Polnocny	LSM		23				
GDR							
Frosch	LST		12	Similar to *Ropucha* class with ramp instead of doors			

Note: A new class of LST is reported to be under construction at Gdansk in Poland, possibly to replace the *Ropucha* class.

PLATE 3.7 Soviet Naval Infantry on the beach with a BTR-60PB armoured personnel carrier in the background, it is armed with a 14.5mm MG and a 7.62MG mounted coaxially. The Brigade in the Northern Fleet is equipped with MT-LB (Multi-Purpose AFV) which has wide tracks for better mobility in snow and swamps, and has a single 7.62mm MG. (*Sovetskiy Voin*)

and this emphasises their concept of launching the landing force as a spearhead which must join up with the main ground forces within a few days; they have little sustainability. Unlike their Western counterpart, they have a good parachute assault capability, and this continues the practice established in the Great Patriotic War of close co-ordination between amphibious and airborne forces in *desants*. Today helicopters are also used, but these are not integral to the Naval Infantry.

The amphibious lift is still heavily dependent upon the older classes which do not have great range. To obtain more reach, the Soviets built the *Ropocha* class from 1976, these are smaller than the *Alligator* but have greater endurance. The largest and most capable amphibious ships are the *Ivan Rogov* class, but only two have been built since 1976. The Soviets also have a formidable array of Air Cushion

Vehicles (ACVs). Like all modern amphibious forces, they cannot carry the full first echelon of the landing force in one lift of specialist ships, but there are many auxiliary amphibious ships, including Roll on-Roll off vessels (Ro-Ros), to provide support.

In the Baltic, the Soviets have worked closely with the other amphibious forces, the Polish and East German. The former maintain the Polish Sea Landing Brigade which operate mainly out of *Polnocny* LSMs. The East Germans are somewhat of an enigma, since they own and run twelve LST of the *Frosch* class, but they do not appear to have any designated landing force. The loyalty of these two 'allies' must, of course, now be in some doubt.

4

A Maritime Strategy for Modern Amphibious Warfare

Amphibious operations are an integral part of a maritime strategy and, as such, are a means of exploiting sea control. An amphibious strategy as a separate entity is, in truth, inconceivable; not only have we seen that historically this is a somewhat ephemeral concept, but it would also deny the interrelationship, the seamless robe, between landings and the full gamut of naval operations.

It might be disputed whether amphibious warfare is an essential element of maritime strategy, in the sense that the Naval Staff of the 1930s and the immediate post-1945 era contemplated 'war as an affair on the high seas'; but this would effectively represent an untenable claim that naval warfare can by itself be decisive. Experience has shown that 'it is almost impossible that a war can be decided by naval action alone'[1] and Corbett, who said this, went on to explain that an overall national strategy must incorporate both the Army and the Navy, writing that, 'the importance of maritime power is its influence on military operations'.[2] The land forces can seize and hold ground, and it is the role of the naval and air forces to make this possible. Admiral Gorshkov developed this view in a manner that must have a wide application, and would have Corbett's approval: he explained that in the past the chief concerns of the navy used to be the defeat of the enemy fleet . . . but

> 'Since the goals of a war were achieved mostly by taking over the territory of an enemy, successful operations of fleet against shore brought a better result than the operations of fleet against fleet. In the first case, the fleet solved a direct *territorial* task, whereas in the second, victory over the enemy's fleet merely created the prerequisites for the later solution of territorial tasks.'[3]

Of course, operations against the shore are not solely amphibious, since maritime power can be projected by nuclear weapons, and by conventional air and missile strikes against ground targets. Moreover, landing operations could only be one relatively small part of a major land campaign.

Despite the recent changes in the international climate, the future remains as yet too uncertain for NATO to lower its guard and in the pages which now follow, the assumption that a threat to NATO from the East remains is sustained. Whether or not that threat becomes diminished, the principles involved in terms of strategic

58   Amphibious Operations

PLATE 4.1 A potent projection of sea power ashore; the battleship USS *New Jersey* firing a *Tomahawk* sea launched cruise missile from one of the eight armoured box launchers; this missile was aimed at a target some 500 miles away . . . (*US Navy*)

and, particularly, maritime doctrine, and hence the case for the maintenance of an amphibious force, are unchanged. As I have already suggested on page 47, in an unstable world, we can be sure of nothing and must be ready for anything.

The European view has been that the battles on the Central Front would be short, brutal and develop into a nuclear exchange within days or weeks, and that 'nuclear deterrence would prevent the USSR embarking on any military adventure, and the higher the risk of escalation to catastrophe, the stronger the deterrence'.[5] An American perspective might place less emphasis upon an early nuclear exchange which would deny Soviet hegemony over Europe but would threaten their own survival. It is beyond my scope to argue the chance of NATO ground and air forces in the Central Region, or to assess the political inhibitions about releasing nuclear weapons, but the longer that any war lasted, the more that naval pressure would tell as the greater potential economic and industrial power of the West, of the United States in the main, would be brought to bear on a global scale. Naval operations would have, in any event, a significant part to play in the outcome of the main battle, since much depends upon the successful delivery of reinforcements, arms and stores by the Sea Lines of Communications (SLOCs) from North

America. At the same time amphibious operations could show the value of 'a limited interference in unlimited war'. Before examining how this might be achieved, let us look at current Western maritime strategy.

THE FORWARD MARITIME STRATEGY

Naval warfare is inherently flexible since the strategic mobility of fleets enables them to contemplate a wide variety of tasks, any one or more of which might be employed in a future conflict. This is an operational strength, but it is also extremely difficult to translate into conceptual argument, especially when these debates are dominated by systems analysis, useful though such methods are. Norman Friedman has encapsulated this dilemma in writing:

> 'Navies usually succeed . . . by capitalising on their flexibility, on the very ambiguity of the threat they present. Analysis typically concentrates on how well naval forces will perform in a given type of engagement, because it is very difficult to model an enemy's response to the range of possibilities inherent in a particular naval force structure. Yet a reading of history strongly suggests that superior strategy, which may amount to an unexpected choice among potential forms of attack, can be decisive. This type of issue tends to arise less often in ground combat because the choices are fewer and more clear cut, due both to the limited mobility of forces and to the nature of terrain.'[6]

In simple terms; until very recently the Army could put its case in words of one syllable, the Royal Navy had a more complex task. The Army was faced with a relatively straightforward calculation in determining the nature of the future battle to be fought by 1 (BR) Corps on the Central Front. The threat was reasonably predictable, yet no less intimidating for all that, and the strength and organisation for the response could be assessed. The Royal Navy, with a wide diversity of potential threats and tasks, found difficulty in articulating its strategy, and for some years the argument went by default. It received so little notice, in comparison with some fixations upon the Central Front, that one was tempted to believe that a soldier feared that he would fall off the edge of the Earth once he ventured North of the Kiel Canal!

During the 1970s the favoured maritime strategy could be described as a combination of convoys to keep open the Sea Lines of Communication (SLOCs), together with a defensive barrier along the line of the Greenland/Iceland/UK (GIUK) Gap. In terms of the means to achieve sea control, this strategy was an expression of *Chokepoint Control* which is but one of four traditional conceptual options (described more fully by Geoffrey Till[7] in the first book in this series). It was an uncertain strategy, an essentially defensive one which, in its caution, appeared to lack the fundamental ability to make a positive response to aggression; from an earlier age, Corbett identified what was missing:

> 'Whatever advantages lie in defence they depend upon the preservation of the offensive spirit. Its essence is the counter attack—waiting deliberately for the chance to strike—not cowering in inactivity.'[8]

Till's fifth option, *Forward Operations*, was emphasised during the Reagan Administration as a global concept for using to best advantage the maritime strength of the US Navy to deter war with the Soviets and to achieve American objectives should deterrence fail. Although the underlying concept is not new, in that there are many examples in history of a broadly similar approach, it has been articulated a

PLATE 4.2 The USS *Nimitz* is one of the nuclear powered aircraft carriers which are an integral part of the US power projection capability. Carrier aircraft are indispensible to a full amphibious capability, and the lack of a Soviet carrier has for some years been an indication of their limited aspirations, although one has now been built. (*US Navy*)

freshness and clarity which has transformed the strategic debate. As described in 1986 by Admiral Watkins USN, then the chief of Naval Operations,[9] it has three main elements; peacetime presence, crisis response and warfighting. The first two of these concern American policy in peacetime and, although we will return to British and American perceptions of these activities in the next chapter, it is the warfighting element that is closely linked to NATO strategy.

Warfighting is divided into three phases; Deterrence and Transition to War, Seizing the Initiative, and Carrying the Fight to the Enemy. The general concept is wholly consistent with the NATO strategy of flexible response, incorporating as it does deterrence, forward defence and coalition warfare; the success of which is entirely dependent upon early political decisions to allow forward deployment both in the Central Region and on the Flanks. This is not intended as an aggressive strategy, since the forces would not be used except if attacked. If an attack took place, NATO's aim would be to resist for as long as possible without using nuclear weapons.

▶ In the first, *Deterrent*, phase NATO would seek to contain, as far north as possible, the Soviet threat from submarines capable of disrupting the shipping in the SLOCs and, in the case of those carrying cruise missiles, launching conventional or nuclear attacks on land targets. Another main aim would be the support of allies in the Northern region, Norway, Denmark and Iceland, by the early deployment of British and allied forces to Northern European Command. Much would also depend upon the prompt despatch of the US carrier battle Groups (CVBG) and amphibious forces into the North Norwegian Sea and its littoral, and this relationship between sea, air and land in this region has been described in these words:

▶ 'The Norwegian Sea and North Norway are inextricably linked; the loss of one could well lead to the loss of the other. Quite apart from the defence of Norway being an imperative in its own right, it is vital to prevent the USSR denying NATO the use of Norwegian airfields. . . . Forward maritime deployment, particularly of the Striking Fleet and submarines, would have a critical impact on deterring or fighting the battle for Norway.'[10]

▶ In the second phase, *Seizing the Initiative*, the aim would be to use US and allied maritime power to dominate the Soviet Navy in the Atlantic, the Pacific and elsewhere. Anti-submarine warfare would concentrate upon the destruction of Soviet submarines, while the CVBGs would secure the air defence of vital areas—Admiral Mustin, when Commander of the Striking Fleet Atlantic, developed techniques for operating carriers in Norwegian Fjords—and might entail conducting air strikes against Soviet bases.

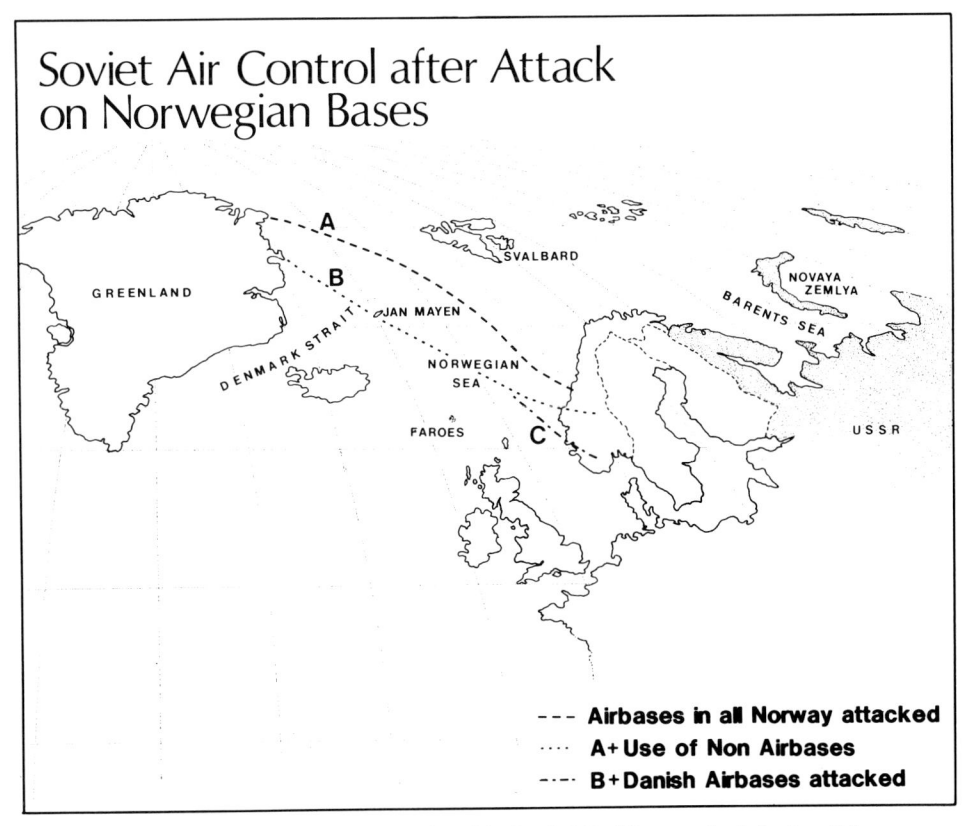

Soviet Air Control after Attack on Norwegian Bases

--- Airbases in all Norway attacked
···· A+Use of Non Airbases
-·-· B+Danish Airbases attacked

MAP 4.1 A series of maps produced by Lt Col Bo Hugemark of the Swedish Armed Forces showed the development of Soviet air control if its forces were to advance into Scandinavia. At the start Soviet air control would be limited to the Barents Sea east of Svalbard, but it could extend to the North Sea if all Scandinavian bases had been secured. This example shows the possible effects of (A) attacking all the Norwegian airfields using Soviet bases, or (B) seizing the North Norwegian airfields, or (C) extending the interdiction to NATO airfields in Denmark. Air power could be projected well to the south of these lines.
(*Source: Clive Archer and others, 'The Soviet Union and Northern Waters'*)

▶ In the third phase, *Carrying the Fight to the Enemy*, the allies would seek to create the conditions for war termination on favourable terms by extending the influence of maritime power to help roll back any Soviet gains.

This is a broad strategy, and its conduct is left to the commanders on the day. It offers a number of opportunities for amphibious forces to fulfil a valuable role in each of the phases, and is a framework for developing maritime support for ground operations by using manœuvre, initiative and offensive tactics. In the next section we will discuss how amphibious forces might be employed, looking not only at the more frequently discussed first two phases, but also postulating how they might continue to fight if a war did remain conventional in the later phases . . . for longer than many Europeans might otherwise expect.

AMPHIBIOUS WARFARE IN THE FORWARD MARITIME STRATEGY

Phase 1: Deterrence and Transition to War

The credibility of an amphibious force as a deterrent depends upon its readiness as a force-in-being; thus it has to be properly structured, organised, combat effective, self-sufficient, sustainable and . . . above all . . . trained. In a time of tension it could be sailed early with the fleet as a sign of national commitment of solidarity with allies, and at very short notice, as the Falklands campaign illustrated. This would probably be a well publicised event, which, in most cases, would probably suit the needs of the Government. In other circumstances, it might be politic to sail the force without publicity, but there must be some doubts whether this could be achieved without attracting the interest of the media.

As a capable force-in-being, it has a deterrent value out of proportion to its size and, like the Fleet, can be deployed forward. Its 'more or less unlimited mobility and ability to advance, withdraw, concentrate or disperse without violating frontiers or abandoning ground'.[11] offers the Government the opportunity to *poise* the force to make a wide range of political and strategic signals to the enemy; *poise* is 'the ability to hold the force in varying degrees of proximity to the objective area, uncommitted but ready to respond'.[12] It could remain in international waters, be recalled to home waters if tension abated, or disembark a landing force to bolster the deterrent value of local forces, one that could be re-embarked rapidly to meet political demands.

Given the Soviet emphasis upon strategic and operational surprise, NATO might not, however, have the opportunity to operate the full range of sophisticated and graduated responses to steadily mounting tension. The main challenge would be to recognise the confused signals of the impending threat in sufficient time to issue the warnings and take the early political decision to mobilise. In this case, speed of deployment *per se* might serve as a deterrent, but the main objective would be to man the forward defences before the first invading forces struck. In this the first task of the Anglo-Dutch and some of the American amphibious forces in the Atlantic Command would still be to mount a convincing deterrent showing alliance intent, but at the same time moving directly into position to help secure the land flank for the NATO fleet operations in the North Norwegian Sea. The UK/NL Amphibious

PLATE 4.3 A good illustration of the harsh Norwegian terrain, with its steep sided valleys, narrow roads, and fjords which offer considerable opportunities to the mobility of amphibious forces. (*Royal Marines*)

Force might be deployed to any part of the North Atlantic or North Sea littoral, but North Norway is a likely option.

The Importance of North Norway

In the 1960s and early 1970s there was a fear of a Soviet land grab in Finnmark, but this faded as it was recognised that the cost/benefit analysis weighed against such adventures, and that the attack in this region was more likely to be dependent upon Soviet aims in the Central Region. Subsequently, the rapid growth of the Soviet Northern Fleet threatened the Atlantic SLOCs, so it began to be realised that the defence of North Norway was fundamental to control of the Atlantic. This area is close to the major Soviet submarine bases in the Kola peninsula and to their bastions for SSBN operations in the Barents Sea. The Russians therefore need to ensure that the NATO fleets cannot operate freely in the North Norwegian Sea and, towards this end, they would wish to capture the surveillance posts, ports and airfields in North Norway. This would give them the opportunity to win air control over that sea, would help their efforts to interdict the passage of American reinforcements across the Atlantic, and would allow them to intercept one of the direct air and missile routes from North America to their homeland. Admiral Staveley has pointed out that, if we lost this area and gave the Soviet Navy free rein

64   Amphibious Operations

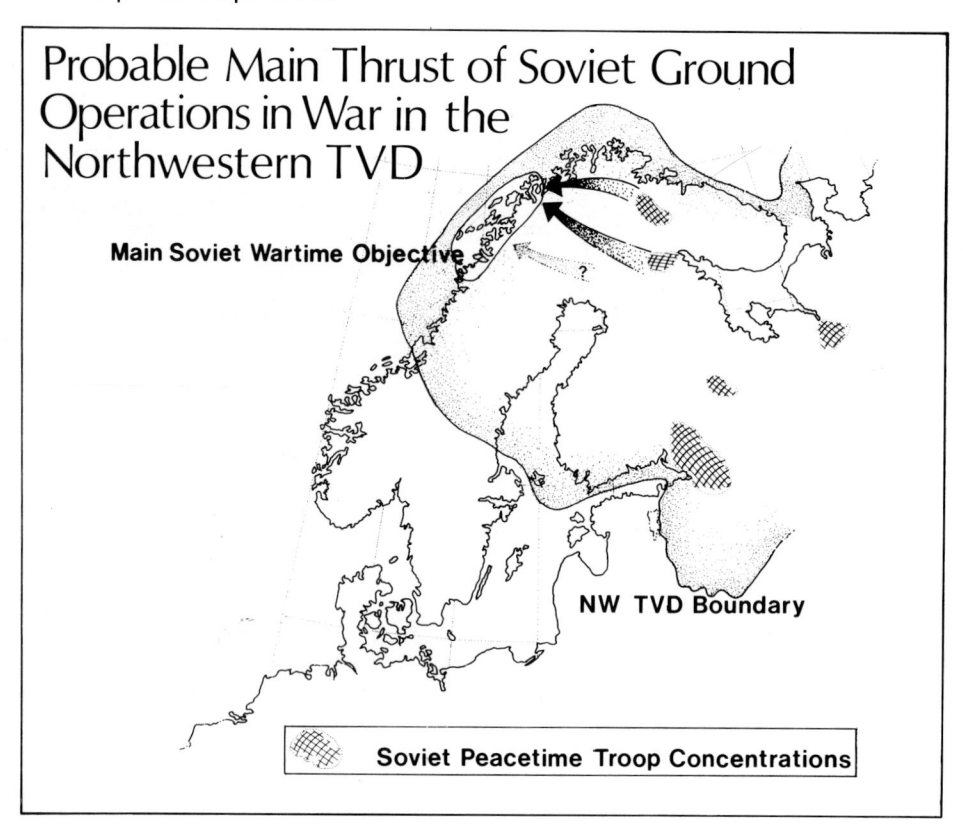

Probable Main Thrust of Soviet Ground Operations in War in the Northwestern TVD

Main Soviet Wartime Objective

NW TVD Boundary

Soviet Peacetime Troop Concentrations

MAP 4.2   Soviet attack options in North Norway. (*Source: Archer*)

north of the Greenland–Iceland–Norway Gap, 'their front line would be closer to this country than the inner German border: that is a prospect I would not relish'.[13] With these perceptions, and with the importance of the forward maritime strategy, there has been a growing realisation in some Defence circles that:

> 'the defence of the Northern European Command would be fundamental to the success of the battle of the Atlantic and therefore, by extension, to any war in central Europe'.[14]

The Re-inforcement of North Norway

In a rapid response to a crisis, one of the first elements to arrive would be the UK/NL Amphibious Force. Shortly afterwards, a USMC airlanded MEB would start to land in Central Norway, marry up with its stockpile of heavy equipment and deploy. Again, a likely destination is North Norway. Given that the Soviets would need some days to move additional forces into the Kola area before launching an attack, these NATO reinforcements would probably be in place in time, but it might be a close run thing. If the Americans can send an airlanded brigade, why should the British and Dutch not do the same?

The Americans would gain a considerable amount of time by an air deployment, ahead of the amphibious forces sailing across the Atlantic, whereas the British would not. Writing in *Jane's Naval Review*, Joseph Porter[15] has estimated that it would take some 500 C-13 *Hercules* sorties to despatch the UK/NL Landing Force to Norway, and even then it would be on light scales without most of its supporting arms. This task would hardly be practicable, given the other commitments of RAF Strike Command at this time. Such a large bill would also severely tax the capacity of the reception airfields in North Norway, especially as they would be overloaded with the national mobilisation forces coming from South Norway, and the reception of Norwegian and Allied air force reinforcing squadrons.

Even assuming that these difficulties could be overcome, by the time that the aircraft had been assembled, the troops moved to airfields in the United Kingdom, the force concentrated after arrival in Norway and deployed to its operational area, any apparent advantages of the flight time over the sea passage would have been lost . . . and the heavy equipment would still have to be sent by sea to be offloaded in the small local ports and moved to joint the main body. There might be a few advantages in establishing stockpiles in the north to avoid the need for this seaborne support, but it would be prohibitively costly to provide a second scale of equipment for the brigade, and it could be rendered useless if Norway proved not to be the chosen theatre; indeed, it would be a hostage to fortune. The amphibious force has considerable advantages in its strategic mobility, its ability to carry the heavy support equipment and main war stocks for the brigade, and its capability to land the operational units for early commitment to tactical operations to meet the local NATO commanders concept, without having to rely on a 'red carpet' of secure ports and airfields demanding a great deal of host nation support.

Liddell Hart summed up the balance between airborne (he was referring to 'airlanded' forces in the modern terminology) and amphibious forces in an article he wrote in 1960:

> 'on a superficial view, airborne forces may be a better counter, as being quicker to arrive. But their speed of strategic movement, and effect on arrival, are subject to many limitations . . . an airborne force is limited in the vehicles, heavy weapons and ammunition it can carry. If it is held up and has to wait for these requirements to arrive by sea, it loses its main advantage, rapidity of intervention.
>
> While it is desirable to have an airborne force, which enables quicker intervention where its use is possible, it is essential to have a marine force, and better that this is to be the bigger of the two. . . . An amphibious force of the modern type, operating from the sea and equipped with helicopters, is free from dependence upon airfields . . . ports and land bases with all their logistical and political complications . . .'[16]

In summary; the UK/NL Amphibious Force, the airlanded MEB, the Norwegian mobilisation forces and the other allied reinforcements complement each other in making use of all forms of transportation to reach a remote but vital area of operations.

Global Mobilisation

A British view tends naturally to concentrate upon maritime operations in the North, but the Maritime Strategy is a global concept. In brief, the US naval and amphibious forces would deploy into the Western Pacific to reassure and defend America's many allies in that area, and to seek to hamper the reinforcement of the Soviet offensive on the Central Front. There are opportunities for amphibious

66   Amphibious Operations

operations on the coasts and islands of the Pacific littoral, although it has been estimated[17] that the Soviet Naval Infantry Division there would be held back to defend important naval installations, to reinforce isolated lightly defended outposts, or to retake territory seized by enemy forces; all essentially defensive operations. In the Mediterranean there is scope for NATO amphibious operations in Turkish Thrace or the Dardanelles—which could also be an objective for the Soviet Naval Infantry brigade in the Black Sea.

Phase 2: Seizing the Initiative

Amphibious Operations in the North

Once they had arrived in North Norway, the amphibious forces might be used to bolster the local ground defences. This would probably be the task of the airlanded MEB since it will not have any shipping, yet its air element, although remaining an integral part of the MEB, will be a welcome addition to the theatre air defences, and its helicopters will give it tactical mobility. It is less certain, however, that it

PLATE 4.4   The two linchpins of tactical mobility for the UK/NL Amphibious Force in the fjords. First, the *Sea King* HC4 which is able to carry some 24 men (less with arctic equipment), or an underslung load such as a landrover or 105mm Light Gun. (*Royal Navy. Crown copyright*)

PLATE 4.5 Secondly, the LCU Mk 9. With its canopy and integral heating system, it can be used for a variety of roles, including deploying forces some distances in arctic weather, as a command post, or for evacuating casualties. (*Royal Marines. Crown copyright*)

would be wise to land the UK/NL Landing Force from the outset, or the amphibious MEB should it be deployed to North Norway when it arrives from the United States some days later.

The terrain in the north favours the defender, with the mountains and steep valleys canalising the attacker so that he cannot use the sweeping armoured tactics which have been designed for the plains of the central Front. There are very few roads and the main one, the narrow and tortuous E6, runs close to the sea for much of its length. Indeed, the sea, with long fjords reaching far inland, is a very telling factor in this area. An advance by land will thus be severely constrained, lines-of-communication for logistics will be long and vulnerable, and much may depend upon the imaginative use of amphibious, airborne, and helicopterborne *desant* operations. The defending forces would be able to establish strong blocking positions at main choke points, but they would also need a mobile reserve.

History has shown the potential value of an amphibious force-in-being, embarked in its ships, or ashore at short notice to move, to present a continuing threat to an enemy's long sea flank. The ships could hide in the fjords, tucked up close to the steep mountains which reach right down to the edge of the water, but moving regularly either to close with the enemy, or as a matter of operational prudence. The landing force could be put ashore from time to time for training, without affecting the force's availability.

Good tactical mobility by helicopters and landing craft enable the UK/NL Landing Force to react quickly to harass the enemy's advance by attacking

68 Amphibious Operations

PLATE 4.6 The escorts fought a brave battle at San Carlos in 1982, but there were casualties, including HMS *Antelope* seen here sinking after being hit and her back broken in an air attack. The crews of the STUFT and Royal Fleet Auxiliaries won praise for their willingness to continue working on the offload during the air attacks, and here are the Ro-Ro ferry *Norland* with the RFA *Stromness* astern. (*Royal Navy. Crown copyright*)

opportunity targets near the coastline, to respond to *desant* operations, or to counter enemy penetration of the main blocking positions of the ground forces. A light, well balanced landing force with its helicopters, landing craft and its readily available logistic support afloat could cause considerable disruption to an enemy seeking to overcome the difficult terrain and weather; this would lead him to exercise caution, and to disperse his fighting units to guard extensive lines-of-communication. An amphibious force could thus be a significant factor in the concept of operations, and this was illustrated by not only the successes, but also the missed opportunities, of amphibious operations in Norway in 1940 and in 1944. As the Allies discovered in 1940, much can be achieved with good intelligence, adequate amphibious resources and a positive approach, but the air threat would be a major concern, and it is essential that both the sea and land elements have a capable integral air defence, to underpin the cover provided by the air forces.

The Vulnerability of Amphibious Forces

The critics of the amphibious capability have pointed out that the ships are vulnerable and, indeed, John Nott has said

A Maritime Strategy for Modern Amphibious Warfare 69

> 'in the age of the stand off missile, we apparently now envisage amphibious landings and command and control, during hostilities with the Soviets, being exercised out of a Norwegian fjord by the successors of *Fearless* and *Intrepid*. No one denies the importance of northern Norway, but replacing the amphibious ships is sheer sentimentality for the traditional role of the Royal Marines; it is unsupportable by rigorous analysis.'[18]

Undoubtedly, there would be risks in despatching the Amphibious Force to Norway if hostilities had already broken out, in manœuvring it around the fjords to conduct landings, and in redeploying it to other parts of Northern European Command. It is sometimes overlooked, however, that *all* armed forces are vulnerable in war, and this leads to quaintly illogical polemics such as the allegation, spotted by John Lehman when US Secretary of the Navy, that navies (capable of steaming at 30 knots) are said to be vulnerable while stockpiles (placed nearer to the enemy and moving at 0 knots) are not. A similar view could apply to the vulnerability of the airfields; they might not sink when bombed, but recently offloaded stores are as comprehensively destroyed as any equipment subjected to fierce aerial attack on any battlefield.

These risks must, however, be weighed in the light of the prevailing situation; the perception of the enemy threat, the geography of the region, the weather and the measure of sea and air control that the allied maritime forces and land based air forces have achieved. At the time of the landings in the Falklands War the Commodore Amphibious Warfare did not have the level of sea and air control that were believed initially to be the prerequisites for an operation of that kind. Yet he had a good feel for the balance of forces and was sufficiently confident of his ability to operate his shipping safely in a hostile environment. Despite the inherent disadvantages, shortage of air defence aircraft, no airborne early warning aircraft, limited ground based air defence and escorts which were not practised in inshore air defence operations, the Task Force succeeded in defeating the Argentinian Air Force. Sadly, some escorts were lost in their brave battle of attrition, but barely anything of significance to the landing force was touched. The chief operational penalty was the time lost in disembarking the logistic support, since the number of amphibious ships in the anchorage had to be kept to the minimum, and the remainder had to be moved away to the 'outfield' for safety.

The challenge in a continental war would undoubtedly be more severe, and use of the open ocean as an 'outfield' would not be possible. It is also unlikely that the Soviets would ignore, as the Argentinians did, the ancient adage for attacking amphibious forces, 'The transports of your enemy are to be your principal objective.'[19] We will consider the methods of protecting the amphibious task force in more detail in Part 2, and Geoffrey Till has also addressed the issue of the vulnerability of surface ships in his introductory volume.[20] But it should suffice to make two points at this stage:

▶ The amphibious forces would be working within the umbrella of theatre air and maritime defences and, indeed, of the one or more powerful carrier battle groups of the Striking Fleet.

▶ The complex geography of the Norwegian Leads offers a great deal of natural protection against even the most predatory enemy. Moreover, this is reinforced by the network of local coastal defences, covered by sophisticated forts.

70 Amphibious Operations

PLATE 4.7 HMS *Fearless* camouflaged and anchored close to the steep sides of a fjord; a difficult target to identify and engage from the air. *(Royal Navy. Crown copyright)*

AMPHIBIOUS OPERATIONS IN NORWAY: SECOND WORLD WAR

British and French Operations: April–June 1940

After the Germans seized the major Norwegian ports with their surprise assault on 9 April 1940 (see Map 2.2), the British responded by dispatching three ill-prepared forces to support the Norwegians. In Central Norway the two brigades, one landing at Namsos and the other at Aldalsnes, were defeated within the month by German forces advancing from Trondheim and Oslo respectively. In the North the allied French and British force fared better at first as the Royal Navy defeated the German destroyer flotilla in the Battle of Narvik. The subsequent operations were conducted in somewhat ponderous fashion and it was not until late May that Narvik was taken, and even then the Allies had to withdraw when the major defeats in France rendered the Northern campaign irrelevant.

In this campaign neither side held any specialist amphibious ships and large over-the-beach assault capability, so landing operations were bound to be small scale unless directed against a weakly defended port. None the less, the example of how to project power ashore was set by the Germans, both in the invasion and

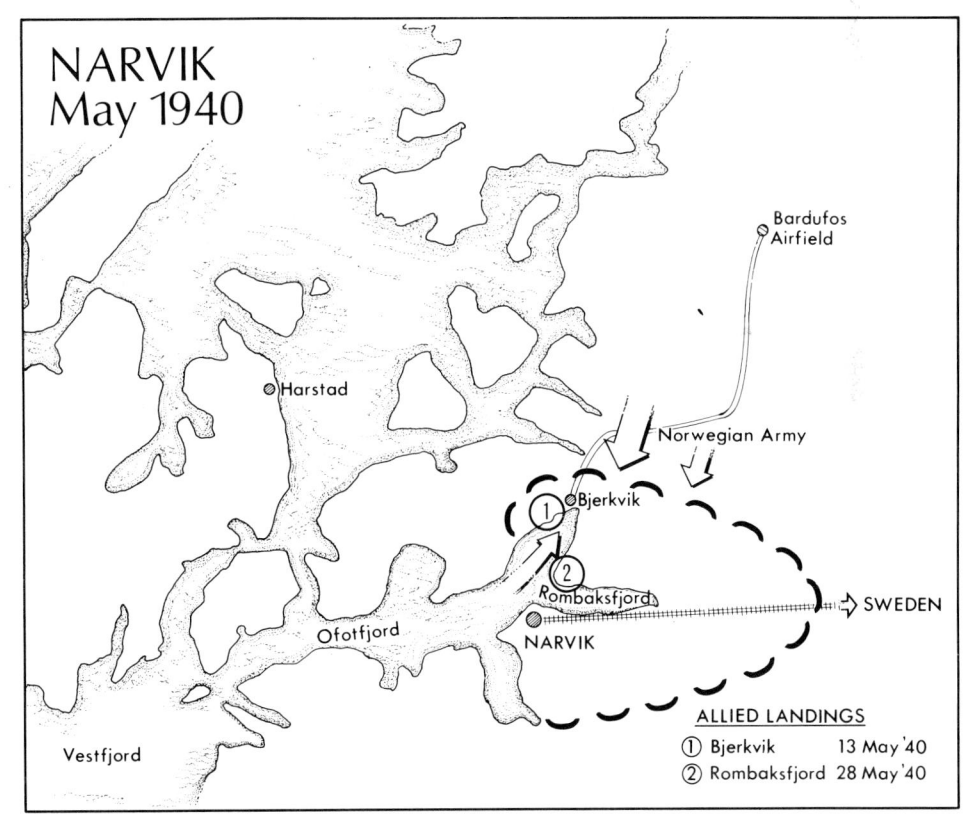

MAP 4.3 The Narvik Campaign 1940

PLATE 4.8 French troops shortly after the landing at Bjerkvik May 1940. (*RM Museum*)

subsequently when they showed a good appreciation of the tactical potential of the sea flank in land operations. The first indication of this occurred during the Namsos battle, when a battalion was landed from a merchant ship to the rear of the British forces. They used this tactic again on the advance north from Namsos when they outflanked the defenders at Mosjoen by landing forces by ship and by seaplane. The British showed less imagination and it was disappointing that they did not make best use of their command of the sea to mount amphibious operations, especially in the fjords of the north.

After the naval battle, the German mountain troops in Narvik were vulnerable to a quick attack, but no contingency plans for such an operation had been made, nor was the fleet trained for landing operations. In these circumstances, an opposed landing in deep snow by a scratch force of sailors and marines would indeed have been a gamble and it is difficult to condemn the British for failing to attempt it.

Once an Allied base had been established at Harstad, Norwegian inshore trawlers, nicknamed 'Puffers', and newly available landing craft were used to deploy Allied troops and logistic support around Ofotfjord. General Mackesy ruled that an opposed landing to assault on Narvik would be unsound but, even if this was a sound judgement, the failure to harrass the tenuous German lines-of-communication was disappointing.

It was not until almost a month later that the first aggressive tactical landing took place at Bjerkvik, and even then the assault force was the Chasseurs Alpins who were trained for desert rather than amphibious warfare. Thereafter the French Foreign Legion conducted a further landing, so at long last Narvik was captured, and the Germans driven up to the Swedish border. These two operations showed, however, what could be done with only limited assets, in this case four assault landing craft and two motor landing craft, provided that the timing and objective were carefully selected to ensure minimal opposition on landing.

Soviet Operations: 1941–44

In August 1941 the Soviets on the Murmansk front used rapidly mobilised ad hoc 'naval infantry'... some army units, but also crews of submarines, naval cadets and shipyard workers... to make two amphibious landings behind the German advance. The second and larger force, at about 1,500 strong, was landed successfully by day from trawlers, patrol ships and launches, and harassed the enemy's rear for some three weeks.

By the time the Soviets launched the attack on Pechenga and Kirkenes in October 1944, the Naval Infantry had been properly formed and, during the weeks before the offensive, there had been intensive reconnaissance of the coastline, rehearsals and preliminary air strikes. Two days after the start of the main ground forces offensive, some 3,000 men of 63 Naval Infantry Brigade (which is still based at Pechenga) landed at night from MTBs and fast submarine chasers to seize Maativuono Bay. The operation included a demonstration landing as a diversion, and gunfire support from land artillery. It was a successful flanking attack, and the Naval Infantry soon fought its way to link up with the main advance. Once the

PLATE 4.9 Soviet Naval Infantry disembark from a trawler on an enemy held coast in 1942; the Soviets did not develop specialist shipping or craft during the war. (*RM Museum. Crown copyright*)

74 Amphibious Operations

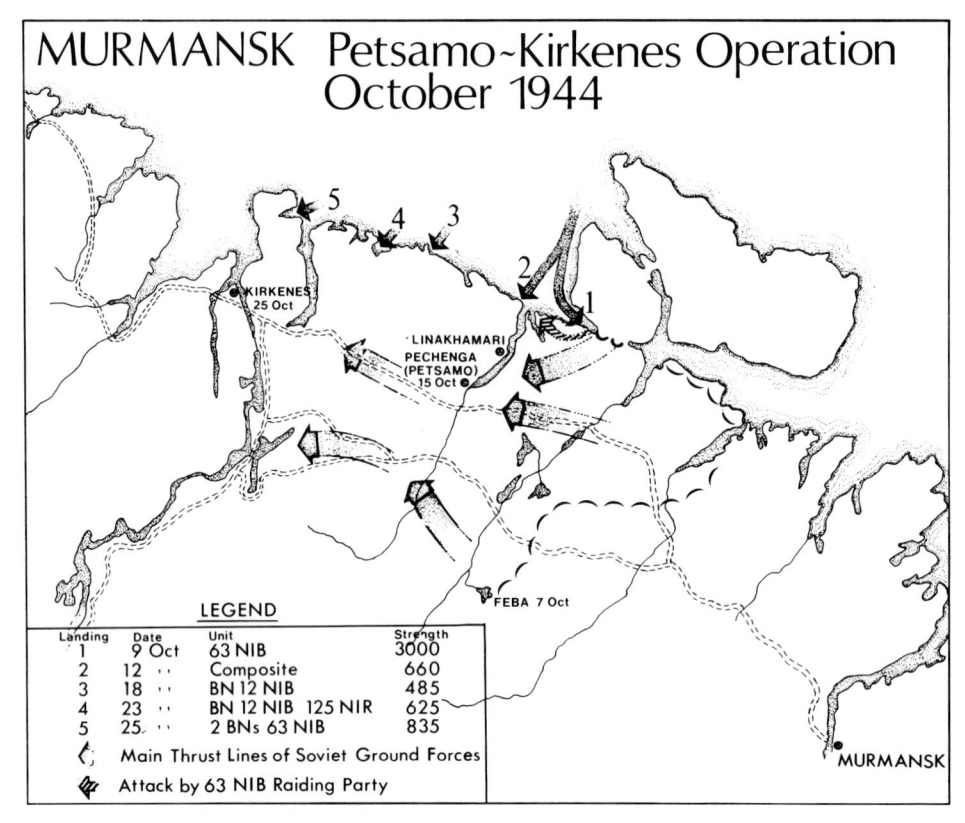

MAP 4.4 The Soviet campaign at Murmansk in 1944; the amphibious operations were closely linked to the main ground forces advance. Note: NIB = Naval Infantry Brigade.

objective had been secured, a 195 man strong raiding party was despatched to seize the batteries overlooking Linakhamari Harbour some 30 km away.

The overall commander, Admiral Golovko, seems to have had a partially formed plan for exploiting the party's success but, surprisingly, no forces were readily available. Undaunted, the Admiral hurriedly assembled an ad hoc battalion-sized force to make the second landing and Pechenga was taken. Thereafter the Naval Infantry battalions were used to conduct three more landings during the campaign, mainly to secure coastal batteries, although one battalion also joined up with a rifle regiment to clear the route west of the Norwegian border.[21]

A Maritime Strategy for Modern Amphibious Warfare 75

Northern Region—Soviet Options

In contingency planning, there is often an apparent and unjustified desire to claim a degree of certainty about the future. The course of events in Phase 2 of the Maritime Strategy will essentially be uncertain, so the timing and level of the commitment of amphibious forces will be the result of many influences. My speculation in the following paragraphs represents only some of the options discussed in open sources.

Even though North Norway is expected to be a most likely scene of operations, it is by no means certain that the enemy would press ahead with a land offensive there. Dr Tomas Ries,[22] for example, has suggested that the Soviets would face stern opposition from the Norwegian Army in the Lyngen area (a natural defensive bastion which the Germans fortified in 1944/45 to block any Soviet penetration after the Wehrmacht's withdrawal from Finnmark and Finland; in the event, no battle was fought there). If the full quota of NATO reinforcements had arrived, this might prove to be a costly operation, so the Soviets might deem it enough to attempt to neutralise the airfields and ports by heavy air interdiction, and not advance overland.

Other possible scenes of conflict could be the Atlantic Islands, such as Madeira, the Azores, Greenland and Iceland[23] which might have to be defended by amphibious or airlanded forces to underpin the Atlantic SLOCs. It might also be necessary to seize Jan Mayen Island, Bear Island and the Svalbard Archipelago, since possession of these could further strengthen the allied ability to prosecute the anti-submarine warfare campaign in the north. The campaign might well encompass South Norway, where the possibility of a major assault in the early stages of the war has been seen as very unlikely but, as CINCNORTH—General Howlett—has observed 'As Sweden's defences weaken, the odds against such an avenue of attack, especially in the air, must reduce, and we should be unwise to ignore the threat.'[24]

In the Baltic, Soviet and other Warsaw Pact amphibious forces could play a part in an attack on Sweden or South Norway, but the more conventional view is that they would support the attack on BALTAP, with the prize of a NATO capital, Copenhagen, in prospect. They could launch *desants* ahead of the main ground forces attack from Pomerania, or land on one of the important islands, such as Zealand, to secure the exist from the Baltic. Success would ensure protection for the right flank of the advance on the Central Front, and would provide airfields from which to mount air strikes against both the centre and the United Kingdom.

South Norway and BALTAP—NATO Responses

For NATO to position forces to face such a plethora of threats to its Northern Flank would demand more troops than are available, so intra-theatre flexibility is essential if the commanders are to be able to concentrate their effort at the critical point. The amphibious forces have an important part to play in this. Should BALTAP be judged to be the more threatened area from the outset, the UK/NL Amphibious Force could be deployed there initially. Alternatively, should it be in

PLATE 4.10 USS *Ticonderoga* is an *Aegis* cruiser, here seen firing the *Harpoon* anti-ship missile. With their long range sensors, fast reaction times, and the ability to track many targets simultaneously, passing the information to other ships, these are the most capable platforms for fighting the anti-air and surface battles. (*Jane's*)

North Norway and the attack there failed to materialise, it could be redeployed southwards as the situation demands. You need little imagination to realise that there is a stark contrast between the type of campaign in Norway, especially north of the Arctic Circle, and that in Denmark and Schleswig-Holstein, where tanks have better going and the flat coastline offers scant protection for amphibious ships. Yet the broken country does not allow armour an easy passage and infantry with anti-tank missiles could fight a sturdy defence. Moreover, the threat from Soviet amphibious and air borne forces puts a premium upon defensive forces with good mobility; just as the aggressor could use the sea flank to further his cause, so could the defender. The landing force would play a useful part in the battle.

The most potent amphibious forces for the campaign would be provided by the USMC, who would be most likely to deploy as MEBs which could be employed singly, or form a MEF. These would include the airlanded MEB which we have already met, a MPS MEB which would fly in to join up with its equipment carried in the MPS squadron, and an amphibious MEB capable of executing an opposed assault from the sea against a hostile shore.[25] The timing for the committal of these forces is a major command decision, and the USMC view is that:

> 'While NATO's armies are containing the assault in Central Europe, every effort will be made to retain amphibious forces for employment at the decisive point and time when the Soviets have lost their momentum and are therefore most vulnerable. This does not preclude the use of Marine Air Ground Task Forces (MAGTFs) to support a NATO defence which is *in extremis* on the English Channel coast. As ever, Marines will fight where they are needed most. We believe, however, that the employment of amphibious MAGTFs in a sustained land warfare role compromises their unique capability for flexible maneuver and, therefore, should be avoided.'[26]

What part could a MEF play in a continental war? The initial fighting will be extremely brutal, and every trained man will be needed. Thus the power of a MEB could be thrown into the balance as soon as it arrives, and certainly the concept of keeping it in reserve is incredible to some pundits who expect that it would be landed to move to the front in a ground holding role. Its flexibility should, none the less, be brought into play, perhaps in a role similar to a Soviet concept; landing a brigade behind the advancing forces to create the time and space for NATO ground forces to counter attack.

Phase 3—Carrying the Fight to the Enemy

One American view [27] is that both sides will expend their sophisticated technological armoury so quickly that, provided the war remains non-nuclear, an impasse will be reached. Thereafter the decision will depend upon which side can reconstitute its forces more quickly, regain the initiative and fight for the conditions which would lead to war termination. There is an underlying conviction in this thesis that NATO *can* stem the initial thrust, although from the outset it may have to be prepared to surrender ground to ensure that it can keep its major forces in being, since, in the long term, it has the advantage of the massive American industrial powerbase to ensure the more rapid regeneration. In this *long war* scenario, which links into the forward maritime strategy, the United States and their allies would expect to achieve widespread sea control.

It would thus justify a decision to keep the amphibious forces in reserve intially, so that they could later exploit the maritime successes by applying pressure of the vulnerable flanks and rear of the enemy, not only in Norway and the Baltic, but also in Thrace and the Black Sea. Such widely separated target areas are not unrealistic, bearing in mind that large naval forces could move up to 500 miles each day. *In extremis*, it might even be necessary to move some or all of the US amphibious forces from the Pacific, to join the British, Dutch and American elements already in Europe, to create 'an enormous maritime Juggernaut' of perhaps three MEFs, one fully amphibious, with rapid reinforcement by the others, able to make a significant contribution at the focal point of a global war. Much would depend upon the relative importance of the Pacific and European theatres and the perceptions of the need to maintain amphibious formations in the Far East where they might be used in operations in, for example, the Kuriles.

Even with such a concentration of amphibious strength, the purpose should remain to constrain the invading enemy forces by unbalancing his strategy. The amphibious task forces, together with supporting battleship surface action groups, could undertake landings to retake conquered territory and seize key objectives in the Soviet rear, which might include the North Cape or the Eastern Baltic.[28] If the aim was to secure the termination of war, then it might not be wise to threaten the homeland itself, with all the diplomatic and military implications of such an adventure.

In the end, as Dr Colin Gray has pointed out; *if* deterrence fails; *if* the battle of the Central Front is lost; *if* intra-war nuclear deterrence holds and; *if* neither side regards that as the end of the matter . . . 'then the maritime perspective provides a framework for the potentially global conduct of hostilities'.[29] Under those almost incredible circumstances, we might again see the build up of the massive amphibious forces which General Bradley had in 1949 consigned to the oblivion of history.

CONCLUSION

The Forward Maritime Strategy has given much greater coherence to the concepts of NATO's maritime forces and, in particular, has led to a realistic development of the employment of amphibious forces. Their value has been long established in the deterrence role, but their role thereafter needed careful consideration; NATO's first requirement is to man the forward defences to repel the initial attacks, but amphibious forces do not easily fit into this stage of the concept, as they are not structured specifically for ground holding against the first echelon (although, in the event, they will, of course, fight where they are most needed). Yet it is fundamentally important to maintain a reserve, and this role offered scope for the employment of mobile forces able to intervene at the pressure points on the littoral, not only at the strategic level, but increasingly—a significant development—at the operational and tactical levels. As the maritime strategy has evolved, and experience has been gained on exercises, so the practical value of this approach (which may have stronger roots in the Soviet *desant* than in the major landings of the Second World War), has been recognised as having a proper place in the overall NATO strategy of forward defence and flexible response.

5
Limited Global Operations

Notwithstanding the overriding importance of preparing to face a continental war, hard experience has taught that conflict must be expected to occur more frequently elsewhere in the world, and that many of these instances have a maritime dimension. Since the withdrawals of the Americans from Vietnam and of the British from East of Suez, Western nations have sought to restrict intervention operations to a more limited, almost surgical concept, not dependent upon politically vulnerable bases which could lead to lengthy and debilitating commitments. The ability to respond in such crises has demanded a greater subtlety of approach and, as Sir James Cable has commented about maritime operations:

> 'Limited naval force is only applicable in particular and rather unusual circumstances. It is not an all purpose tool, but a screwdriver and, as such, can be a miserable failure in hammering home a nail.'[1]

Navies can conduct a wide range of lower level peacetime operations without recourse to amphibious warfare; their programme of ships visits can reinforce diplomatic links, the deployment of ships to sensitive areas can play a deterrent role as a part of coercive diplomacy, and there have been several instances, such as the international operation in the Gulf, where disagreements have been expressed chiefly through the purposeful use of limited naval force on the high seas. But, if they wish to be able to project influence ashore in peacetime, then amphibious forces provide the flexible tool they seek. Those characteristics that we have seen in the NATO role apply with equal, and perhaps greater, effect to peacetime operations:

▶ A relatively small amphibious force can be used to make resounding political signals when a crisis disturbs the peace. It can be sailed to demonstrate national resolve, can poise during negotiations and be diverted, withdrawn or committed as the situation demands.

▶ The force need not be used offensively, and its tasks might include disaster relief, the evacuation of nationals, international peacekeeping, and as a deterrent in contingency support of friendly governments under threat.

▶ The force could be used to apply whatever level of pressure best serves the diplomatic interest. It could mount small special forces operations or land

80　Amphibious Operations

PLATE 5.1　Port visits are an integral part of the practice of maritime diplomacy, and here HMS *Beaver* is illuminated on the Far East deployment *Global 86*. She is a Batch 2 Type 22 and has no gun; as a result of experience in the Falklands, the ships in batch 3 of the class were each fitted with a gun to provide naval gunfire support. (*Royal Navy. Crown copyright*)

balanced and logistically sustainable forces without having to rely upon local ports or airfields. The structure of the formation can be tailored to meet the type of conflict; perhaps depending largely upon infantry for counter-insurgency operations, or a heavier force with armour and artillery for more conventional use. Once the task is complete, they can be withdrawn rapidly. Sir James Cable has commented that

> 'Amphibious operations do not have to attempt total conquest to exert their impact and, the smaller the scale, the easier they would be to launch.'[2]

The ability to conduct any of these operations from a base at sea eliminates the political, economic and social damage that can be provoked by the presence of large support elements ashore. The tactical elements of the landing force can be kept to the essential minimum, relying on logistic backup by helicopters, hovercraft or landing craft. This reduces the need for infantry units to guard shore bases, denying insurgents a prime target, and thus helping to ensure the security of the force.

PLATE 5.2 MPS ships are a rarity amongst civilian ships adapted for military use, as they have been specially tailored to the task; they are roll-on/roll-off multi purpose ships that can each carry part of a MEB's combat equipment and stores including ammunition, diesel fuel, aviation fuel, petrol and some 1,400 vehicles. They have a good cargo handling capability, including five 40-ton cranes, a fully slewing stern ramp, ten cargo causeways, a warping tug, two LCM-8s and a helicopter platform for CH-53E. They can discharge their cargo most effectively at a pier but they could also land it across the beach, taking some 5 days for the process. Here a shipboard crane is unloading motorised pontoons. (*US Navy*)

For all these advantages, amphibious forces are quite slow to transit to a far distant crisis and might not be available on the spot with the alacrity that Governments demand, unless they are already deployed forward; the Americans maintain an Amphibious Readiness Group in both the Mediterranean and the Pacific (this was moved to the Indian Ocean to provide contingency cover for naval operations in the Gulf). To help speed the response, these forces are often closely linked with airmobile and airborne forces to provide a full reaction capability. The British Out of Area forces could be found from any part of the Armed Forces, but the military forces would probably be drawn from 5 Airborne Brigade and 3 Commando Brigade RM, who are both trained in this role. The Americans have a mix of light, airborne and amphibious forces available, including the Maritime Prepositioning Ship (MPS).

BRITISH PERCEPTIONS

British views on operations out of the NATO area range from the sceptics who dismiss the concept of global reach as a nostalgic wish for the days of Empire, and those who believe that Britain and, indeed, other NATO nations should be prepared to assist the United States in the tasks of containing the Soviet threat worldwide; a balanced view would see it as an ability to protect national interests or to support Third World allies. The discussion often concentrates upon defence resources, rather than strategic or diplomatic interests, in the mistaken belief that we devote certain assets to this mission alone. One correspondent has suggested that the CVS and the amphibious ships comprise the Navy's intervention capability which is 'a luxury the country cannot afford'.[3] But these ships and formations have a primary role in NATO which is the justification for their existence. Their secondary intervention role makes them even more cost effective and, to confirm the position, the Defence policy is:

> 'Although we do not maintain forces exclusively for operations outside the NATO area, we can (after consultation with our NATO allies) deploy substantial and well balanced forces that could operate, if necessary, anywhere in the world.'[4]

US PERCEPTIONS

The Americans have little doubt about the global scope of their responsibilities, and Admiral Watkins said that 'One key goal of our peacetime strategy is to further international stability through support of regional balances of power.'[5] This would entail playing a full part in providing a peacetime presence and crisis response, as illustrated in *The Spectrum Of Conflict* graphs (Figure 5.1).

This illustrates the development of the forward maritime strategy, but it is considered to lay too much stress upon high intensity global conflict, and a '*knee*' has been inserted in the curve (Figure 5.2) . . . at least by the USMC . . . to reflect the view that 'It is the Third World, the so-called low-intensity conflict arena, where we are most likely to be committed this decade.'[6] This is not a lone opinion, and the Commission on Integrated Long-Term Strategy, appointed by Caspar Weinberger when he was Secretary of Defense, reported in its publication *Discriminate Deterrence* that:

> 'We need to fit together our plans and forces for a wide range of conflicts, from the lowest intensity and highest probability to the most apocalyptic and least likely.
>
> The Pentagon must give preference to more mobile and versatile forces—forces that can deter aggression by their ability to respond rapidly and discriminately to a wide range of attacks.
>
> To defend its interests properly in the Third World, the United States will have to take low intensity conflict much more seriously.
>
> . . . we will always need to deter the extreme contingencies. But it does not take much nuclear force to destroy a civil society. We need to devote our predominant effort to a wide range of more plausible, important contingencies.'[7]

Discriminate Deterrence has not been accepted as national policy, but these elements calling for a greater concentration on low and medium intensity operations have begun to influence priorities. In his report to Congress in 1988 the Commandant of the Marine Corps, General A. M. Gray, announced that 'The

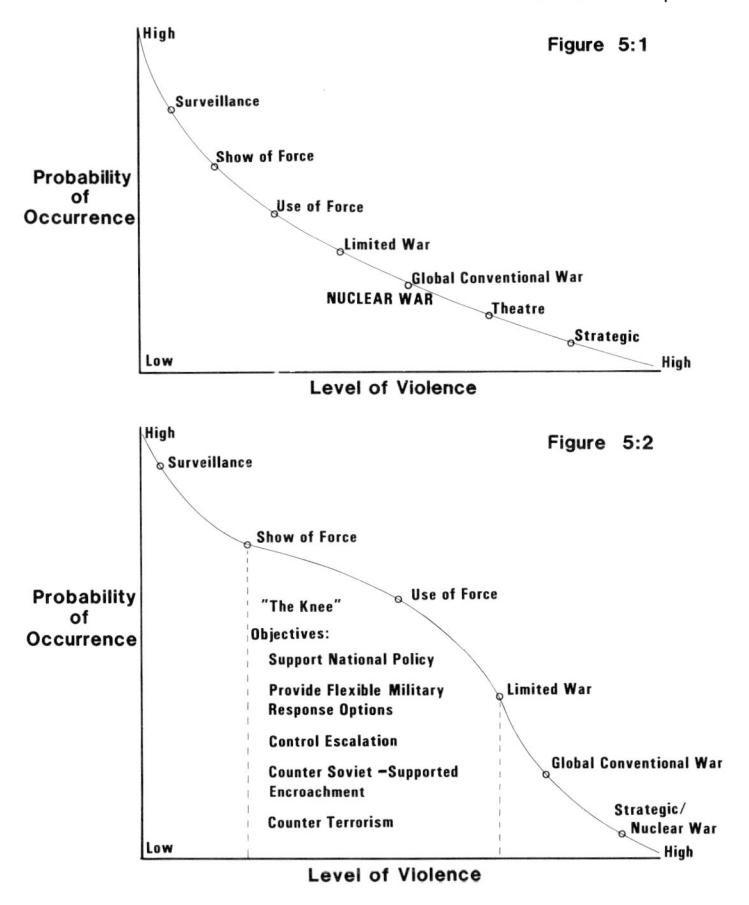

FIG. 5.1 and FIG. 5.2   Spectrum of Conflict Graphs

reason the nation has a Marine Corps is to project power into areas where we do not have forces stationed in peacetime. Our amphibious capability, our seaborne mobility, and our expeditionary nature make us uniquely suited for the task; this is the major contribution we provide the nation.'[8] To mark the change of emphasis, he has redesignated the USMC units and formations as 'expeditionary' rather than 'amphibious'. Thus the old 'Marine Amphibious Brigade' has become the 'Marine Expeditionary Brigade'. Furthermore, the MEUs deployed in the Mediterranean and the Pacific have been given a special operations capability. This shift reflects a deeply ingrained conviction within the Marine Corps, and General Trainor USMC, now the Defense Correspondent of *The New York Times*, probably captured the consensus when he wrote:

> 'To get a measly slice of the defense pie, the Marine Corps claimed a NATO role for itself in Norway on the Alliance's northern flank. In their hearts, however, Marines knew that they would fight many places before they ever fired a shot in Norway or any place else in Europe. Wisely, the Corps resisted entreaties to specialize in warfare on NATO's flank in favour of a more general worldwide role.'[9]

84   Amphibious Operations

PLATE 5.3   Airlanded forces are an important element in USMC deployments. Here a Light Armoured Vehicle (LAV) is being driven off a massive *Galaxy* aircraft. The LAV carries a squad of 9 men including the gunner who fires the 25mm chain gun, and gives the MAGTF a light reconnaissance capability. (*US Navy*)

SOVIET PERCEPTIONS

Have the Soviets sought a global capability for amphibious warfare? Admiral Gorshkov wrote at length about the American ability to project sea power ashore during the Korean and Vietnam campaigns. He conducted a detailed examination of landings, air strikes, bombardments and the value of sea transport. As Geoffrey Till has written 'Interestingly, Gorshkov offered no comment about all this, apart from some low key and ritualistic remarks about the disgraceful use to which this power was put; no doubt he expected the figures to speak for themselves. His dead pan analysis perhaps suggests that the Soviet Navy would like to develop this kind of intervention capability for itself one day.'[10]

Looking at the development of Soviet amphibious forces out of area in recent years helps us to assess whether Gorshkov made any progress. They have indeed played a part in the extension of the Soviet Navy's global reach over the past 25 years. Amphibious ships have been used to transport military equipment to client countries, notably Angola in 1973 when an *Alligator* class amphibious ship was conveniently available in the Gulf of Guinea when required, and to move friendly forces to the war area, such as the South Yemenis to help the Arab cause in 1973. The Soviet Mediterranean Squadron used to include 2 or 3 amphibious ships although these may not always have had any Soviet Infantry embarked. An interesting recent development has been in the Far East where the Soviets have their most modern and effective amphibious capability. There they have a small division of Naval Infantry embarked. An interesting recent development has been in the Far East where the Soviets have their most modern and effective amphibious capability. There they have a small division of Naval Infantry, two LPDs, the LASH container ship which could transport some 260 tanks (sufficient for a motor rifle division) and there are now two small aircraft carriers, which could give

PLATE 5.4 The LPD *Ivan Rogov* is the most capable Soviet amphibious ship which can carry about 520 troops and 20 tanks. It has helicopter platforms fore and aft, and can carry landing craft or *Lebed* ACVs in the dock. (*Jane's*)

86 Amphibious Operations

support to amphibious operations with their 20 *Hormone* helicopters and 13 *Yak 36 Forgers*. Indeed in 1984 the LPD *Ivan Rogov* with 500 Naval Infantry and the *Minsk* took part in the first Soviet-Vietnamese naval exercise south of Haiphong. Air support was provided from that valuable but now diminishing strategic facility, Cam Ranh Bay. Notwithstanding these indications of interest, it currently seems more unlikely than ever that the Soviets will challenge the Western global capability. The absence of a large amphibious shipping programme and the configuration of their new carriers as air defence ships, coupled with their lack of underway supply ships, indicates that they are not likely to develop a long range amphibious intervention capability. As James Cable has commented:

> 'In peacetime, even when Soviet warships have undertaken some distant deployment, they have seldom ever used, seldom even threatened limited naval force for political purposes. When contrasted with the addiction of the United States to gunboat diplomacy, the Soviet attitude has been cautious to the point of timidity.'[11]

THE UNCERTAIN FUTURE

Public perceptions of the threat in Europe are changing rapidly as the influence of *Perestroika* and *Glasnost*, steps towards nuclear arms control, together with Soviet and American statements about conventional force reductions, tend to diminish the danger of war. There will, however, be difficult questions to answer about the force levels in the central Region which could have an indirect effect upon future amphibious roles.

There could be pressure from the Soviet Government for arms control measures to be extended beyond the armour and aircraft of the Central Front to the maritime sphere. In a speech at Murmansk in October 1987, Gorbachev suggested a co-operative security regime for the Arctic to include confidence building measures in adjacent waters. Other Soviet proposals have included calls to reduce maritime activity in the Baltic, Norwegian and Greenland Seas and to limit the number of exercises to about one per year. There is undoubtedly a Soviet concern about the threat to its own territory from carrier and amphibious forces, which the West may regard as extreme, but Soviet memories recall the intervention in support of the White Russians in 1919 much more readily than we do. To an extent, this concern may have been recognised in the Stockholm Agreement under which amphibious exercises are notified if more than 3,000 troops are to cross the beach, which is a lower level than is required for other military activities.

NATO has made it clear that the amphibious forces are deployed entirely in a deterrent and forward defensive posture, and that reinforcements for the defence of Norway are best deployed by a mix of amphibious and airlanded means. It has also successfully refused to include naval forces (except land based maritime aviation) in the Conventional Stability Talks. Most of the Nordic countries have reacted cautiously to the Soviet initiatives, with Norway and Denmark explicitly refusing to break NATO ranks on this issue. It is too early to say whether there might eventually be a reduced or indeed enhanced commitment for amphibious forces in Northern European Command, but the experiences of the Norway 1940 campaign and the bonds that have developed in recent years make the retention of an amphibious capability a sensible long term insurance policy. Moreover, any

PLATE 5.5 Royal Marines on a helicopter landing site during an Out-of-Area exercise, *Saif Saira*, in Oman. (*Royal Marines. Crown copyright*)

withdrawals of ground forces from Europe could place a higher premium on amphibious reinforcement.

There has already been some speculation in Britain about the potential impact of any force reductions in NATO, including a report that 'Senior officers... are increasingly drawn to the creation of a dedicated overseas intervention force' the elements of which '... already lie ready to hand in the parachute and commando brigades'.[12] Improved East-West relationships will very probably change attitudes to global commitments.

In the past, there have certainly been suggestions that there will be no further call for amphibious forces to intervene; that the British will never fight another Falklands War, or the Americans another Grenada. Western policies will continue to give priority to diplomatic, material, technical and training support to friends out of the NATO area, so the use of military power will undoubtedly be an exceptional event. It might be argued, however, that an increasingly multi-polar world, with less emphasis upon the politics of Bloc confrontation, might create other pressures to endanger peace and security. But this will not change the fundamental case for a mobile and versatile intervention capability which has existed for some time, and will continue for many years to come:

> It is a potent deterrent against potential aggression. One of the causes of the Falklands War was the Argentine perception that the UK lacked both the will and the capability to intervene.
>
> If deterrence fails, then there must be a force in being able to react to the unexpected. Experience shows that these operations rarely occur in areas covered by contingency plans, so we must be ready to react to a surprise move.
>
> The crisis is likely to have a maritime dimension and include a call for amphibious power projection.

The difference is that these fundamentals could be more readily recognised if there are lesser demands for the Central Region. With the assumption that the amphibious reinforcement of Northern Europe will continue to retain its value, separate measures would have to be taken to cater also for a global capability which offers a wide range of options for crisis management and the controlled use of force. Under these circumstances, the amphibious force would have to be strengthened or expanded to meet increased responsibilities.

Part II

The Conduct of Amphibious Operations

6

Broad Principles and Command

'Amphibious operations are a very specialised form of warfare. They have "to fit together like a jewelled bracelet", as Churchill once said. . . . The business of war would be far less complicated, if only purely military considerations had to be taken into account.'

Lord Ismay[1]

MAIN PRINCIPLES

Is an amphibious landing the most complex operation in war? There are organisational and technical challenges, fraught with potential sources of friction, in co-ordinating and sustaining a wide range of different elements; such as the carriers, land based air, landing craft, helicopters and the landing force itself. There are the natural hazards of the surf, rocks and sandbars close to shore which soldiers and sailors alike find alien to their normal fighting environment. Faced with these problems, the planners have developed a set of apparently idiosyncratic procedures. So the prospect appears daunting and, in the past, this has provoked a view in the single Services that joint amphibious operations were not their proper employment.

Perhaps the secret of success lies in realising that the interface of sea, air and land is not a sharp divide, but is a zone within which diverse activities must be co-ordinated and managed. The fundamental requirements for fighting within that zone are based on standard naval, air and military practices suitably adjusted for the special situation but, to avoid a repetition of the debacles of Gallipoli and Norway 1940, the necessary resources, techniques and expertise must be made available. General Moulton—who, after staff experience of amphibious warfare at Dunkirk and Madagascar, commanded 48 Commando RM in Normandy and at Walcheren in 1944—has taken a more catholic view than Lord Ismay:

> 'With a suitable adjustment, the requirements would apply to almost any contemporary operation of war. Nor does it seem to me that, historically, joint operations proved to be more difficult than others; an infantry attack in 1916–17, a Russian or North Atlantic convoy in 1942–43, the strategic air offensive when things were going wrong, any of these, surely, made technical demands at least as exacting as those of opposed landings and were a good deal rougher at the point of contact.'[2]

PLATE 6.1 A wet landing, one of the more uncomfortable aspects of amphibious operations! (*Marine Corps Gazette*)

In this part of the book I will describe the conduct of modern amphibious operations, discuss some future developments and give a few historical illustrations (mainly as inserts); it is a general overview which might serve as an introduction for those who have only seen part of the process, or have not come across it at all. I will concentrate upon the structure and operations of the UK/NL Amphibious Force but will draw upon US amphibious practice when necessary, and will consider Soviet methods from time to time, as far as they are known; to avoid having to make somewhat pedantic changes in terminology, I will continue to use the title UK/NL Amphibious, or Landing, Force throughout.

There is no specific scenario, and these methods could apply to landings, possibly with allies, during Phases 2 and 3 of the Forward Maritime Strategy, or on Out of Area (OOA) operations. I will pay most attention to the essentially amphibious elements, which might lead the reader to conclude that some very important aspects such as the naval and air battles—have been given short shrift, but other books in this series are designed to complete the full picture.

As we have heard, the doctrine for amphibious warfare was established by the Marine Corps Schools at Quantico and in the United Kingdom during the 1930s, and were honed to a fine pitch during the Second World War. The majority of the general principles in the American *Tentative Manual for Landing Operations* and the British *Manual of Combined Operations 1938* still hold good today, and can be read in their modern counterparts, the US LFM-01 and the almost identical NATO version ATP-8. These principles can be summarised as:

▶ Local maritime and air superiority are essential for the passage of the force and the landing. They enable the beachhead to be isolated from enemy reinforcement and attack, so that the ships can be unloaded swiftly and in relative safety, and allow the landing force to have continuous naval and air support during the operation.

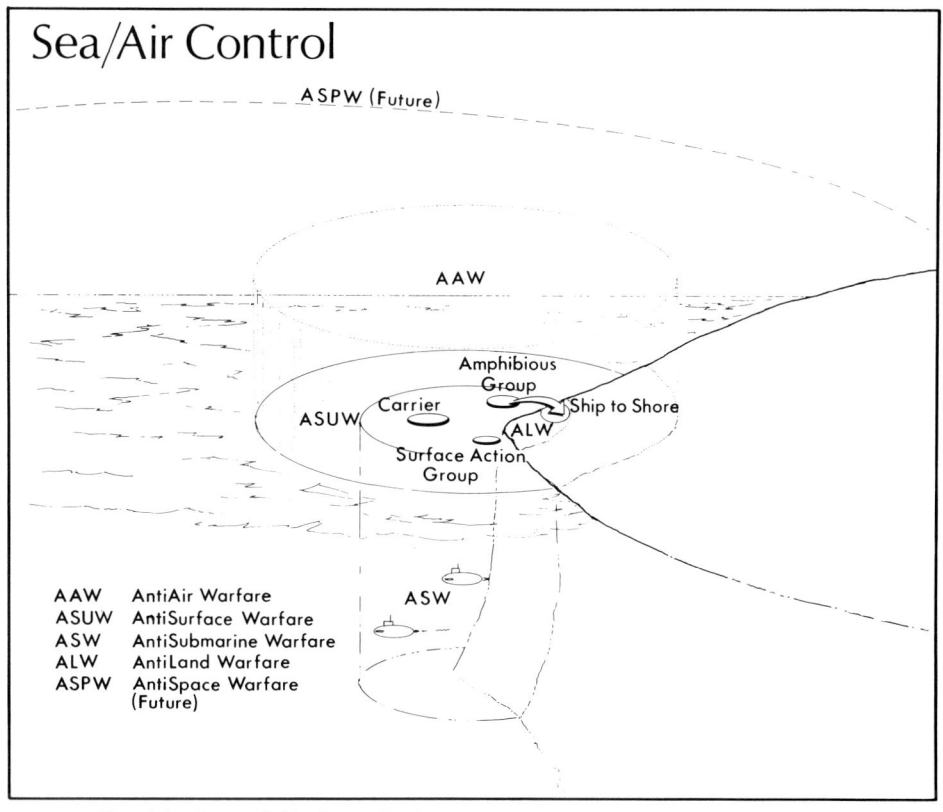

FIG. 6.1 Sea and Air Control. This illustrates the five elements (including the increasingly important one of Space) which comprise the protective shields for an amphibious operation

PLATE 6.2 USS *Nassau* (LHA-4) firing the anti-aircraft missile *Sea Sparrow*. The air defence of the landing must be layered, with the amphibious ships able to contribute to the inner layers. (*US Navy*)

▶ The landing force must have substantial superiority over the enemy forces ashore in the objective area. In an opposed landing this would require an advantage of about 3-to-1, but such a precise calculation would not apply to an unopposed landing when the force needs only to be able to overcome any minor and unexpected opposition, and to defeat the immediate enemy counter attack. Moreover, the sum should take into account the additional naval and air fire support available to the force.

▶ There must be clear and unambiguous arrangements for the command of the force. Overall command is vested in a naval officer because this is essentially a maritime operation, and the problems of the security of the task force are naval ones. The landing force commander is responsible for the selection and execution of landing force objectives, so he is a vital partner in the planning process, and is usually of equal rank. In NATO parlance, the two are known as Commander Amphibious Task Force (CATF) and Commander Landing Force (CLF) respectively, and their personal relationship is crucial to the success of the operation. Hence we will address command first, before looking at the procedural and material issues.

COMMAND

'War consists of two independent wills confronting each other.'[3]

In his excellent book *Command in War*, Martin van Creveld points out that uncertainty is the central fact that all command systems have to cope with, and he suggests that the role of uncertainty should be the decisive factor in determining the command structure. This, as you will have realised, applies with redoubled vigour to amphibious warfare, in which the development of the command system has faced two particular problems:

▶ First, the need to bring together the command elements of two and, occasionally, three Services to campaign in harness. Sometimes the 'two independent wills confronting one another' were as likely to be the naval and army commanders as the two warring sides.
▶ Secondly, the need to resolve the balance between what van Creveld calls 'function orientated' and 'output orientated' systems of command or, broadly, this could be expressed as; what is the role of uncertainty?

Unified and Joint Command

In the past, governments and senior commanders had three main options when deciding how combined operations should be commanded:

▶ *Joint Command*, in which the commander of each Service has also a joint responsibility for the enterprise as a whole.
▶ *Unified Command*, in which responsibility for the whole operation is vested in a combined Commander-in-Chief, with the commanders of the Services taking part as his subordinates
▶ *Command by One Service*, in which the commander of the Service playing the chief part is given overall command.

When they were determining their doctrine, the USMC had little difficulty in deciding upon the third method, since their forces would normally be despatched as part of a naval task force under the single command of a flag officer who would hold overall responsibility throughout. This worked well, although it had to be amended through experience during the Second World War, especially to allow for the command of operations ashore to be transferred to the landing force commander at an appropriate time.

For many years British combined operations were conducted under joint command. Neither the general nor the admiral, by tradition and upbringing, could admit that the other was qualified to give orders outside his own element. Therefore collectively they were responsible for the success of the enterprise as a whole, while, individually, each was responsible for the control and employment of his own forces. Success depended upon a willingness to work in close harmony, and it was a well proven system, although at times it could be inefficient, as at Gallipoli, or it could founder on misunderstandings, as at Narvik in 1940 (see insert).

COMMAND AT NARVIK 1940

In April 1940, the two commanders for Narvik, Admiral of the Fleet Lord Cork and Orrery and Major-General Mackesy, were appointed under unfortunate circumstances when the Chiefs of Staff struggled to assemble a force to respond to the surprise German invasion:

> 'The Chief of the Naval Staff and the Chief of the Imperial General Staff acted with sturdy independence. They appointed their respective commanders without consultation with each other; and, worse still, they gave directives to those commanders without harmonising them. Thereafter they continued to issue separate orders to them. Thus was confusion worse confounded.' Lord Ismay.[4]

Contrary to normal practice, the joint commanders did not sail together, and their first contact after Mackesy's arrival on 14 April was a signal from Lord Cork, delayed in transmission, ordering an amphibious attack on Narvik the next day to capitalise upon the naval victory. There was too little time to comply, but from thereon operations against Narvik were bedevilled by the clash of personalities between these two independent commanders as they disputed whether to assault the town.

Cork had orders to conduct the early assault, and argued strongly that this should be undertaken after a naval bombardment. Mackesy's separate orders from the War Office included the sentence; 'it is not intended that you should land in the face of opposition',[5] apparently contradicted by the advice from the CIGS Ironside that 'you may have a chance of taking advantage of naval action and you should do if you can. Boldness is required'.[6] Once on the ground, however, Mackesy's view was that the troops could not operate in deep snow, that '... the naval bombardment cannot be militarily effective, and that a landing from open boats ... must be ruled out absolutely'.[7]

Should Mackesy have attacked Narvik? The Germans thought that the Allies had far overestimated the strength of their enemy[8] but, faced with a situation demanding bold action, he had only partially trained men and inadequate equipment for an opposed landing. His view, however, won no support in London and on 20 April he was placed under the direct command of Lord Cork and was replaced by General Auchinleck on 13 May.

Other commanders might have resolved their differences. But with Cork and Mackesy the disparity in their ranks and personalities, their determination not to establish a joint headquarters (the Admiral remained at sea while the General stayed in Harstad) and their licence initially to report independently to their respective single Service COS, militated against a solution.

At a higher level, the Americans had also employed joint command, until Pearl Harbor exposed 'the inherent and intolerable weaknesses of command by mutual cooperation',[9] so it was decided to adopt the unified command system, with one man commanding an entire theatre—air, ground, and ships. It did not take long for this concept to cross the Atlantic when the sheer size of operations, and American influence, demanded the appointment of a Supreme Commander.

The system of command in force today has evolved from all these influences. The higher command system in NATO is unified, and this is described more fully in another book in this series.[10] Thus, for example, at an appropriate moment in the transition to war, the UK/NL Amphibious Force would be placed under the operational command of the Supreme Allied Commander Atlantic (SACLANT), who would delegate operational control to one of his subordinate commanders. Once, however, the UK/NL Landing Force is completely ashore, when the amphibious phase of the operation has been completed and the force is ready to take part in the subsequent land campaign, the operational command would switch to the Supreme Allied Commander Europe (SACEUR). He, in turn, would delegate operational control to an appropriate local subordinate.

Amphibious operations themselves, however, are commanded by an amalgam of the old joint system and the single Service command used from the outset by the USMC. Although the overall command is vested in the Naval CATF, he is, in some respects, really the *primus inter pares*, since the CLF afloat 'will retain an equal status with the commander of the amphibious task group in whose ships he is embarked with regard to planning amphibious operations'.[11] In simple terms, the commanders are co-equals responsible for making plans for their own services, although these are co-ordinated by CATF and, in the last resort, the buck stops with him! In these arrangements, much still depends upon the compatability of the commanders, and the advice of the 1938 *Manual of Combined Operations* still holds good:

> 'the commanders must be suited both by temperament and experience to co-operate with each other. They must not only be able to enjoy each other's confidence and to work as a team but each commander should have a broad knowledge of the capabilities and limitations of the other Services.'[12]

Functions and Output

The root of the second main difficulty was described in blunt terms by Edward Luttwak in his criticism of US amphibious operations, in that:

> 'The landing routine is so complex in its choreography that by the time that the ballet is done there is no attention left to devote to the enemy and respond to what he does.'[13]

Amphibious operations do indeed present problems for the commanders, since the planning process for the loading and offloading of ships, the latter probably under fire, demands what Martin van Creveld calls a function-orientated, or logistic, command system. Of necessity, this must be more centralised and mechanised than an output-orientated, or operational, system which is designed for fighting the enemy. Van Creveld comments that:

> 'the command system that makes possible the successful completion of preparations may be inadequate or even positively harmful once that undertaking is under way. It is vital, in other

98 Amphibious Operations

words, for the structure of any command system to be adapted to the measure of uncertainty involved in the performance of the task at hand.'[14]

MODERN SOLUTIONS

The solution has to be a synthesis, achieved by establishing a sound staff system to cope with the functions, and superimposing on this a flexible and responsive command system which is prepared to delegate responsibility to best effect (we will return to this aspect in Chapter 14). Then ensure that the whole is closely harmonised, sound and well practised.

The harmony must start at the top. In the UK/NL Amphibious Force the CATF, the Commodore Amphibious Warfare, and the CLF, the Commander, 3 Commando Brigade, Royal Marines and their staffs have been co-located at Stonehouse Barracks, Plymouth. Thus there is a proper management and training organisation working closely together and the two commanders come to know each other well; when deployed they always sail together. Major General Thompson summed up his

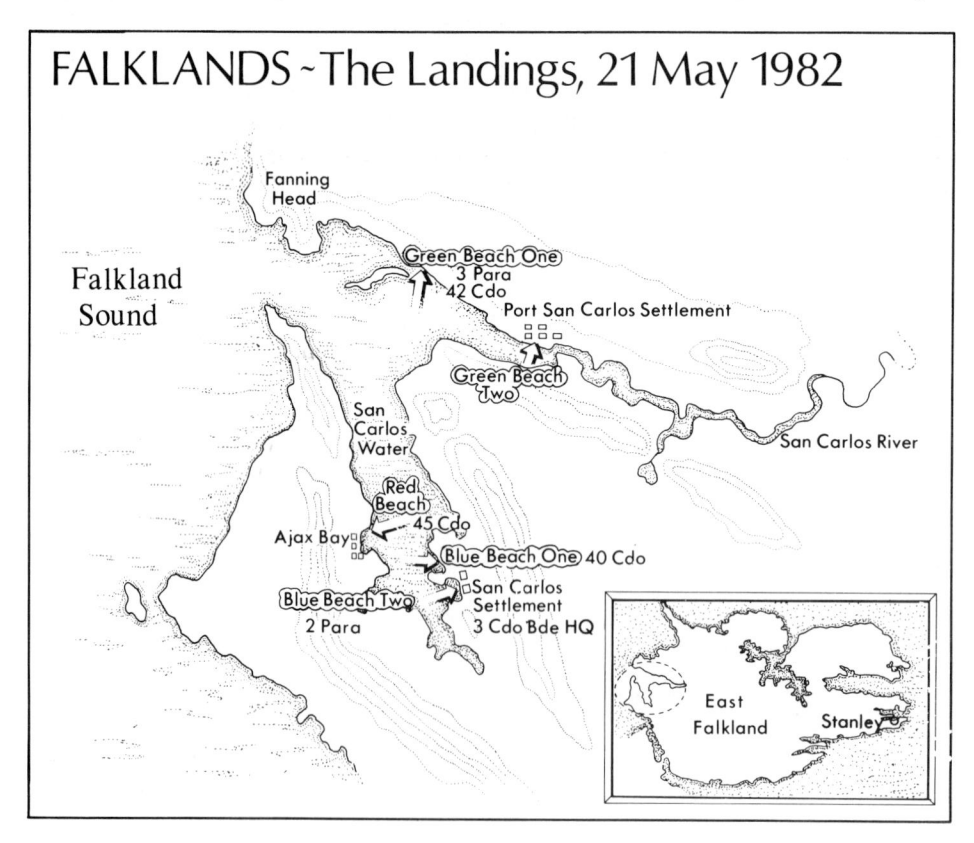

MAP 6.1 The landings at San Carlos on 21 May, 1982 provide a number of examples throughout the book on the conduct of amphibious landings, especially as valuable lessons were learned for the refinement of command and control procedures. The initial landings were entirely by landing craft, as there was not a specialist helicopter ship available, and they were virtually unopposed.

PLATE 6.3 SS *Canberra* was known as 'The Great White Whale' during the Falkland Islands campaign. This luxury liner was converted at short notice to carry units of 3 Commando Brigade RM and two helicopter platforms were fitted. On the forward one is a *Sea King HC4* with its blades folded, and there are 'Chacon' containers of stores on the upper deck forward of the funnel.
(*Royal Navy. Crown copyright*)

relationship with Commodore Clapp during the Falklands Islands campaign when he wrote:

'It was also fortunate that Clapp and I got on so well. In each other's company almost constantly and involved in long discussions until late each night, there was plenty of scope for bickering and recrimination, but harmony was the order of the day ... (we) were totally frank in exchanging our views and understood the problems of amphibious operations.'[15]

The Americans have several examples of similar close links, with the Commanding General Fleet Marine Force Atlantic (who is also the commander of II MEF), for example, being co-located at Norfolk, Virginia with SACLANT and the Commander of the Striking Fleet. At a lower level, the Commodores of the Amphibious Readiness Groups in the Mediterranean and the Pacific live and work very closely for long periods with the USMC commanders of the embarked MEUs. It is very noticeable, and hardly surprising, that standing command arrangements such as the UK/NL Amphibious Force and the ARG/MEU develop a confidence in the procedures and in the joint capabilities of their forces which ameliorates much of the potential *friction* of these complex operations. This mutual confidence, of course, enables the commanders to concentrate upon the main issue; outwitting the enemy.

It is less easy to ensure the smooth running of larger formations, involving two brigades or a division, although the modern arrangements far outstrip those of the past. As a lesson from the Falkland Islands campaign, a revised system was introduced for British national amphibious operations out of the NATO area. At the higher level there has been no significant change, since operational command would be normally vested in the Commander-in-Chief Fleet who has his headquarters in Northwood. The innovation was to make standing arrangements for the delegation of operational control to a 2-star commander at sea, the Rear Admiral Flag Officer Third Flotilla (FOF 3) who, as Joint Force Commander (JFC), would work in close concert with the landing forces' commander—Major-General Royal Marines Commando Forces. Once his forces are securely established ashore the Major General would assume the role of JFC. His divisional size headquarters would be assembled from various sources specifically for the operation, with the nucleus coming from his own staff and from a Joint Service organisation called the Joint Force Operating Staff whose peacetime task is to plan and prepare for these contingencies.

The command and control procedures are practised regularly on relatively small scale exercises, but in November 1987 the largest British amphibious force gathered together since the Falkland Islands campaign took part in Exercise *Purple Warrior* off the West coast of Scotland. This was one of comparatively few opportunities for the British higher command to practice this level of operation with all the forces deployed since peacetime constraints, especially costs, preclude frequent repetition.

On major NATO exercises, the allied amphibious forces, such as a MEB and the UK/NL Amphibious Force, work together under the command of the Commander of the Combined Amphibious Task Force (CCATF), usually an American. Much is gained from the regular contacts and wide ranging discussions between the amphibious forces and with their NATO commanders in the lengthy preparatory planning phase. The exercises offer a good chance to work out procedures and evaluate equipment, and might lead to such lessons as CINCNORTH's recent observation on the impact of the arrival of large naval and amphibious forces to support land operations as part of the forward maritime strategy:

> 'Command and control arrangements are possibly more complicated in the North European Command than in other regions of ACE . . . and when the Striking Fleets arrive in the areas, the command and control arrangements, particularly air space management, become very complex. I am concerned that we do not yet have the necessary physical means of communications and transmission of information to overcome the potential difficulties and make use of all our assets.'[16]

With the higher commanders facing such challenges, it is perhaps understandable that large exercises tend to concentrate on the formal and procedural aspects, and offer few opportunities to practise the commanders at all levels in the management of uncertainty. This has been recognised, and the Commander of 3 Commando Brigade RM has commented:

> 'What is required is the understanding that confusion and chaos are an essential characteristic of war. Our training should reflect this.'[17]

None the less, the exercising forces are sometimes surprised by the turn of events, and a good example was given in a response to Edward Luttwak's earlier criticism.

PLATE 6.4 HMS *Illustrious* was used in the amphibious helicopter (LPH) role during Exercise *Purple Warrior* in 1987, carrying 40 Commando Group with its stores and support weapons. Here a stick is moved up from the assembly area in the hangar to the flight deck by the lift, to load on to *Sea King* helicopters. On that exercise, another CVS, HMS *Ark Royal* was used as a strike carrier and the command ship for the Joint Force Headquarters. (*Royal Navy. Crown copyright*)

102   Amphibious Operations

PLATE 6.5   USS *Mount Whitney* is the command ship (LCC) for Striking Fleet Atlantic, and is fitted with a wide range of integrated command, control and communications equipment for sea, land and air commanders in amphibious operations. There are 3 computer systems to support the Naval Tactical Data System, the Amphibious Command Information System and the Naval Intelligence Processing System. (*US Navy*)

On an exercise in the Pacific:

> 'After successful operations ashore, the elements of the MAGTF commenced re-embarkation aboard amphibious shipping. Approximately two-thirds of the way through re-embarkation, the MAGTF commander issued, with no advance notice whatsoever, an order requiring his forces to conduct a noncombatant evacuation operation (NEO) of a fictional embassy located on a different island. Within two hours the operation was planned by Navy and Marine Corps planners: the task force moved within striking distance, and the NEO was undertaken. Within four hours of receipt of the order, the operation was successfully completed.'[18]

One cannot overstate the value of training and exercises in creating the expertise in managing complex procedures under stress, since it effectively creates the space for commanders to concentrate upon the main issue of running the tactical battle. This process should not only rely upon practical experience, it is also important to have an intellectual base. For the single Services this base is provided, to a significant extent, by their staff colleges, and in America the USMC Command and Staff College at Quantico meets the needs of amphibious warfare. After the decision to close the National Defence College at Latimer in 1982, it was feared that there would be no future provision for joint warfare training in Britain, but it was subsequently decided to establish the Joint Warfare Staff at Poole which now acts as a focal point for teaching and developing, among other joint subjects, amphibious warfare doctrine.

THE STAFFS

'. . . the success of a combined operation will depend largely on close and cordial co-operation not only between the commanders of the Services and their staffs but also between all subordinate commanders and other personnel whose duties bring them into contact or communication with each other'.

Manual of Combined Operations 1938

Another main factor which enables the commanders to concentrate upon the conduct of the battle, rather than upon the mechanics, is the structure of their staffs. In the UK/NL Amphibious Force the planning of the landing is carried out jointly by the Staff of COMAW and the Staff of Headquarters 3 Cdo Bde RM. In this organisation the CATF staff consists of two teams; a naval one which is mainly responsible for the maritime defence and movements of the Amphibious Task Group, and a military team which plans and controls the loading and offloading of the ships. The CLF staff is constructed in the same fashion as an army brigade headquarters, although it is slightly larger than its army counterpart, since the landing force usually operates in a more independent fashion; it is not part of a division and does not have the support which would come from a national superior headquarters deployed with it.

For planning his operations ashore, the CLF draws advice from his senior staff officers, plus the members of his Rover Group. This consists of the supporting arms commanders, of the artillery and engineers, plus other regular specialist advisers covering helicopters and landing craft. To give a flavour of the way a well worked up team might operate, Brigadier Thompson commented that:

> 'The Rover or R Group was well practised in working together and for over a year this same team had been taking part in reconnaissances for several exercises and possible operations; as a result they were totally 'in the Brigade Commander's mind'—an ideal situation . . . the planning team . . . was summoned together either as individuals or together to spend hours in my cabin in the *Fearless* poring over the maps and dissecting the options before being sent away to prepare yet another outline plan. It would be hard to overstate the achievements of the R Group or the Staff. Their hard work, professionalism, flexibility and abiding cheerfulness under great pressure for seven weeks before D-Day and throughout the campaign was second to none. No Brigade Commander could have been better served.'[19]

The commanders and their staffs have to orchestrate a large cast of sailors, marines, airmen and soldiers—with a wide range of equipment—and in the next chapter we will look at the initial planning procedures which represent the cornerstone of an operation. In subsequent chapters we will consider the craft and ships that could make up the amphibious force, and then the many elements of the landing force before, finally, discussing the maritime battle and the landing itself.

7
Planning

INITIAL PLANNING

Each amphibious operation is complete in itself and consists of five main phases; planning, embarkation, rehearsals, movement to the objective area, and the assault. Many of the chief constituents of the operation are determined in the initial planning phase.

From the loading of ships, often in several different ports, to the planning, timing and execution of the tactical offload, an amphibious operation demands staff work of the highest quality. Major General Thompson has summarised the procedure as

> 'Identify the tasks (mission), find out all you can about the enemy (intelligence), make the plan, stow your ships so that the men and loads will come off in the sequence you want to meet your plan; then land.'[1]

If the amphibious task group is already deployed well forward, time for planning will be short and many of the main ingredients, such as the size and composition of the force, will be pre-determined, but we will consider the full process for a force being mobilised from a base port. The first stage is mainly the responsibility of the superior headquarters, although the CATF and CLF staffs will be fully consulted. The result will be the *Initiating Directive* which gives the force's mission, the arrangements for command, the composition of the naval, land and air forces and sufficient information for the detailed planning process to start.

The most important decision is the overall *Mission*. For NATO operations it may well be relatively simple to direct the force to undertake one of the Maritime Contingency Force Atlantic (MARCONFORLANT) plans.[2] Other operations will demand a discrete political decision as part of the crisis management process, and experience has shown that the objective must be stated very clearly. There was a prime example of confusion at Narvik in 1940 and, in their book *Battle for the Falklands* Max Hastings and Simon Jenkins reported that there was a failure to give Brigadier Thompson clear orders to press inland after the initial landing.

In determining the mission and in all subsequent stages of planning, good *intelligence* is vital; where is the enemy, how great is his strength and what is he going to do next? This concerns not only the land forces, but also the surface, submarine and air forces on passage and in the objective area. A major difference between normal military operations and an amphibious landing is the sheer physical separation of the main opposing forces until the last minute. Routine patrols cannot readily be sent across the forward edge of the battle area to discover

PLATE 7.1. AWACS aircraft are one part of the sophisticated reconnaissance and surveillance structure that supports the fleet. (*Jane's*)

enemy positions, but means have to be found to overcome this problem without compromising surprise.

Today much can be achieved by electronic means, including satellites and communications intelligence, or by any friendly forces in the area. These sources would have to provide the basis for the first tentative plans, but it will be essential to update information continually, to obtain some specific data about the beaches and their defences, terrain, weather and, essential to achieving an unopposed landing, where the enemy is not holding in strength. Therefore an early decision will be whether to mount an *advanced force operation* to insert Special Forces and other reconnaissance teams into possible landing areas. This phase could also include anti-submarine tasks, minesweeping, air strikes and naval bombardment.

With some idea of the opposition, a decision can be made about the size of the *landing force*. It is one of the cardinal rules of the USMC that they tailor their MAGTFs to suit the mission in hand, fitting together the ground, air and combat service support elements as circumstances dictate. On the other hand, the UK Landing Force is permanently constituted (with the NL elements immediately available for NATO operations) although, when there is the scope, additional infantry, supporting arms and specialist support units may be added to the strength. The size and composition of the force will ultimately depend upon the capacity and type of the amphibious and civilian support ships available.

Then there are the ships, which might include: the transport group carrying the landing force; the control group with ships with command and communications

PLATE 7.2 The Ro-Ro ferry *Mercandia*, one of the STUFT used on UK/NL Amphibious Force exercises. Here a *Mexeflote* has been manœuvred up to the stern ramp for offloading. (*MOD (Navy). Crown copyright*)

facilities; the fire support group which provides naval gunfire or guided missile support to the landing force; a support carrier force or screen to provide air/anti-submarine warfare defence during transit and air superiority over the beachhead; a screen consisting of ships, submarines and aircraft; a mine warfare group to clear the shallow water approach to the shore; and lastly the underway replenishment group to resupply the task force during the operation.

Another important early decision will identify the *Amphibious Objective Area (AOA)* which, as its title suggests, is the venue for the landing. This is usually a large envelope of sea, land and air within which the CATF is responsible for controlling all the forces involved in the landing. He must, as soon as possible after arrival, ensure the defence of the AOA against attack, so that the landings can be made in the most favourable circumstances. The concept of the AOA was conceived by the Americans for their operations in the Pacific, where a large circle could be drawn around an island and the CATF designated as commander of all he surveyed within it. This procedure is not as simple in continental Europe where the dimensions of the AOA must be planned in close conjunction with the host nation and the local NATO commanders, and the activities of any other friendly forces within the envelope must be co-ordinated by the CATF in the interests of safety. The process of establishing, running and then dis-establishing the AOA is well practised during amphibious exercises.

PLATE 7.3 The amphibious task force forms up in a Norwegian fjord for exercise *Cold Winter 89*, with a mixture of specialist, auxiliary and STUFT shipping. HMS *Ark Royal* in the helicopter role is in the foreground. (*Royal Navy. Crown copyright*)

The plan itself is conceived by the CATF working closely with the CLF. Before embarkation the CLF will determine his tentative concept of operations for the landing and operations ashore. This guidance enables the staffs to marry up the naval and landing force requirements so that CATF can allocate assets and issue his outline plan. At this early stage, this plan needs to be precise enough to meet tactical objectives yet flexible enough to cope with the changes that will inevitably occur; arising from political imperatives, intelligence, the vagaries of the weather, the composition of the force, logistics and the terrain.

By the end of the initial planning phase, the many naval, air and ground elements must have a clear idea of the plan and how it is to be executed. Once the detailed *Staff Tables* of all the men and equipment have been drawn up, the ships can be loaded so that the landing forces can be offloaded fully prepared and ready to conduct operations ashore, with troops, weapons, vehicles, ammunition and stores properly stowed. Increasingly, the complicated calculations which make this possible are being carried out by information technology.

This might sound marvellously ordered, but in reality it represents a period of frenetic activity. The call for amphibious forces would probably be sudden and urgent, and the mobilisation of men and, in particular, war maintenance reserve stores, which are kept in depots throughout the country, would impose considerable demands on all those servicemen, civil servants and dockyard workers who have any dealings with the force. Doubtless, the nature of the emergency will call for the ships to sail at the shortest possible notice. Everyone's concerted efforts should ensure that the planned time for embarkation is considerably shortened, although this might prove more difficult during a general mobilisation when there would be many demands on overall national resources to meet a number of contingencies. Under any circumstances, it would be a very fortunate staff that has had the foresight to stow everything to match the commander's final plan, and it may well be necessary to pause in some convenient haven, if time allows, to restow in order to achieve the desired solution. This may well be linked in to the rehearsal landing, a normal part of the movement phase, and is designed to ensure that the plan is sound, especially the timings, and that everyone knows their part.

PLANNING SHIP TO SHORE MOVEMENT

Once at sea, the commanders would continue their detailed operational planning, which we will return to in Chapter 13. As they are deciding *what* to do with the amphibious force, their staffs concentrate upon *how* it is to be done, and in this section we will consider a simplified explanation of the procedure.

The aim of movement planning is to ensure that the landing force reaches the beaches and landing zones ashore in the right tactical order to meet the commanders' concept of operations. The operation takes place in two main parts: first, the assault and initial tactical offload whilst the landing force is striving to establish its first foothold. The plan must therefore be designed to provide an immediate response to demands for reserves and equipment. The second part is the general offload, after the beachhead is secure. In this phase it is important to deliver a large volume of supplies, equipment and stores to build up to maximum strength; thus it is essentially a logistic exercise using all the movement resources.

Once the CLF has produced his outline plan, the units work out how they wish to land to fulfil their part of it, and submit detailed proposals for the order of landing. These the CATF and CLF staffs match to the available helicopters and landing craft. To assist control, especially when wishing to make urgent changes, a *serial number* is given to each unit, sub unit or tactical grouping in the assault and initial landing; all the elements of each serial would be embarked on the same ship, and would be destined to land in the same place at about the same time. With this information, the CLF staff would compile a *Landing Priority Table* to plan the build up of the troops and supplies ashore, arranging them into these categories:

> ▶ *Scheduled Waves*, which contain the men and weapons in the first assault; a wave of helicopters or landing craft will normally form up in to a formation which allows the units to be landed in a coherent group. A limiting factor at present, with the heavy dependence upon STUFT, is the need for a preliminary cross decking programme to ensure that the assault units are moved to a ship capable of operating helicopters or landing craft before the operation is launched.

Planning   109

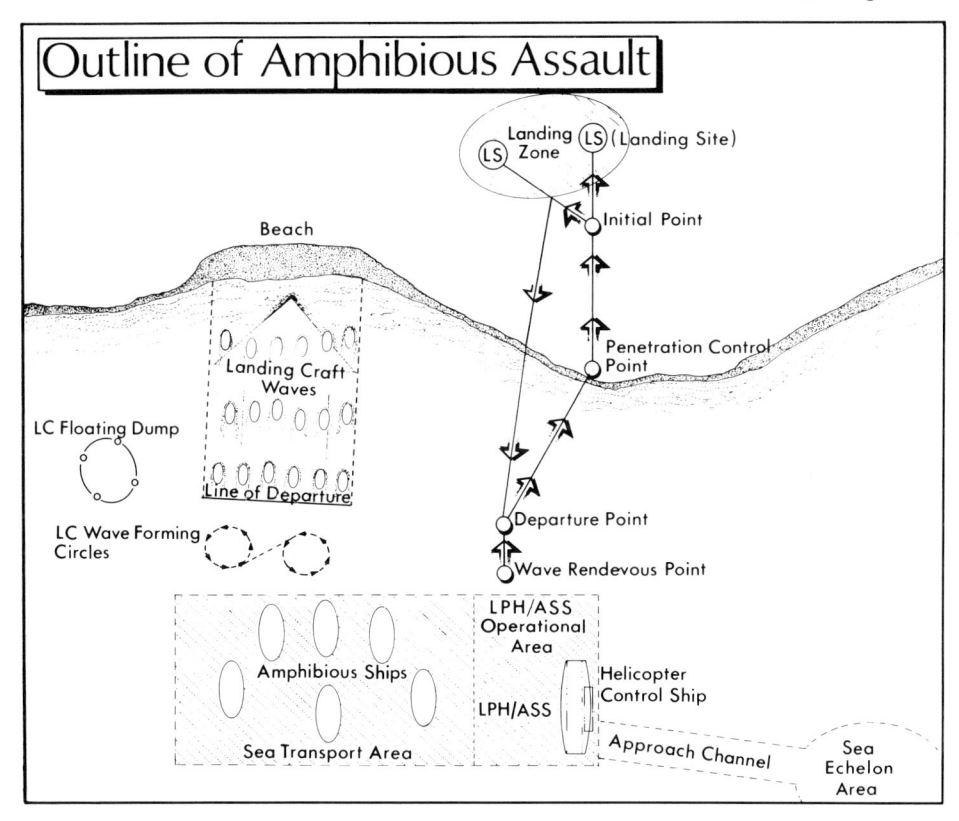

Outline of Amphibious Assault

Fig. 7.1

Plate 7.4 40 Commando RM cross decking by helicopter and landing craft before the San Carlos landing. (*Royal Navy. Crown copyright*)

110 Amphibious Operations

▶ The *On-Call Waves* include a relatively small number of units which are required ashore shortly after the assault, but whose time and place of landing depend upon the commander's reading of the operation. In a similar category are the *Emergency Prepackaged Supplies* which are on-call stores ready to be sent forward at short notice. These might be kept as floating dumps on board landing craft, or pre-packaged for rapid helicopter lift.

▶ The remainder of the landing would be conducted in stream, with the helicopters and landing craft moving singly or in small groups, carrying the *Non-Scheduled Units*. These are the combat units not required initially, probably including the balance of the engineers, artillery, and all the logistic units. The final category would be the *Landing Force Supplies*. This term is self explanatory and represents the main part of the general offload. It is potentially by far the largest category if everything is to be offloaded. However, under what is known as a *sea basing* concept, much might be kept at sea.

Each marine must know how and when he is going ashore, and the staff tell his commanders through two detailed tables, the *Surface Assault Schedule* for landing craft (Americans would recognise this as the *Landing Craft and Amphibious Vehicle Assignment Table*; the UK/NL Amphibious Force does not have any amphibians) and the *Helicopter Employment and Assault Landing Table (HEALT)*. These documents show which serials are going where, in which landing craft or helicopter, in which order and, where this is applicable, the time of launch. These two landing timetables are the core of the ship-to-shore movement planning and control, and their production, which is gradually being computerised, keeps unit adjutants and the staffs extremely busy during the passage.

At the same time, the CATF staff plans the defence of the AOA, the deployment of the amphibious shipping for the offload, and the employment of the helicopters and the landing craft. For example, there would be an *Assault Area Diagram* showing where each ship is to be located during those critical hours, and a *Landing Diagram* which is a graphic representation of the movement of landing craft.

LANDING CRAFT AND HELICOPTER CONTROL

Landing Craft

Control of landing craft in the UK/NL Amphibious Force is a good deal more simple than for the US Amphibious Forces with their substantial assets. The key individual is the Primary Control Officer who controls the tasking and movement of the landing craft to meet the needs of the Surface Assault Schedule. He advises the CATF staff upon any changes needed to meet urgent demands from the landing force if they face difficulties ashore.

The craft themselves would be loaded as ordered in the Assignment Table and launched from amphibious ships, usually underway, to circle near the parent ship until the complete wave was formed; at the appropriate time, the Boat Group Commander would order the wave to cross the *Line of Departure* towards the beach, sailing in formation. The wave might be guided by radar from the parent ship, depending upon the policy for emission control that is in force, or by lights set up by Special Boat Service teams sent ashore as part of the Advance Force. At the

PLATES 7.5 and 7.6 The Beach Armoured Recovery Vehicle (BARV) is part of the Amphibious Beach Unit and can wade in two metres of water or more. In the top picture it is warding off a LCU which has broached to, and in the bottom picture it is towing off a grounded LCVP Mk IV during trials at the Amphibious Trials and Training Unit (ATTURM) in North Devon. With its aluminium hull, the LCVP Mk IV is lighter than its predecessors, and has stronger engines giving it a speed of about 18 knots. It has an arctic canopy and protected wheelhouse, and can carry a landrover or about 30 troops—fewer if they are wearing arctic equipment. (*Royal Marines. Crown copyright*)

beach, the craft would lower their ramps, the troops would exit and the ramps would be raised again for the craft to retract from the beach as quickly as possible, avoiding the next incoming wave of craft. After the initial assault, the control and management of the beach would be in the hands of the *Amphibious Beach Unit* which we will discuss later.

Helicopters

The assault helicopter lift is monitored and co-ordinated from the Amphibious Operations Room in the LPD by the *Helicopter Co-ordination Section*, which is part of the CATF staff. Ideally, the detailed control would be carried out by the *Helicopter Direction Centre (HDC)* which would normally be on board the senior helicopter-capable ship. However, with the demise of the LPHs *Bulwark* and *Hermes*, this capability is lacking in the UK/NL Amphibious Force until the ASS joins the fleet. In the meantime, the task is carried out in the cramped conditions of the LPD.

For the helicopter programme, the landing force is organised into *sticks*, each of which comprise the men and equipment making up one helicopter load. The procedure is very similar to the waterborne move. When the helicopter has loaded its *stick*, it will fly to the *Wave Rendezvous Point* to join the other helicopters, possibly from different ships, to assemble up into formation, before flying inland as shown in Figure 7.1. Once the initial assault has been completed, *Mobile Air Operations Teams (MAOT)* would be set up to control LZs, and these have an especially valuable role in night operations.

Rehearsals

Once all this basic planning has been completed, there should always be a rehearsal to confirm the mechanics and timings of the operation. This enables everyone to practise their personal routine for the landing, from the individual rifleman with his heavy load of equipment, who has to familiarise himself with the route through the ship from his messdeck to his disembarkation point, to the staff in the Amphibious Operations Room whose task is to ensure that the timings are all realistic. The rehearsal usually goes as far as the landing but, if time is short or no landing is possible, the drills can be rehearsed at sea in what is called a *Turnaway Landing*. For their attack on Iwo Jima in 1945, the Americans had a thorough training period and two rehearsals, in Hawaii and the Marianas. Lack of rehearsal can lead to unfortunate delays in the main landing. In 1982, through no fault of their own, 2 Para had not been able to rehearse the night landing drills in Ascension. As a result, there were difficulties in loading the craft at San Carlos and the operation fell an hour behind schedule.

SOVIET METHODS

The Main Stages of a Soviet Amphibious Assault

Although we do not know the procedures for Soviet amphibious operations in the same detail, we do know that they pay similar attention to the basic principles for local sea and air control, superiority of landing forces and good command and control. Their procedures emphasise the importance of surprise, speed and heavy fire support for the landing itself.

The command of Soviet amphibious operations would be vested in the Commander-in-Chief of the Theatre of Military Operations where it is being carried out. He would assign the forces and appoint a commander from the Army or

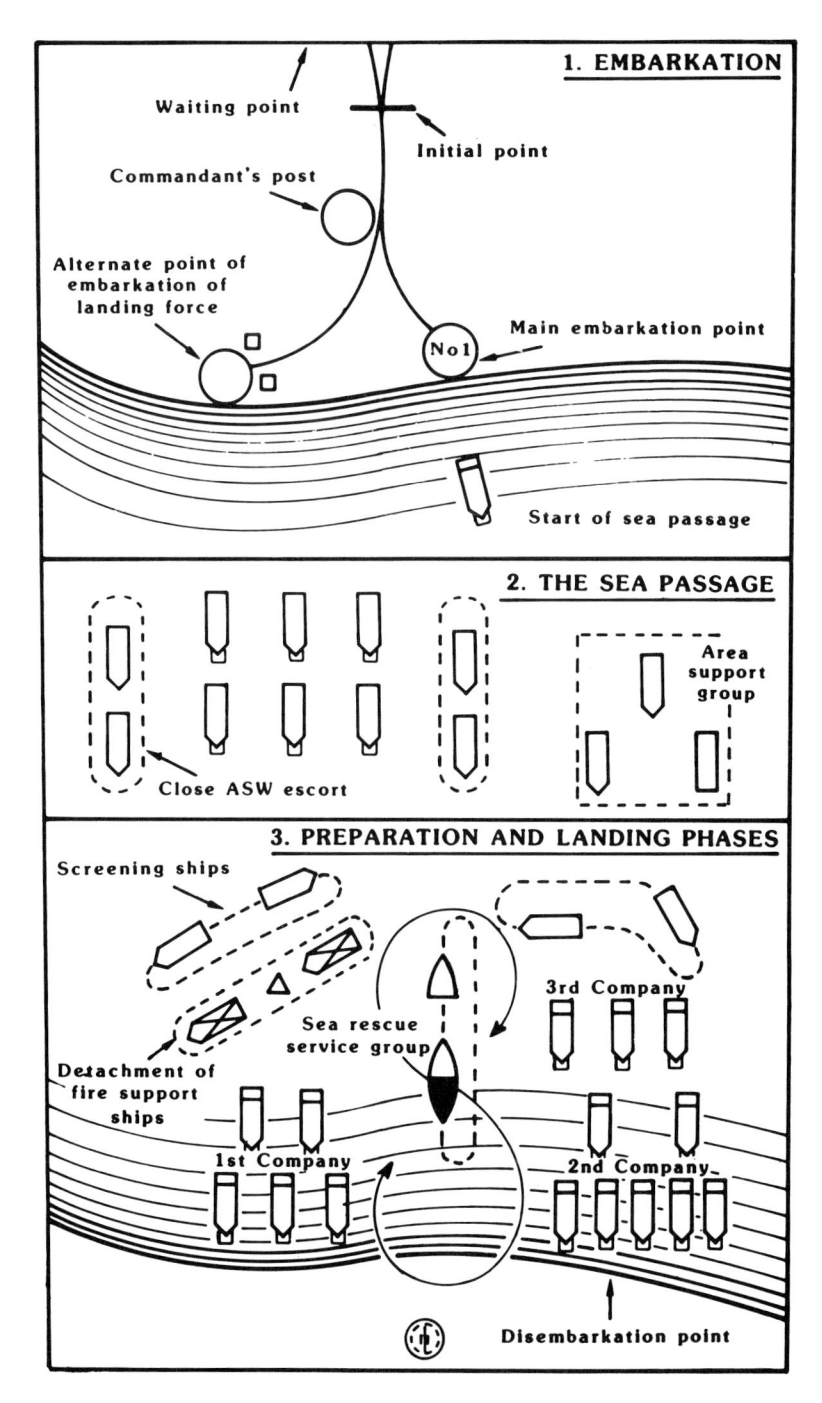

FIG. 7.2 The main stages of a Soviet amphibious assault at battalion strength. (*Source: C. Donnelly* et al., *Soviet Amphibious Warfare, Soviet Studies Centre, Sandhurst 1985. Crown copyright*)

PLATE 7.7   The *Aist* was the first of the large Soviet ACVs. It is powered by two gas turbine engines, has a top speed of about 80 knots and can carry some four medium tanks and 50 troops. It has a ramp at the stern as well as the bow ramp shown here. (*Sovetskiy Vion*)

Navy who would be responsible for the safe embarkation, passage and landing. The naval and surface forces, assault force and support units would be subordinated to him. The commander of the landing force would be responsible for the Naval Infantry and any Army units taking part in the operation; the Naval Infantry would be used in the initial assault, with the remainder as follow-up forces. It would appear that there are no standing staffs for amphibious operations, although the General Staff Operations Group for the operation would consist of specially trained staff officers, with responsibilities for co-ordinating the various arms and services, including air support.

Tactical level Soviet amphibious operations are often mounted at short notice from comparatively close range, and consist of four main stages:

▶   *The Waiting Area*, close to the coast and probably not far behind the main front line. It must be a secure area where the landing force can be dispersed and concealed.

▶   *The Embarkation Area*, which would be a port, bay or estuary where the landing force would join up with the amphibious ships. There would be a number of embarkation points where the ships could beach, or come to a slipway, so that the vehicles could be driven on board.

▶   *The Passage*. The length of the passage would depend upon the ground and the state of the battle, but the doctrine is said to require it to be conducted entirely at night. Given that the Soviets also plan to land at night, this limits the length of the passage considerably, although operational level forces launched from the main bases against North Norway or in the Baltic would clearly require a longer passage. We assume that the hovercraft would deploy separately and join the slower surface shipping at a rendezvous from which they would move to the *Tactical Deployment Line*, some 12 miles off the beach, to form up into an assault formation.

▶   *The Landing*. For an unopposed landing, the amphibious ships and hovercraft would normally beach so that the armour can drive off rapidly, but if opposition is encountered, the amphibians would disembark out of machine gun range from the shore, and swim to the beach. The landing would probably be co-ordinated with an airborne or helicopter borne desant, usually mounted from land bases; we do not believe that the Soviet amphibious ships have a capability to carry more than a small helicopter assault force.

AMPHIBIOUS OPERATIONS IN GRENADA 1983

On 20 October, 1983 the amphibious task force[3] consisting of five amphibious ships (LPH, LPD, LSD and two LSTs), and carrying 22nd MAU, was off Bermuda en route for the Mediterranean when it was diverted towards Grenada. This was a first contingency response to the political unrest on that island following the murder of its Prime Minister, Maurice Bishop, by soldiers of a hard line Revolutionary Council that had ties with Cuba and the Soviet Union. On 23 October, the Organisation of Eastern Caribbean States formally requested United States assistance, and the American Government agreed, especially in view of concern about the safety of some 1,000 American citizens there, that action was called for.

On board the task force there was scanty intelligence about the enemy and the beaches. The initial plan developed during the passage was to land one company in AAVs across Grand Anse Beach, while a second company was to carry out a heliborne assault into Salines airport and the third was to remain on board as the reserve. The key documents for an amphibious assault were duly completed.

On 23 October, however, less than 30 hours before the scheduled landing, the ATF learned that Army Rangers and elements of 82nd Airborne would be

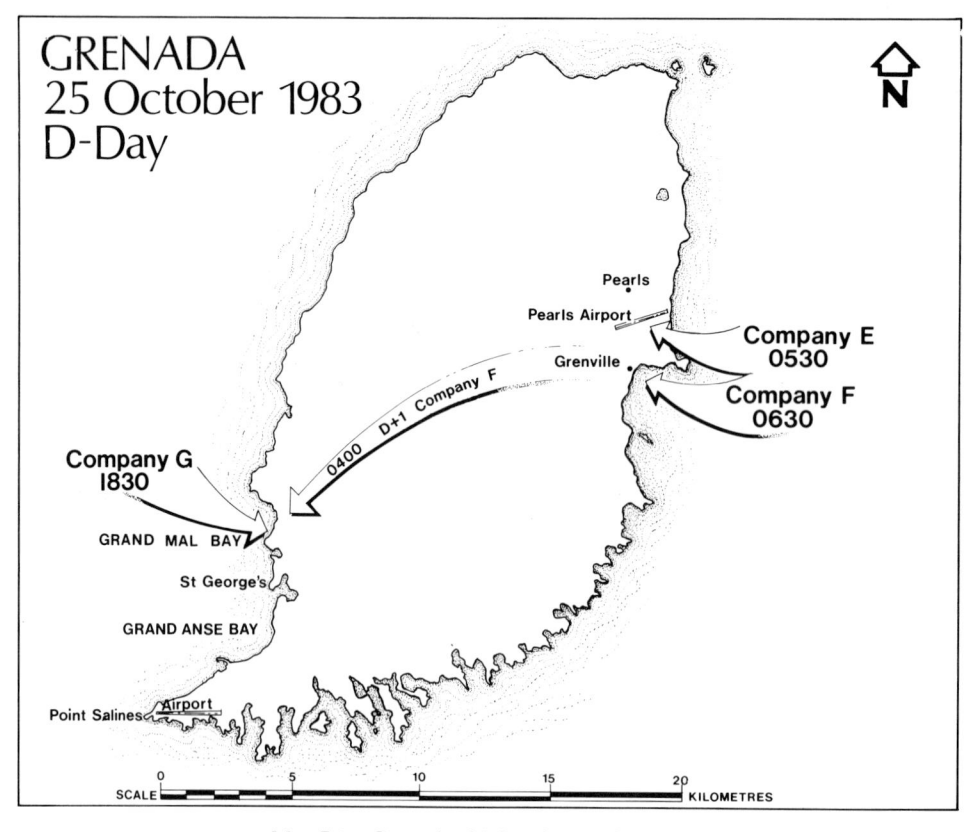

MAP 7.1   Grenada: 25 October 1983—D-Day

responsible for the southern portion of the island, and that the Marines' task was to secure Pearls Airport and Grenville. The enlargement of the force to include these Army elements provoked some overall command and control problems, but we will concentrate upon the amphibious aspects.

Opposition to the landing was expected from the Grenadian People's Revolutionary Army, numbering about 1,200 men, plus a militia of up to 5,000 men, with the most effective resistance expected from the anti-aircraft batteries equipped with Soviet designed 12.7mm and 37mm guns. Furthermore there were some 750

PLATE 7.8 US Marines loading into CH-46 *Sea Knight* on USS *Guam* during Operation *Urgent Fury* at Grenada. (*US Navy*)

Cuban civilians, construction workers and military, of whom the latter constituted about 25 per cent.

The revised concept of operations was for a combined AAV and heliborne assault, but a SEAL* Team reconnaissance on the night of the landing reported at 0200 hrs on 25 October that the beach was unsatisfactory. In consequence, the CATF directed that the assault would be exclusively by air. The first company started to take off at 0315 hrs in four divisions of assault helicopters and one escort division of Sea Cobras *as escorts, totalling 21 helicopters, all equipped with night vision goggles (NVG).*

It was just still dark when the first helicopters reached the landing zone south of Pearls Airport at 0530 hrs, and the pilots saw through their NVG that the first site was covered with high brush and tall palm trees. The Squadron Commander rapidly directed the helicopters to the relatively clear northwest corner of the zone. The gunships silenced some anti-aircraft guns which had fired from the hills near the airport, but the landing was otherwise unopposed. Again, when the second company was flown into Grenville one hour later, the Squadron Commander had to make a rapid change to the landing site, this time using a soccer pitch for an unopposed landing in the centre of the town.

In subsequent operations, two Sea Cobras *were lost in actions at St George's, and the ATF sailed round to the west of the island. There they landed the reserve company by AAV and LCU after first light on 25 October in Grand Mal Bay. Here it was reinforced during the night by the company redeployed by helicopter from Grenville. The next day, the Marine helicopters carried Rangers to Grand Anse Bay to rescue American students from the Medical School there.*

St George's was secured on 27 October and the island was in the hands of United States and Caribbean forces the next day. At 0530 hrs on 1 November the ATF launched yet another AAV and helicopter assault on Carriacou, an island some 30 miles north of Granada, where they received a friendly welcome from the locals. Even though the resistance was light, with three combined assaults and several other helicopter operations over six days, Commodore Erie as CATF was justified in his comment that 'Grenada demonstrated that a Navy-Marine ATF is capable of fast, flexible combat operations in support of joint task force operations.'[4]

* *SEAL is an acronym for Sea Air Land, and these teams are the USN's special forces.*

8

Means of Delivery

The major technological changes affecting amphibious warfare have naturally been linked to significant developments in doctrine, tactics or strategy. The classic example has been the creation of the United States amphibious capability in the 1930s when the logical progression of thought; *strategy*; *doctrine*; *tactics*; *equipment*; constituted the ideal critical path. More often, however, it has been developments in the technology affecting the means of amphibious delivery, the landing craft, helicopters and amphibians, that have driven the pace of tactical change.

The refurbishment programmes of the 1960s in America and Britain, for example, were heavily influenced by the introduction of helicopters. This led to the concept of vertical envelopment, which meant that assaults would no longer be confined to beaches, as the CLF had the option to outflank the defence, seize vital ground inland, and then secure the beachhead through which to offload his heavy equipment. That concept led, in turn, to the development of the specialist helicopter ships. Today, we are at another crossroads in the development of amphibious warfare, with the United States developing a new concept of over-the-horizon (OTH) landings to exploit the tilt rotor aircraft and hovercraft, and the Soviets pressing forward with wing-in-ground-effect craft.

FH70 & PRIMEMOVER LOADING TRIAL ON LCU(R).

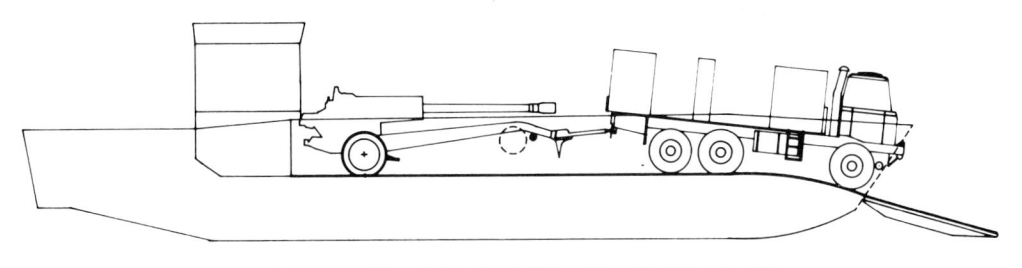

NO CLEARANCE. WILL REQUIRE UNHITCHING TO FIT.

FIG. 8.1 During trials of the FH-70, the graphics computer at ATTURM examined whether the gun and its prime mover could be loaded into a LCU ready to be driven off; it could not, and they have to be carried decoupled

LANDING CRAFT

The ubiquitous landing craft can be found fulfilling a variety of roles in most navies and, worldwide, they are probably used more on administrative, logistic and ferry tasks than they are on amphibious operations. They come in many sizes and types, most being dayboats with little seagoing capability, but the larger ones are very capable and there is little to choose between them and the LSTs. We know them as the workhorse of the amphibious fleet, designed expressly for the mundane task of shuttling men, vehicles and stores from ship to shore; the basic craft is a shallow draft, flat bottomed boat fitted with a bow ramp, and with the ability to carry a good load. A comment by a USMC officer in 1939 about the excellent Higgins boat which became the core of the US wartime landing craft fleet, captures the essence of the requirement, 'It has more speed, more manœuvrability, handles easier, and lands troops higher on the beach than any other craft evaluated.'[1]

The engine is sited aft to give ballast for beaching, and to allow the maximum deck space forward for cargo. The act of beaching is clearly a hazard to machinery, especially propellers, rudders and cooling systems. Several measures can be taken to overcome these problems; the rotatable *Kort* nozzle, which does not project below the hull, protects the propeller and provides very good steering; water jet propulsion is an alternative method. Another precaution would be to fit a *Keel Cooler*, which is an internal fresh water engine cooling system preferable to the normal external salt water system liable to blockages from debris ingested near the beach.

Successful landing craft operations depend upon good intelligence of the beach area, weather and tides. The beaches should have sufficient capacity, adequate

TABLE 8.1

Characteristics of Some Landing Craft

Type	Displacement (tons)	Dimensions (metres)	Speed (knots)	Range (nm)	Capacity
UNITED STATES					
LCU 1610	375	27.5 × 6.8	10	1200	170 tons, 3 tanks
LCM-8	105	22 × 6	9	190	60 tons, one tank
LCM-6	60	17 × 4	9	130	30 tons, 80 troops
UNITED KINGDOM					
LCU Mk 9 (RM)	176	28 × 5.5	10		120 tons, one tank, or 4 × 4 ton vehicles, or about 120 troops
LCVP Mk 4 (RM)	16	13 × 3	18		Landrover or 30 troops
LCL-4001 (RCT)	1663	72 × 15	10.3		350 tons, or 5 tanks or 11 × 8 ton vehicles
SOVIET UNION					
ONDATRA	145	24 × 6	10	500	One tank
FRANCE					
CDIC (replacing EDIC)	872	59 × 11	10	1000	1000 tons. Designed to work with TCD-90-Foudre

Means of Delivery 121

approaches, an acceptable gradient, a surface which vehicles can traverse, and exists for vehicles on to routes inland. The landing craft must have a clear run to the beach, and not be grounded on reefs or shoals some way off, as occurred with dire results in the Tarawa landings. A steep gradient gives a better chance of a dry landing and there is less danger of the craft being stranded on an ebb tide than with a shallow gradient. Classic amphibious landings are conducted on wide beaches which allow a large wave to land in line abreast, but the UK/NL Amphibious Force has become practised in landing on the small, and often rocky, beaches of Norway.

Waterproofing. All landing craft should be able to ground in no more than 4′ 6″ on a shallow gradient beach (they would do better on a steep gradient) so it follows that, allowing some room for 'sinkage', vehicles must be able to negotiate 5′ of

Rover 90 – Waterproofed items

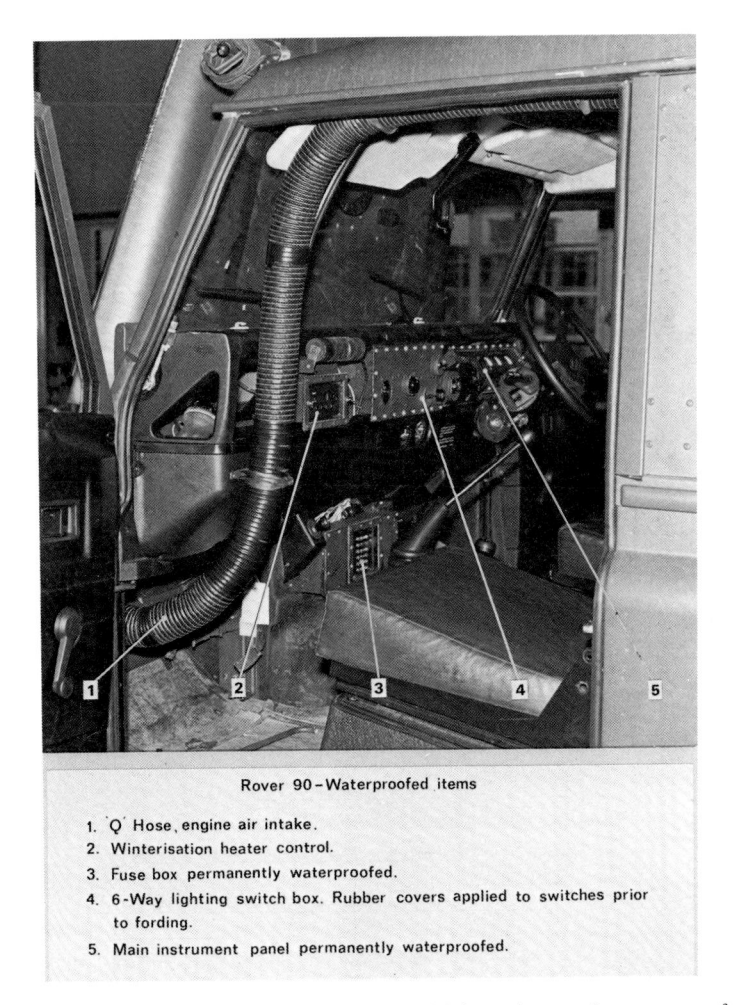

1. 'Q' Hose, engine air intake.
2. Winterisation heater control.
3. Fuse box permanently waterproofed.
4. 6-Way lighting switch box. Rubber covers applied to switches prior to fording.
5. Main instrument panel permanently waterproofed.

PLATES 8.1, 8.2 and 8.3   Plate 8.1 shows which items have to be waterproofed in the cab of the new Rover 90, while in Plate 8.2 a vehicle mechanic is at work on the engine. The result must be able to withstand the deep wade from a landing craft shown in Plate 8.3. (*Royal Marines. Crown copyright*)

Plate 8.2

Plate 8.3

water. Waterproofing is a complex, and sometimes lengthy, process that ensures clean dry air to the engine, allows the gases to escape, and makes sure that the ignition system and electrics continue to function. Waterproofing kits have to be specially designed for all types of vehicles; some of which have the equipment built in, while others have semi-permanent systems which do not take long to prepare for wading. The rest have to be specially fitted with appliqué kits before an operation, and that takes time and training. The penalty, of course, for bad waterproofing or bad driving in a wade is a *drowned vehicle* which would have to be rescued by the *Beach Armoured Recovery Vehicle* (*BARV*) of the Amphibious Beach Unit.

Landing Craft in the UK/NL Amphibious Force

Perhaps the best known of the smaller craft is the Landing Craft Vehicle and Personnel (LCVP)—an American title now used by the British who once called them *Landing Craft Assault* (the title still used by the Dutch). Thousands were built during the Second World War, and the basic design survives today, despite many efforts to make improvements. They were certainly proved in a hard school, and General Holland Smith, who commanded the landing force at Saipan, commented that the LCVO '... did more to win the war in the Pacific than any other single piece of equipment....'[2] The present British version, the LCVP Mk IV, was introduced in 1985/6 (see Plate 7.6).

Landing craft are an integral part of an amphibious ship and, indeed, in the United States they are manned by the Navy. In the UK/NL Amphibious Force the Royal Marines man the assault craft, the LCVPs and *Landing Craft Utility* (*LCU*) which are carried by the LPD. The Royal Corps of Transport man the support craft, the self-deploying *Landing Craft Logistic* (*LCL*), the *Ramped Craft Lighter* (*RCL*) and the two types of powered pontoons, the *Mexeflotes* and the *Ramped Support Pontoons* (*RSP*). The last three types are carried in LSLs or STUFT and provide a very useful back-up to the landing craft for carrying heavy loads, albeit slowly in the case of the pontoons, for the general offload.

There is also an unusual unit which provides discrete support to the UK/NL Landing Force (so is commanded by the CLF rather than the CATF). 539 Assault Squadron RM was formed as a result of experience in the Falklands war, based on a concept of operations which had been developed and trialled for some years in Norway. Its craft include arcticised LCVs and LCVPs, both equipped with glass fibre removable igloos, heating and enhanced navigation systems, so that they can operate at extended ranges carrying troops and equipment in the Arctic. The squadron also has some 15 knot inflatable raiding craft, and Rigid Raiding Craft (RRC).

The LCVs could make their own way across the North Sea to operational areas in Northern Europe, but normally the whole squadron would be deployed as deck cargo in heavy lift shipping or preferably in the dock of a semi-submersible. Once in the AOA, 539 Assault Squadron will be used in the assault landings, but its main task in subsequent operations would be to assist the landing force to use the sea flank for tactical operations such as raids, to provide a mobile command post, and to reinforce the logistic life. One advantage that it offers is that landing craft can continue to operate in weather conditions in inshore waters that would deter

PLATE 8.4 The 40 knot Rigid Raiding Craft are capable of carrying 5 arctic equipped troops. These craft have a relatively limited range, but they can be deployed over some considerable distances towed behind LCUs, which carry the troops in the protection of the arcticised canopies, and can load and dispatch the raiders close to the objective. (*Royal Marines. Crown copyright*)

helicopters and other forms of movement. The squadron can also take under command the Dutch LCAs, other allied landing craft, local fishing boats, coastal shipping and anything that could give additional waterborne mobility to the force . . . so, with this wide variety of craft, there is a long list of tasks for this versatile squadron in any operational area that has a challenging coastline and difficult terrain restricting movement ashore.

AMPHIBIANS

Amphibious Assault Vehicles

The *Amphibious Assault Vehicle (AAV-7A1)* series[3] is the core of the USMC opposed assault capability, and these vehicles are also used by several allied amphibious forces, but not by the British. The range includes the standard troop carrier, a command vehicle and a recovery vehicle. They are lightly armoured, and armed with a 0.5 machine gun and a 40mm automatic grenade launcher, but there is at present no version armed with an assault gun to give close support as the wave

PLATE 8.5 The AAV-7A1. The driver is forward on the port side, with the commander behind him, and the gunner mans the .5″ machine gun in the starboard turret. The AAV comes in command and recovery variants as well as this personnel carrier. (*Marine Corps Gazette*)

closes the beach. As there are also no landing craft which can provide this support, there appears to be a serious capability gap; at San Carlos the British improvised by placing two CVRTs (or light tanks), a *Scorpion* and a *Scimitar*, side by side in a LCV ready 'to blast at any enemy on the beach over the bow ramp lowered just before the start of the run-in'.[4]

AAVs can be launched from the stern of a LST which is moving at some 12 knots; they drive like lemmings into the sea, plunging apparently to destruction, then bob

126   Amphibious Operations

up to reveal only a few inches of freeboard to form up at the Line of Departure some 4,000m from the beach . . . an awe inspiring sight! They have a speed of 8 knots in water, and have good cross country mobility in the armoured personnel carrier role ashore, although their performance is not as good as other infantry fighting vehicles. The size required for buoyancy and weight constraints for flotation conflict with features desired for land combat, such as smaller size and heavier armour. The replacement of the present generation by vehicles that can be absorbed into the developing OTH concept is causing some concern, but we will return to that in Chapter 13.

WALCHEREN—NOVEMBER 1944

As the Allies advanced into the Low Countries, the Island of Walcheren blocked the entrance to the Scheldt and Antwerp, and was strongly defended. Most of the centre of the island lay below sea level, so it was decided to breach the retaining dykes by bombing, leaving a saucer of dry ground with the centre flooded, except for the main towns. The assaulting forces were 4 Commando Brigade RM from the sea at Westkapelle and 4 (Army) Commando at Flushing, mounting from Ostend.

PLATE 8.6   During the Second World War a wide variety of close support craft were developed, including this LCT (G) firing more than 1,000 rockets. (*RM Museum*)

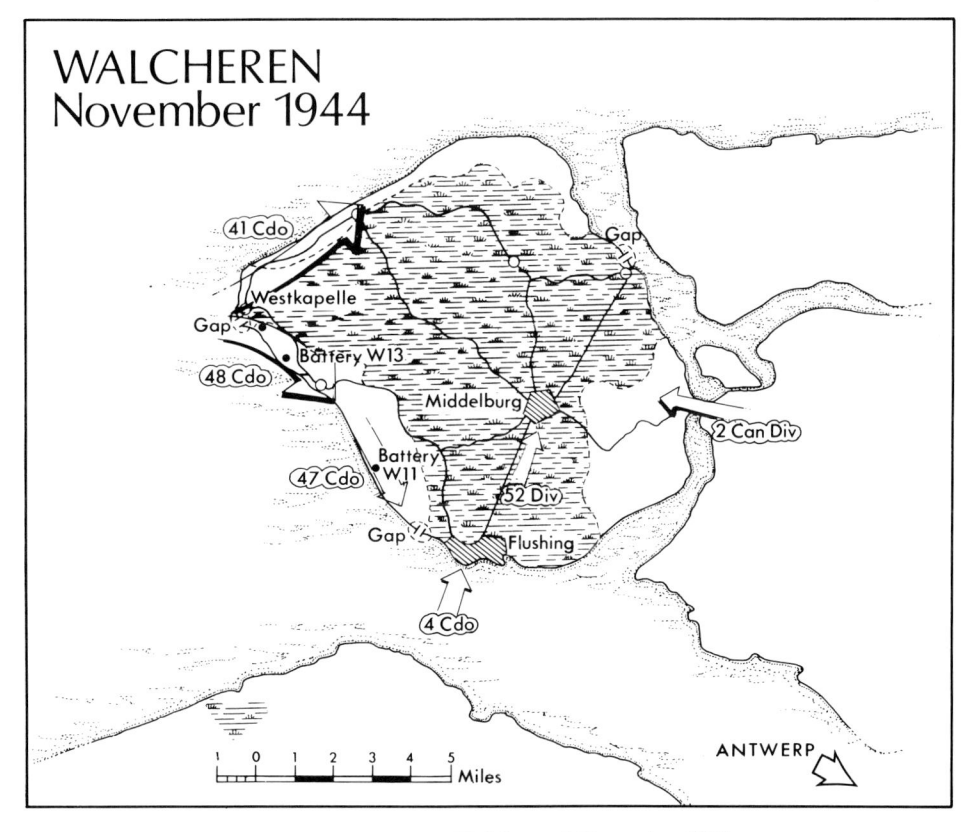

MAP 8.1   Assault on Walcheren 1 November 1944

> *H-hour was 0945 hours on 1 November, 1944. Initially, the main problem was to draw the fire of the strong shore batteries away from the approaching landing craft. The shallow coastal waters would not allow destroyers to approach, so the task was given to the Landing Craft (Gun) and other varieties of support craft of Support Squadron Eastern Flank (SSEF) which gallantly sailed in close to the shore to engage the enemy. The price was heavy, and of 28 craft in the action, nine were sunk; one captain of an offshore craft wrote: 'I cannot conclude without saying how much I and my ship's Company admired the sustained fighting of the inshore craft. They were an inspiring sight'.[5]*
>
> *The diversion succeeded and the commanders landed; two units in LCI (Small) for the first wave . . . but Moulton, commanding the third, 48 Commando RM, had insisted in having the more powerful LCTs and LVTs (called* Buffaloes *by the British) in his first wave, instead of the second (a lesson he had learned in Normandy).[6] The battle to capture the many batteries was hard, and the* Buffaloes *proved their worth on the difficult going on the dunes. The island was secure by 8 November.*

AIR CUSHION VEHICLES (ACV)

ACVs, or hovercraft, appear to have all the attributes of the ideal amphibian. They can achieve high speeds in calm seas, can operate in waters denied to other ships, have low acoustic, magnetic and pressure signatures for mines, their air cushion makes them virtually immune to underwater explosions and torpedoes, and they can land on many more beaches than other landing craft, rapidly taking their cargo or passengers clear of the potentially hazardous beach areas. They have, unfortunately, a number of significant disadvantages which have deterred some amphibious forces from using them in large numbers. They suffer from high fuel consumption and much reduced performance in rough water, and the welter of spray possibly creates the most testing conditions for high performance gas turbines, so maintenance can be difficult. ACVs have a low payload, although their speed can compensate for this, they are noisy, which might compromise tactical surprise, and they are much more expensive than landing craft in comparative terms. For the UK/NL Landing Force they have had only a limited attraction for operations on the stormy Atlantic littoral and, although they can traverse ice, they often cannot find a way up the steep and narrow exits from the Norwegian beaches.

For possibly the same reasons, there are few ACVs in the Soviet Northern Fleet, but the operating areas in the Far East, the Black Sea and the Baltic are well suited for these craft and, especially in the Baltic, the flat hinterland offers good opportunities for deep penetration. Thus the Soviets have been the leaders in using ACVs for amphibious warfare since the early 1970s, and they have increased the numbers by some 50 per cent since 1980. Their lighter craft can be carried in the *Ivan Rogov* but, generally, ACVs would be used from shore bases in relatively

TABLE 8.2

ACV Characteristics

Type	Displacement (tons)	Dimensions (metres)	Speed (knots)	Range (miles)	Capacity	Remarks
UNITED STATES						
LCAC	170	27 × 14	40	200	60 tons one tank	Carried in amphibious ship. Programme for 90
SOVIET UNION						
AIST	250	47 × 17	80	350	4 tank & 50 troops	
LEBED	87	25 × 11	70	100	40 tons 2 light tanks or 120 troops	Carried in LPD
TSAPLYA	105	26 × 13			1 tank & 80 troops	Carried in LPD. LEBED successor?
UTENOK	70	23 × 11	65		1 tank	
GUS	27	21 × 7	60	185	25 troops	
POMORNIK	350	57 × 20	50		100 tons One tank, 80 troops	

* All are gas turbine driven.

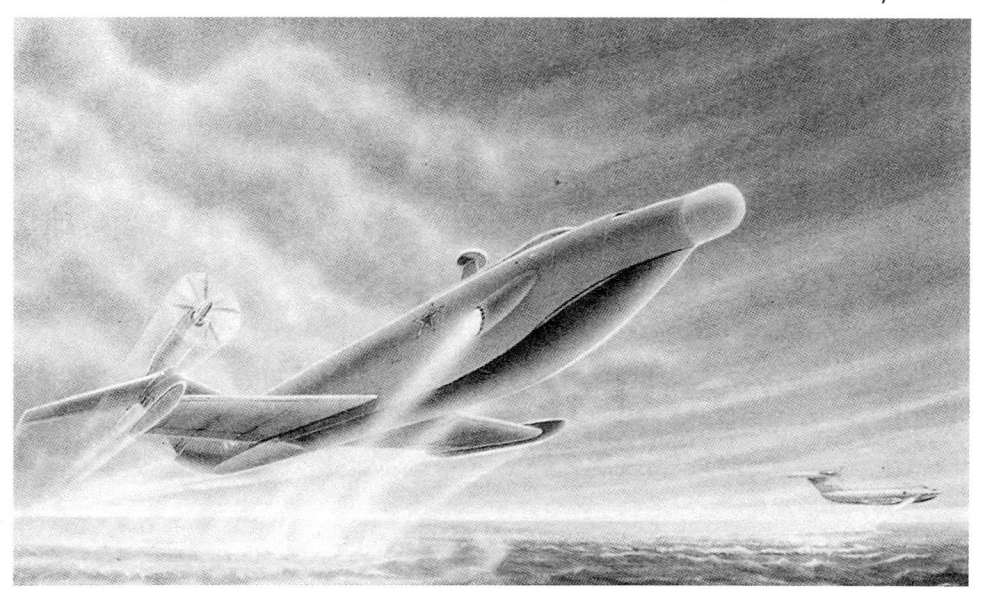

PLATE 8.7 An artist's impression of the Soviet Wing-in-Ground Effect (WIG) craft. (*US Department of Defense*)

short range operations. A new generation is now being introduced, which includes the 350 ton *Pomornik*, and there may be a trend towards large ACVs suited for independent operation.

The Americans concentrate upon different characteristics. They are, of course, mainly interested in a hovercraft that can be deployed strategically, therefore it has to be carried in an amphibious ship. Their *Landing Craft Air Cushion* (*LCAC*) has made best use of high cushion pressure to achieve a more compact design than other hovercraft. Some old hovercraft traits remain, however, as the performance is degraded in rough weather, they are noisy and they take up a lot of shipping space compared to landing craft.

Among the developments in this general area which might affect amphibious warfare in the future, the Soviets have a large *Wing-in-Ground-Effect* (*WIG*) craft on trial, or perhaps even in production. A WIG looks like an aircraft (see Plate 8.7), but flies very close to the surface. At this height the lift/drag ratio of the wings can be doubled, giving a significant improvement in aerodynamic efficiency. In practice, it is an aircraft which produces its own air cushion. The cushion effect is lost at the height of one wingspan, so it follows that WIGs tend to be large because the bigger the wingspan, the higher the flight and the more chance of avoiding waves at sea. It is difficult to get a relatively heavy sea-based aircraft airborne without providing excessive power, so the *Power Augmented Ram WIG*, or PAR WIG, system has been developed whereby the propulsion engines are redirected downwards to augment wing lift at low speed. The Soviets have used this concept to produce a craft which is believed to have a speed of some 300 knots and an impressive lift of about 900 troops. Theoretically the PAR WIG is very efficient and cost effective, but there is great technological risk, and we can only speculate about

130   Amphibious Operations

PLATE 8.8   The Slingsby Aviation SAH 2200 has a single diesel engine which powers both lift and thrust, can carry up to 24 people (about 16 troops in arctic equipment), and has a speed of 40 knots and a range of up to 500 miles. (*Slingsby Aviation*)

its true potential for amphibious warfare. It is unlikely to be used for an assault, but its speed and capacity could make it extremely useful for rapid reinforcement of a beachhead in the later stages of an operation.

At the other end of the scale, Western forces are continuing to search for hovercraft that can fit into amphibious ships and replace landing craft effectively. There are hopes that diesel driven hovercraft, made of composite materials and using advanced skirt technology, can be developed further. They offer ease of maintenance, have a rugged design and are relatively quiet, but the payload does not yet rival the LCU. They might, however, soon compare favourably with the LCVP in terms of cost, size, sea going ability and capacity . . . to which must be added their speed and amphibian characteristics.

ASSAULT SUPPORT HELICOPTERS AND TILT ROTORS

Since the 1950s, the helicopter has been an essential means of tactical deployment, and has given amphibious forces a vertical envelopment capability. The concept of using unarmoured medium lift helicopters as the first elements of an assault is well proven, but it entails a degree of risk. Good intelligence can help to ensure an unopposed route and landing, and protection can be provided by attack helicopters and fixing wing aircraft (see Chapter 10), but the medium life helicopters must be agile enough to fly low and evasively (called 'nap-of-the-earth' flying). They should also have a self-protection suite which might include one or more of: a radar warner, a short range air-to-air-missile (preferable 'fire and forget'

TABLE 8.3

Assault Support Helicopter Characteristics

Type	Name	Speed (mph)	Range (miles)	Weight (lb)	Capacity
UNITED STATES MARINE CORPS					
CH-46E	Sea Knight	137	190	15,800	30 troops
CH-53A/D	Sea Stallion	150	250	23,600	8,000 lb
					37 troops
CH-53E	Super Stallion	170	480	33,200	16 tons
					56 troops
UK/NL AMPHIBIOUS FORCE					
CH-4	Sea King HC4	169	246	12,300	24 troops
SOVIET					
Mi-8	Hip	160	250	16,000	28 troops, or 8,000 lb. Also used armed
Mi-6	Hook	186	385	60,000	26,000 lb

or laser guided), machine guns, chaff and flare dispenser, infra-red jammer and armoured seats. There also needs to be a good balance between lift capacity and numbers of helicopters; a few relatively large helicopters (carrying, say, over 40 troops) might be attractive in economic terms, but the implications of any losses are that much more serious, so it is much better in tactical terms to have greater numbers of smaller helicopters (carrying some 20–30 troops) to ensure operational redundancy in the squadrons. An ideal helicopter force would include a preponderance of smaller support helicopters, together with some heavier lift helicopters for vehicles, equipment and logistics.

The British rely upon the *Sea King HC 4-Commando*, which will be in service until the turn of the century. With a capacity to carry 24 men—rather less when all are wearing arctic warfare equipment—it is a satisfactory troop lift helicopter despite some lack of agility and self protection. The 24 helicopters available enable the deployment of a two company group of some 300 men with their support weapons and ammunition—this is the minimum force which is judged to be necessary to secure an initial lodgement ashore[7]—but there is no heavy lift helicopter available. In the Falklands, the one *Chinook* remaining after the loss of the *Atlantic Conveyor* did sterling service, and doubtless such helicopters would be welcome in future, but they are too big for the planned amphibious ships and special provision would again have to be made for their deployment to the AOA. Another lesson from 1982 was the formation of the Commando Helicopter Operations and Support Cell (CHOSC) to improve the co-ordination of tasking and planning, which is particularly important ashore where the helicopters would be dispersed into a number of Forward Operating Bases (FOB). Indeed, these operations present the RN pilots (there are a few RM) with a considerable challenge, as they are trained for maritime, usually ASW, operations, and have to adjust to the somewhat alien demands of the land battle, which they have done with great success over the years.

132   Amphibious Operations

PLATE 8.9   The *MV-22 Osprey* during one of its first test flights. (*Bell-Boeing*)

The Soviet Naval Infantry do not have any integral support helicopters and the amphibious ships cannot mount a large assault wave, but short range helicopter *desants* might well be mounted, from behind the ground forces FEBA, to support amphibious landings. For this they would use the Mi-6 *Hook* which can carry 70 troops or a BMD, or the Mi-8 *Hip* which has several roles including carrying 24 troops.

The Americans, as one would expect, have the full gamut of medium and heavy lift helicopters, with the mighty *CH-53E Super Stallion* having a lift of 16 tons, able to move the 155mm M198 howitzer and its prime mover, or the Light Armoured Vehicle. During the 1990s the present generation of medium lift helicopters was to have been replaced by the revolutionary *MV-22 Osprey* tilt rotor aircraft. This concept has some impressive characteristics; it is more efficient than conventional helicopters in the cruise, where a speed of 250 knots can be achieved carrying 24 combat-ready troops over a radius of 200 miles; the conventional helicopter is more efficient only in hovering flight. Its cost, however, and limited constituency turned the Department of Defense against it and only Congressional support might keep it alive. Confirmation of its cancellation would be a major blow to the USMC.

SOVIET NAVAL INFANTRY AIRBORNE FORCES

One step removed from assault helicopter operations are airborne landings; the Soviet Naval Infantry has integral airborne elements as part of its assault force. On Exercise *Zapad 81*, an entire naval infantry battalion was landed by parachute in support of an amphibious landing and on another exercise three companies were landed, each by different methods; shipping, helicopters and airborne, with BMDs being dropped as well, possibly from the Mi-26 *Halo*, which is an all weather heavy

PLATE 8.10 Like the USMC, the Soviet Naval Infantry recruits women marines, and apparently deploys them on airborne operations. (*Sovetskiy Voin*)

lift aircraft which can carry 86 men or two BMD light armoured vehicles. This is a concept not widely used elsewhere; although 5 Airborne Brigade shares the out-of-area role with 3 Cdo Bde RM, airborne operations are not generally an integral part of NATO amphibious operations, at least on any scale beyond the insertion of small parties.

9
Amphibious Ships

The core of the amphibious capability is the specialist shipping; large, expensive and somewhat idiosyncratic vessels built on utilitarian rather than heroic lines. Classes and types and the balance of fleets vary from country to country, but there is much in common in the broad criteria for determining the shape and size of the fleet, and in the design of the ships.

PLANNING CRITERIA

Ideally, a nation's fleet should enable the full landing force and its stores to be embarked in specialist amphibious ships. As we have seen, cost and defence priorities militate against the ideal and this leads to what Geoffrey Till calls 'the attenuation of means'; an acceptance of compromise which is by no means peculiar to amphibious warfare. So some national priorities have to be calculated:

▶ *First*, decide what to do with amphibious forces as part of the maritime strategy. As we saw in Part I, the Americans want a strategic force able to undertake opposed landings. The Soviets appear to want a strike force for operational and tactical level *desants*, but with little strategic capability. The British have decided upon a force with strategic reach for out-of-area tasks, and with an operational capability optimised for the Northern Flank.

▶ *Secondly*, design the landing forces. Generally, the organisation and equipment will be based on the nation's ground forces suitably adapted for amphibious operations.

▶ *Thirdly*, make an essential decision about the minimum amount of the landing force and its first line logistic support that has to be put ashore early for tactical operations; that determines the outline requirement for specialist amphibious shipping. The United States capability can now cater for the assault echelons of one MEF, although the planning target is to increase to one MEF and one MEB in the mid-1990s, or roughly two MEBs on each of the East and West coasts, but this requires the ambitious building programme to be continued throughout an era when there is mass obsolescence of the present ships. The UK/NL Amphibious Force should, in future, be able to land about 2/3rds of the fighting element of the force from specialist shipping, which is possibly about the same as the Soviet capacity.

▶ *Fourthly*, calculate whether and how to move the balance of the force by

136 Amphibious Operations

other means for rapid reinforcement, by less capable shipping or by air. The Americans call the element that moves by commercial shipping the assault follow-on echelon (AFOE) and the air element the fly-in echelon (FIE).

▶ *Finally*, counter the cost and design the ships. It would cost (at 1986 prices) about £500 million for an American multi-purpose Assault Ship (LHD) of the *Wasp* class, about £200 million for a new British Landing Platform Dock (LPD) and some £105 million for the ASS. In this market place economists and writers search for a cheaper solution, such as this British suggestion:

> 'Instead of building two amphibious ships, the . . . Government might choose a makeshift option, arming a couple of container ships at a third of the cost, crewed by twenty-five not 500 men. In principle, each would require only a minimum armament of Phalanx guns for use against sea skimming missiles; and high velocity missile systems against low flying aircraft.
>
> Since the Marines would need at least eight helicopters to take off simultaneously, carrying 240 soldiers, the containers would have to be adapted accordingly. Given the present range of heavy lift helicopters, the ships which might carry them could probably remain over the horizon. The idea of converting merchant shipping in this way is actually very attractive.'[1]

There is certainly a need for economy, but it must be realised that ships that are to be used successfully on hazardous operations in war need to meet certain criteria.

PLATE 9.1 After the Falklands campaign, the RFA *Reliant* trialled the *Arapaho* system of containers so that she could operate aircraft and helicopters. Relatively cheap platforms such as this could have value as force multipliers, to back up specialist amphibious ships. The Soviets may also be experimenting with operating VTOL aircraft, *Forgers*, from specially configured Ro-Ro ships.
(*British Aerospace*)

SPECIALIST SHIPS

Specialist ships are normally built to warship standards to stand a reasonable chance of surviving the passage to, and operations in, the AOA; have the capacity and technological capability to embark, carry, maintain and, essentially, disgorge the land force rapidly to conduct the initial assault in tactical formation; and thereafter help to sustain the force ashore. Some ships should also have the facilities to command the maritime battle, and for the embarked force to plan, command and execute the landing.

Survivability

Survivability on passage is mainly a tactical issue, dependent upon the operations of the escorts, but an amphibious ship should have:

- ▶ *Local protection* such as surface-to-air and close in weapon systems (CIWS). Some may have relatively little but the most capable new American LHD, *Wasp*, will have a full range (see Table 9.1).
- ▶ *The speed, endurance and sufficient manœuvrability* to operate with her escorts. With the speed of the convoy being that of the slowest vessel, it is important to have a reasonable minimum within an amphibious fleet, and the USN aims for 20 knots. The Western navies and, increasingly, the Soviets, expect these ships to be capable of deployments of some 8–10,000 miles range. Important, too, is the ability to manœuvre slowly in difficult waters close to the shore.
- ▶ *Inbuilt Damage Control Systems* to enable her to withstand a degree of damage and still carry out her task.
- ▶ *Nuclear, Chemical and Biological Protection* through the ability of warships to achieve gas tight integrity in the citadel, which is a group of interconnecting compartments (possibly most of the ship) with a gas tight boundary impervious to NBCD agents. There should also be 'pre-wetting' systems to cleanse the upper deck of contaminents, and cleansing stations inside the citadel to allow people to move in and out about their business.

One of the most telling factors in her survival, however, is the speed and efficiency of the disembarkation so that she can spend as little time as possible exposed to the most extreme hazards close to the beach area while the landing force is securing the objective.

Capacity and Capability

An important aim in designing an amphibious ship is to allow her to embark a complete fighting unit, or a coherent group of units, with their weapons, vehicles, ammunition and stores, and to carry the aircraft, helicopters, hovercraft and landing craft to put them ashore and support them. The more the unit group/ship identity can be fostered, the more efficient the landing. Unfortunately, but understandably, design constraints and resources and, indeed, operational and tactical demands on the day, often prevent the ideal balance.

TABLE 9.1
Amphibious Shipping Characteristics

Type & Class	Displacement (tons)	Dimensions (metres)	Speed (knots)	Armament	Hels[1]	LC[1]	Capacity/troops
UNITED STATES							
LPH Iwo Jima	18,000	183 × 25	23	2 Sea Sparrow 4 × 3in 2 Phalanx	Spots 7 Hangar 20 CH-46	nil	1746 pax[2]
LHA Tarawa	39,300	250 × 40	24	2 Sea Sparrow 3 × 5in 2 Phalanx	Spots 12 Hangar 26 CH-46	1 LCAC 1 LCM-8 6 LCM-6 4 LCU 1600	1700 pax
LHD Wasp	40,533	257 × 40	23	2 Sea Sparrow 3 Phalanx	Spots 9 Hangar 42 CH-46	3 LCAC or 12 LCM-6	1894 pax
LPD Austin	16,900	174 × 30	21	2 × 3in 2 Phalanx	Platform 6 CH-46 Small telescopic hangar	2 LCAC	930 pax
LSD-41 Whidbey Island	15,726	185 × 25	20+	2 Phalanx	Platform, no hangar	4 LCAC or 21 LCM-6	338 pax 17,500 sq ft for cargo transport
LST Newport	8,450	159 × 21	20	4 3in 1 Phalanx	Platform, no hangar	AAVs	420 pax
UNITED KINGDOM							
LPD Fearless	12,120	158 × 24	21	2 Sea Cat 2 Phalanx 2 Bofors 40/60	Platform, no hangar	4 LCU 4 LCVP	380 pax
Sir Galahad	8,451	140 × 19	18	nil	Platform	2 Mexefloat	340 pax

(Compared to the early LSLs, the new Sir Galahad and the rebuilt Sir Tristram have strengthened flightdecks and steel superstructures: Sir Galahad is 29 ft longer)

Amphibious Ships

SOVIET UNION						
LPD Ivan Rogov	14,000	158 × 24	25	SAM: SA-N-4 twin launcher 2 SA-N-5 quad launchers 2 × 3in BM-21 multi-barrelled rocket launcher	Platform	LCM 2 Lebed	522 pax 20 tanks
LST Alligator	4,700	111 × 15	18	3 × SA-N-5 2 × 57mm twin BM-21	nil	nil	300 pax 20 tanks
LST Ropucha	3,800	113 × 14	18	4 × SA-N-5 4 × 57mm (2-twin)	nil	nil	225 pax 20 tanks
LSM Polnochny Group C	1,150	82 × 10	18	4 × SA-N-5 2 × 30mm 2 × 40mm RLs	nil	nil	180 pax 6 tanks
FRANCE						
TCD 90 Foudre	11,800	168 × 22	21	SAM: 2 × Matra Sadral sextuple launchers	Spots 2 Hangar: 4 Super Puma	2 CDIC	470 pax (100 vehs)
TCD Ouragan	8,500	149 × 23	17	2 × 120mm mortars 4 × 40mm Bofors	Spots 4 Super Frelon	3 LCVPs 2 EDIC	343 pax 120 AMX tanks
BTMs Bougainville[3]	5,600	113 × 17 × 4.3	15		Spots 2 Super Puma	2 CTIM (similar size as US LCM-8)	500 pax
ITALY						
LPD San Giorgio	7,667	133 × 20	20	1 × 76mm	Spots 2 2 × Oerlikon 20mm	3 LCMs 3 LCVPs	516 pax 36 APCs

(1) Helicopter and Landing Craft details are illustrative; there are many permutations.
(2) pax = passengers (troops).
(3) Bougainville was built to support the Pacific nuclear test site and is rated as an auxiliary.

140   Amphibious Operations

The various ingredients to be considered in the design are:

▶ *Troops.* The ship should be able to accommodate formed bodies of troops, say eight or nine hundred for a battalion/commando group that consists of the infantry with its supporting weapons, artillery and engineers, or about four or five hundred for smaller logistic or signals units. The LHDs and LHAs can accept nearly 2,000, while the ASS is planned to take 800, and the British LPDs and LSLs can take under 400 each. All these ships can accept a higher number of troops under overload conditions for short passages; on occasions the British LPDs have been overloaded by as many as 1,000 men.

The ship must be designed to administer, accommodate and feed these men for long periods, and give them space for training so that they do not lose their edge during transit.

To ensure a quick disembarkation, the routes—from assembly areas in the messdecks through the passageways, past stores and armouries to collect weapons and ammunition, to a waiting area for embarkation in the landing craft, AAV, LCAC or helicopter—must be planned in the initial design of the ship. The routes have to be as straightforward as possible, well marked and, on operations and exercises, well practised.

PLATE 9.2   An artist's impression of the LHD USS *Wasp* which was commissioned in 1989. (*US Navy*)

▶ *Helicopters*. The helicopter-capable ship, such as an LHD, LHA or ASS should be able to launch, without undue delay, assault support helicopters with their accompanying attack or light helicopters. The ASS, for example, will carry 12 *Sea King* and 6 light or attack helicopters and really ought to be referred to as a LPH (which I will do from here on). The *sticks* must be loaded and the helicopters despatched rapidly, so 6 will be launched simultaneously from operating spots. The next 6 helicopters would be ranged on parking spots with engines burning but rotor blades stowed and these would be moved to the operating spots as soon as the first group has left for the *rendezvous point*. At the same time, any further helicopters would be moved up one of the two lifts to the parking spots. Moving up the scale, the LHD has 9 operating spots and can carry 40 helicopters of all types.

It is, of course, technically feasible to put together an assault force from a number of ships in a task group each with one, two or three spots, but these would be the most basic heliborne operations, giving the commander little chance of achieving concentration and surprise, and the potential for Clausewitzian *friction* (or Murphy's Law) is great. The lack of helicopter-capable ships was one of the factors leading Brigadier Thompson to rely upon landing craft for the assault at San Carlos in 1982, and it is still a limitation for the UK/NL Amphibious Force.

The value of the helicopter capable ship does not end with the assault, since an immediate reserve force, sometimes called an Eagle Flight, could be held on board until required, and then deployed rapidly from the ship. She will also play an important role in the build up and maintenance of the force ashore, especially as she has the command and control facilities, technicians, stores and fuel to run, maintain and repair the helicopter force during lengthy operations. Even when a forward operating base has been established ashore, the second line support from a ship is still important.

▶ *Aircraft*. Since their experience in the Second World War when their integral air wings rarely operated from the supporting carriers, the USMC have been trying to ensure that their close support aircraft were available for the assault. The acquisition of the STOL AV-8 *Harrier* solved the problem, and the LHDs and LHAs are now designed to operate these aircraft. There must be, however, a trade off between *Harriers* and helicopters in deciding the mix for any operation, depending on the balance of amphibious firepower and troop lift needed. The Americans usually have the luxury of this choice, but the British must also face it when using one of the CVS such as *Ark Royal* as an amphibious ship in the quick dash role.

▶ *Landing Craft, Hovercraft and Amphibians*. The chief means of disembarking tanks, large vehicles and heavy equipment is still by landing craft and, increasingly for the Americans, the LCAC. They are also important alternative means of disembarking troops.

> The LCUs and LCMs are usually carried in the docks of ships such as the LHD and LPD which can ballast down, flood the docks and open their stern doors. The craft can enter or leave while the ship is under way at about 5 knots. The stern docks are designed so that vehicles can be driven straight on board the craft from the vehicle decks.

PLATE 9.3   AAVs splash into the water from the LST USS *Frederick* during a joint exercise with the Australians in 1987. (*Marine Corps Gazette*)

The normal design of the dock, as in the British LPDs, has a central barrier which allows four LCUs to be docked down in pairs. The Italian LPD *San Giorgio* has a different system (see Plate 3.6).

To ensure that the first vehicles can be offloaded as soon as possible at the beach, the landing craft remain fully loaded in transit. It is a particular advantage if the craft can have a ramp at both ends, to give a roll-on roll-off facility, so that vehicles can be manœuvred in and out of the craft during passage if it is necessary to alter the loading plan before the landing. The British LCUs do not yet have this capability, but will in future designs.

The modern American ships are being built to carry LCAC, and an LHD can accommodate three. Again, there must be a trade off, and in this case the LCAC would replace the 12 hard working but less exciting LCMs. The LCACs can, however, enter and leave the dock without the ship flooding down as, of course, do the AAVs.

The LCVPs are carried hanging from davits on the British LPDs and will be in their LPH (ASS).

▶   *Vehicles, Tanks and Guns.* The ships must be able to embark and secure for passage the large numbers of vehicles used by the landing force and, to give planning flexibility, there should be facilities to enable the crew to reorganise the vehicle decks to match adjustments to the landing plan during passage. The design also needs to ensure that high vehicles and low, heavy and light can be stowed with good access to the various exits, which include the dock, the flightdeck, and a bow door with a built-in ramp capable of reaching onto a dockside or down onto a *Mexeflote*.

▶ *Stores, Fuel and Ammunition.* The assault ships would carry the main combat supplies for the first echelon during the early stages of landing, with the support ships carrying the bulk of the war maintenance reserve. For efficient operation, modern simultaneous loading and unloading stores pallet ports are needed.

▶ *Hospitals.* Many amphibious ships have good hospital facilities, and the LHD will have 600 hospital beds and 6 operating theatres.

C3-Command, Control and Communications

Experience in the Second World War showed that amphibious operations should be commanded from a specialist command ship rather than from a warship which had a primary fighting role. This is still a valid argument today and the Americans have two specialist ships in the *Blue Ridge (LCC)* class, one in the Atlantic and the other in the Pacific. The *Mount Whitney* is often used on Striking Fleet Atlantic tasks. However, in most cases, command of amphibious operations is exercised from a LHD, LHA or LPD. This arrangement has disadvantages since the assault ship does not have as good a communications fit as the LCC, and she needs to be close to the beach, whereas the CATF should not be committed so far forward if he is to take a balanced view of the AOA. It has, however, to be made to work and the UK/NL Amphibious Force is commanded from the LPD, which means that her construction should include good communications facilities and the space for naval and landing force operations rooms. The CATF and CLF staffs need to be adjacent to one another, close to their commanders, and have separate spaces for planning and for running the operation.

A FORCE MIX

A logical solution for the design of a modern assault ship would be, as you have probably gathered from the frequent mention of the LHD, to provide all the helicopter, landing craft/LCAC and command facilities in one ship. The Americans built specialist helicopter ships in the 1960s, the LPHs of the *Iwo Jima* class which reflected the dominance of helicopters in tactical thinking at the time. In the 1970s they opted for the more balanced approach of the general purpose ship in the LHAs of the *Tarawa* class. They have continued to develop this concept in the new design of the LHD and, undoubtedly, they give the commander a number of options for landing his assault force. The LHA/LHD is, however, too large and expensive for other amphibious nations to consider.

The LPDs such as the British *Fearless* and the US *Austin* are direct descendants of the dock ships of the Second World War, with the after dock covered over to

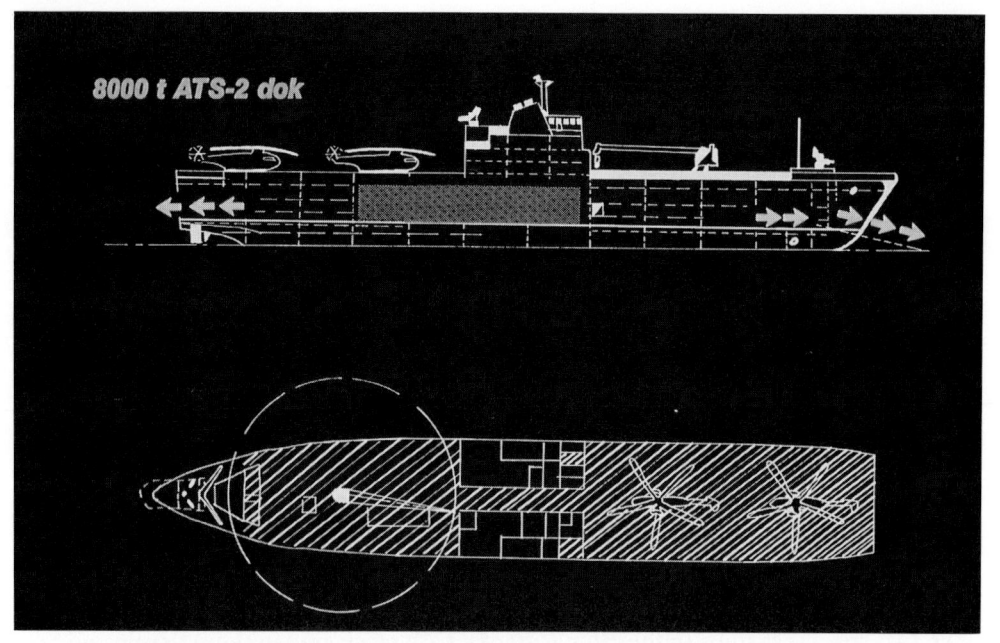

PLATE 9.4 The Dutch ATS is planned to have a dock capable of carrying six LCAs, a ro-ro vehicle deck, a platform for two helicopters, two *Mexeflotes*, be defended by the *Goalkeeper* air defence system and to lift two-thirds of 1 ACG. (*MOD (NL)*)

PLATE 9.5 An early artist's impression of the ASS . . . or LPH . . . which shows six operating spots for helicopters, but there is no room for six parked aircraft. The self defence was limited to four single 30mm gun mounts *Sea Gnat* chaff dispensers and IR decoy launchers. A later version of this picture included a smaller island and enlarged deck to allow parking space and a *Seawolf* air defence missile system. The design produced after the present tendering process may incorporate further changes. (*Hart Fenton*)

provide a helicopter deck. They are the well proven mainstay of the assault category, providing good command facilities and the ability to carry and offload much of the transport needed early in an operation. In the USN they are complementary to the LHA/LHD classes, but they are the cornerstone of several other amphibious fleets, such as the British, the Soviets'—the *Ivan Rogov* class— the Italians'—*San Giorgio* class—and the French with the new *Foudre* class. Thus they will be part of the amphibious fleets for some time to come; the *Austin* class will be given a further 10 years life by a Service Life Extension Programme (SLEP), and the British are examining whether to SLEP the LPDs or to build new ones ... we wait to hear the outcome, hoping for a new build which would give qualitative improvements, including a smaller crew, improved vehicle and personnel lift, modern communications and command informations systems fits for both the CATF and CLF staffs, and 25–30 years life. The planned Dutch amphibious ship is also expected to fall into this category, although it will be called an *Amphibious Transport ship (ATS)*.

The idea for the British LPH (or ASS) stemmed from the conversion of the 28,000 tonne Ro-Ro civilian container ship *Contender Bezant* into the Air Training Ship *Argus*. It was planned at first to convert the sister ship *Contender Argent* as a very economical replacement for the *Hermes*, but subsequent studies showed the advantages of building new to provide many of the facilities expected of a specialist ship and, at the time of writing, the Government is awaiting tenders from industry

PLATE 9.6 The Landing Ships Dock (LSD) are similar to the LPDs in their basic construction, but optimised for tanks, vehicle and stores for the assault echelons. The USS *Germantown* is one of the new LSD-41 *Whidbey Island* class which have a flight deck and carry either four LCACs or a number of LCMs. A cargo variant is being developed. (*US Navy*)

PLATE 9.7 A cargo ship (LKA); some of this class can carry two LCACs, but all carry 360 troops, some landing craft and have a helicopter deck. (*US Navy*)

for designs. Some might argue that, by opting for a specialist helicopter ship rather than a multi-purpose ship with a dock, the British have decided to continue using an outdated concept. With the multi-purpose ship being so expensive, however, gaining the ability to launch a mobile commando group from an economical and versatile platform, by helicopters and the four LCVPs, would still be a very significant step forward for the operations for the UK/NL Landing Force.

Then there are what the USN would call support ships, although they are often involved in the assault phase. These include the new LSD-41, the supply ships (LKA) and, finally, the LSTs which are the descendants of those wartime ships derived from the Maracaibo oilers. They include the American LSTs of the *Newport* class, the British LSLs, and the Soviet *Alligator, Ropucha* and the small 700 ton *Polnocny* classes. All these four types can be beached for rapid unloading, sometimes during the assault (today only a Soviet practice) but, more often, once the beachhead has been secured. There is the danger that the ships might be grounded on an ebbing tide, but this is reduced by the ingenious ways that have been designed to bridge the water gap between the ship and the shore.

Amphibious Ships 147

PLATE 9.8 The unusual US *Newport* class LST has a conventional dock for the AAVs and LCUs, but it is the bow that is unique. To reach a speed of 20 knots, the old design of bow door opening below the waterline could not be used, so these ships unload onto a pontoon or the shore by a 112 ft ramp over the bow; the ramp is supported by the derrick arms which give the class its unique signature. Here the USS *Schenectady* beaches and lowers its ramp. (*Marine Corps Gazette*)

148   Amphibious Operations

PLATE 9.9 The British LSLs were built to the less exacting, and cheaper, commercial standards. They have a helicopter platform aft, and a second amidships if no vehicles or chacons are being carried there. They carry one or two *Mexeflotes* whose main purpose (notwithstanding its value as a slow landing craft) is to provide a link between the ship and the landing craft, or with the shore; here an RSP is acting as the link while the *Mexeflote* waits to be loaded in its 'landing craft' role. There has been some reluctance to beach these ships, partly because of the requirement for dry dock inspection thereafter. On recent exercises, however, LSLs have started to be beached more readily; this is undoubtedly a much quicker and safer way to unload in war . . . one experienced amphibious warrior pointed out that, in the 1960s, the old LSTs were put ashore in the Gulf five times a day! At present the LSLs have no integral armament and urgently need some; they could only be defended by the hand held air defence weapons of the landing force during passage, but these *Javelin* would have to be withdrawn at a critical time when the landing takes place, a most unsatisfactory solution. These ships are now some 20–25 years old and one has been withdrawn already. The replacement or SLEP of the remaining four will have to be addressed soon, although no announcement has yet been made.
(*Royal Navy. Crown copyright*)

PLATE 9.10 The most modern Soviet LSTs in the *Ropucha* class are smaller than their Western counterparts, and are designed as ro-ro ships. In some respects they are more capable than the earlier *Alligator* class which were built to mercantile standards and were also fitted with a bow and stern ramp, but they provide significantly less space for loading. (*Royal Navy. Crown copyright*)

NON-SPECIALIST AMPHIBIOUS SHIPS

Virtually any ship or craft can be used in amphibious operations to offload men and stores. Aircraft carriers can be transformed into LPHs without great delay, and the British exercise the CVS in this role regularly. Destroyers and frigates can carry a company group and, with their speed, defensive capability, gun armament and, especially, their excellent C3I, they can be a most effective means to put ashore a small force for a special mission, a raid, or as part of advance force operations. Fast patrol boats, fishing boats and submarines may be used to insert Special Forces, and the Soviets lay sufficient stress on the value of covert submarine operations in the Great Patriotic War to imply that they still view this as one of the important facets of projecting seapower against the shore. Warships have, of course, a fundamental role in winning sea control, so they should only be tasked in an amphibious fashion if there is no other means to get a force ashore and the mission is of the highest priority.

Ships Taken Up From Trade (STUFT)

Thus the main alternatives to specialist amphibious ships are civilian ships taken up from trade, or STUFT, and the MV *Norland* and the MV *Elk* were among others which served with distinction in the Falkland Islands campaign. STUFT will continue to have an important contribution to all amphibious operations of the UK/NL Amphibious Force and, indeed, they take part in most of the exercises.

Given the shortfall in specialist amphibious ships to carry the assault echelons, all amphibious forces must call upon the services of STUFT for major operations. It has been calculated[2] that some 30 civilian ships would have to be taken up by the USN's Military Sealift Command to carry the Assault Follow-on Echelon (AFOE) of a notional MEF. The AFOE might contain about $\frac{1}{3}$ of the personnel—19,000 troops—half of the transport, and $\frac{3}{4}$ of the stores—over 5 million cubic feet—of the landing force. Thus the shipping would have to include 7 troop ships, one aviation support ship, one crane ship, 4 LASH, 9 container and 4 each of roll-on/roll-off ships and tankers. Both the Americans and the British, however, face increasing difficulties in procuring ships suitable for supporting amphibious operations, as shipping lines have tended to concentrate upon building large container ships, and many sail under flags of convenience. The Maritime Pre-positioning Ships, however, help to alleviate any American shortfall.

The Soviets also incorporate their merchant fleet into their planning and, unlike the West, the ships are built with military uses in mind. It has been calculated that they have the capability to transport five motor rifle divisions at any one time, thus they could lift the follow-up motor rifle regiments used in an amphibious operation without significant difficulty. Among their one hundred or more amphibious auxiliaries they have six classes of Ro-Ro ships, a large diesel-powered barge carrier, the 60,000 tonnes displacement *Aleksey Kosygin* based with the Pacific Fleet, and a nuclear powered sister ship in the Black Sea.

Operating with STUFT

STUFT present the commanders with a number of problems, after all, these ships are not designed for operations close to the shore, possibly under fire. They have no damage control facilities and, as the tragic sinking of the *Herald of Free Enterprise* revealed, Ro-Ro ferries cannot survive a serious accident. Most of them are fast enough, but some have difficulty manoeuvring at slow speeds and, in particular, the short sea crossing ferries have limited endurance and very limited fresh water capacity. Little can be done to alleviate these inbuilt deficiencies except to try to select ships for STUFT duties with considerable care.

Other deficiencies can be put right in the short time available between mobilisation and sailing, including communications for working with the task force, integral air defence, and helicopter platforms. Ideally, containerised communications should be available at short notice, but it is more likely that only small portable sets can be provided. As with the LSLs, hand-held guided weapons or, at the least, machine guns could be deployed to give some rudimentary air defence. Helicopter platforms can be fitted at comparatively short notice in port before sailing, as with the *Arapaho* system. Further modifications might include additional accommodation, temporary water tanks, and fittings for underway replenishment and refuelling. The extra accommodation would be for an embarked naval party to man communications circuits and to provide advice on convoy and operational procedures, or it might be to allow the drivers to travel with their vehicles. This work could be implemented very quickly, and in April 1982 took only four days for the first ships.

PLATE 9.11   The heavy lift semi-submersible *Este Submerger II* which is used to carry 539 Assault Squadron. (*Royal Navy. Crown copyright*)

Experience on exercises with the UK/NL Amphibious Force has shown that the masters and navigators of STUFT vessels adapt very readily to the demands of operating with the amphibious task force. The most challenging task, however, is the offload. These ships suffer from constraints in rough seas, especially the large LASH types of submersibles carrying landing craft or barges pre-loaded with vehicles which have some difficulty in docking down when a sea is running. In such conditions the ferries too may not be able to offload troops or open their bow doors to accept landing craft. On one recent exercise off the west coast of Denmark, a ferry could not carry out its part of the landing and had to sail into port to unload; hence the need for crossdecking assault troops to specialist ships.

None the less, given good planning, reasonable weather, and careful selection of anchorages, these ships can make a valid contribution to the build up of the force. It takes some experience and skill to achieve success, so one of the first tasks after sailing is normally to carry out a rehearsal to practise the drills, such as ensuring that the STUFT crews know how to make the essential link between their ramps and the *Mexeflotes* and Ramped Craft Lighters. Even under the most favourable conditions, however, the rate of unloading on to a beach from these ships is comparatively slow, some 20 tons per hour, compared to some 90 tons per hour from specialist dock ships.

CONCLUSION

The success of an amphibious operation depends upon a sufficiency of specialist ships to land a force quickly enough to achieve its objective, and to ensure a rapid build up thereafter. The UK/NL Amphibious Force has a limited capability at present, but the developing plans for an overall combination of two LPDs, two LPHs and the Dutch ATS show promise of an improved balance and effectiveness in the future.

10

The Landing Force and its Fire Support

The raw material for the CLF's plan is the combat strength of his landing force. Whether the formations are as light as the UK/NL Landing Force or as heavy as a MEF, the main objective is to achieve a balance of weapons able to fight effectively on a modern battlefield. None of these forces have the sheer power of the armoured divisions on the Central Front, but naval and air support can help to make them formidable opponents. Naval gunfire, air, attack helicopters and artillery play a part in all the stages of the operation; supporting the advanced force operation, bringing down preliminary fire on the main or alternative objectives, covering the landing, and prosecuting the land battle, and we will look at them in turn.

AMPHIBIOUS INFANTRY

Before we concentrate upon the support, a point of principle; all Marines are essentially amphibious infantrymen. In the Royal Marines all officers and men, from pilots through vehicle mechanics and signallers to swimmer canoeists *et al.* . . . all do their basic training as infantrymen at the Commando Training Centre Royal Marines at Lympstone; 30 weeks for recruits and 15 months for young officers, including the Commando Course. Furthermore, Royal Navy and Army officers and men do the Commando Course to earn the Green Beret which they wear while serving with 3 Commando Brigade RM. Much of the quality of the British and Dutch troops derives from their $2\frac{1}{2}$ months of Mountain and Arctic warfare training and exercises in Norway each winter. Let Max Hastings comment on the results in the Falklands:

> '. . . the Royal Marines and the Parachute Regiment did everything that had been expected of them, and more. The war proved that British military training is good, and re-emphasised the case for elite infantry forces, trained and equipped for exceptional exertions on the battlefield.'[1]

A similar quest for excellence characterises the USMC and the Soviet Naval Infantry. In both forces, Marines man a wide variety of equipments and weapons, and the US Marines man their own air wings as well. But their fundamental skill is still as an amphibious infantryman, and General A. M. Gray USMC summed it up when he said:

> 'In today's environment, there are no rear areas; every Marine must know how to fight as a rifleman. All Marine training will be based on that concept.'[2]

LAYERED DEFENCE

In his plan, the CLF will wish to achieve a synthesis of the combat and fire support available to him, and this is illustrated in Figure 10.1. It is a layered system which is closely associated, and dependent upon, the air defence matrix which we will consider in Chapter 12. To take the anti-armour battle as a brief example of this:

▶ The outer layers would be provided by air interdiction and long range artillery and naval gunfire.

▶ As the attack closed in, these would be joined by close air support, attack helicopters and, in the foreseeable future, anti-armour mortars.

▶ The inner layer is the most crucial... if the enemy breaks through the basic ground defences, then all the sophistication of the outer layers is for nought. As well as those long range systems we have already mentioned, the close combat battle will depend upon armour, mines and anti-tank guided weapons.

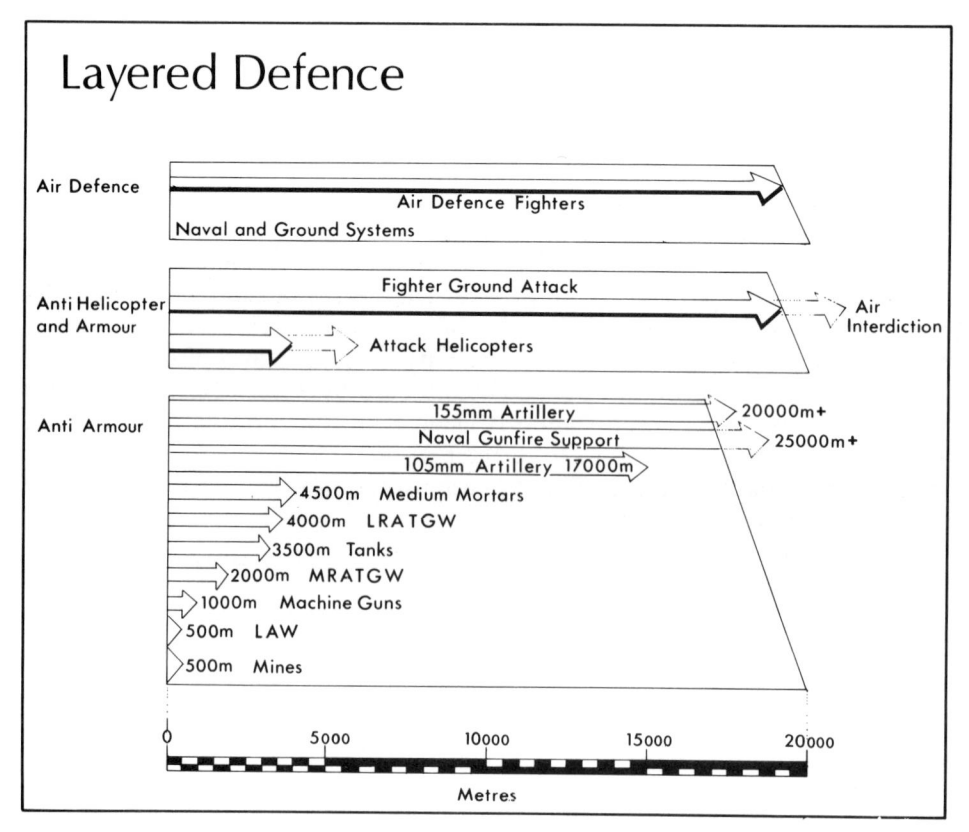

FIG. 10.1 Layered Defence

The Landing Force and Its Fire Support 155

PLATE 10.1 The USMC will soon have the M1A1 *Abrams* tank replacing the ageing M60A1, although with a total of only some 160 tanks in the Marine Corps, the MAGTFs do not rely on armour to the same extent as the equivalent Army formations. The main armament of the MIAI is a 120mm smooth bore gun with a range of 3,500m. (*Marine Corps Gazette*)

PLATE 10.2 To back up the *Abrams*, the USMC have the new series of *Light Armoured Vehicles* (*LAV*) which give them an armoured reconnaissance and covering force capability. There are a number of LAV variants, and this is firing a 90mm gun. (*Marine Corps Gazette*)

PLATE 10.3   Each Soviet Naval Infantry brigade is equipped with T-72 medium tanks and amphibious light tanks, the venerable PT76, so it has an adequate armoured capability. (*International Defence Review*)

PLATE 10.4   The core of the defensive minefields laid by the combat engineers are the relatively heavy anti-tank mines such as *Barmine* which take some time to emplace, even by mechanical layers. Here is an Arctic Barmine Layer, towed behind a BV 202. For the future, *Scatterable Mines* are being introduced which can be delivered rapidly by artillery, helicopters and vehicles, and these are particularly valuable for creating the early defences after a landing, or for reacting quickly to enemy moves. (*MOD (Army). Crown copyright*)

The Landing Force and Its Fire Support 157

PLATE 10.5 A good balance of ATGW would include long range—3,500m—weapons, such as the USMC's TOW2 as mounted on the HMMWV *Hummer* here. (*Marine Corps Gazette*)

PLATE 10.6 In the future an alternative long range anti-armour system may be provided for the infantry by smart weapons such as the British Aerospace *Merlin*, which is fired from an 81mm mortar. This is a relatively light munition and a longer range and heavier 120mm mortar version is also under development. (*British Aerospace*)

158 Amphibious Operations

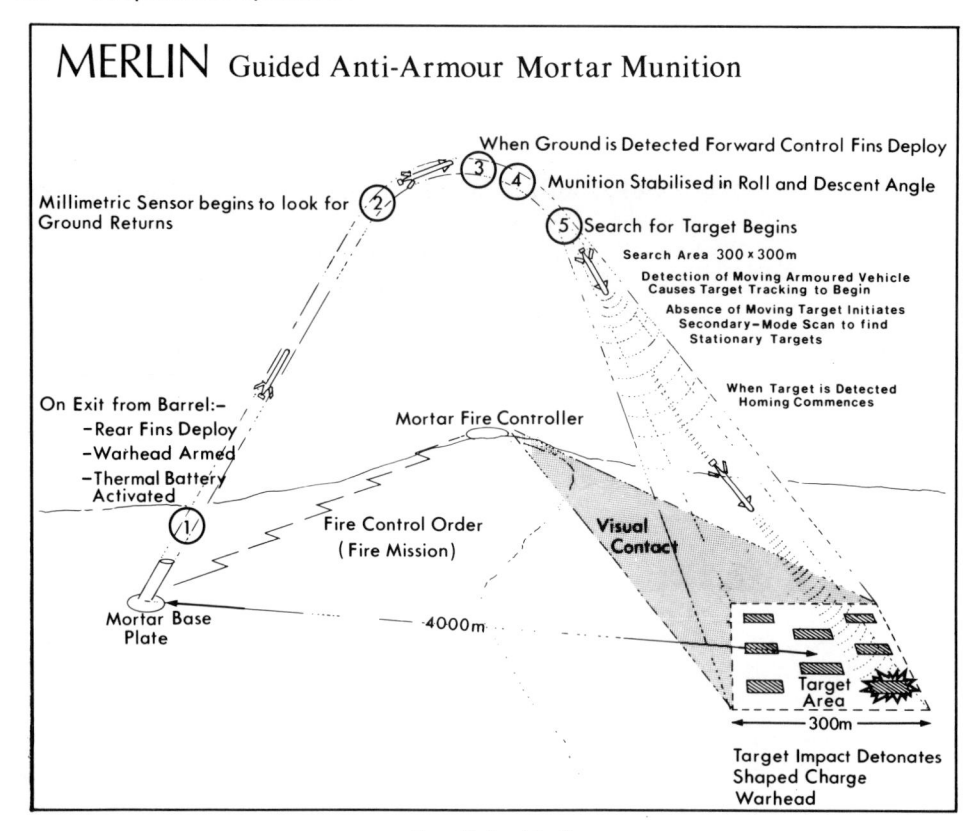

MERLIN Guided Anti-Armour Mortar Munition

When Ground is Detected Forward Control Fins Deploy
Munition Stabilised in Roll and Descent Angle
Search for Target Begins
Search Area 300 x 300m
Detection of Moving Armoured Vehicle Causes Target Tracking to Begin
Absence of Moving Target Initiates Secondary-Mode Scan to find Stationary Targets
When Target is Detected Homing Commences

Millimetric Sensor begins to look for Ground Returns

On Exit from Barrel:-
— Rear Fins Deploy
— Warhead Armed
— Thermal Battery Activated

Mortar Fire Controller

Fire Control Order (Fire Mission)

Visual Contact

Mortar Base Plate

4000m

Target Area
300m

Target Impact Detonates Shaped Charge Warhead

Fig. 10.2 *Merlin*

Plate 10.7 There should also be medium range—2,000m—AGTW, such as the UK/NL Landing Force's *Milan* shown here, and *Dragon*. In the last ditch are the unguided short-range weapons like the *Light anti-armour Weapon* (*LAW*), manned by riflemen. (*Royal Marines. Crown copyright*)

FIRE SUPPORT-CONTROL AND CO-ORDINATION

Central control of the fire support is entrusted to the CATF's Supporting Arms Co-ordination Cell (SACC) consisting of teams responsible for each type of support, whose task is to carry out the detailed fire planning and the allocation of targets. The SACC has to ensure that the best available weapon is employed for each target, avoid duplication, task and brief the ships and flight leaders, make sure aircraft do not fly through artillery or naval gun lines of fire, and so on. In the UK/NL Amphibious Force, this cell would move ashore with the CLF's headquarters to form the Fire Support Co-ordination Cell (FSCC) ashore, leaving a liaison officer on board. In the USMC, the SACC and FSCC are separate organisations (the privilege of size).

Although there are specialist controllers for each system, there has to be a tremendous cross fertilization of skills to get the best out of all. Most of the specialists can control the other systems if necessary so, for example, light helicopter pilots acting as forward aircraft controllers would also be able to call for and direct artillery fire. With good training, all commanders down to corporals at section level should be able to call for fire support.

The quantity and quality of supporting firepower available to the US amphibious forces far outstrips any other nation's, and in allied operations the MEF or MEB can provide welcome support to neighbouring formations. A control agency is also supplied in the form of the Air/Naval Gunfire Liaison Company (ANGLICO) which is attached to the allied brigade or division to give it the same level of expertise that is integral to a USMC formation.

NAVAL GUNFIRE SUPPORT

Naval Gunfire Support (NGS) has always been an essential part of amphibious operations, although Nelson's maxim 'A ship's a fool to fight a fort' illustrates the reserve felt about its effectiveness until the Second World War. In the optimum conditions of the Central Pacific campaign, with almost complete sea and air control in the later battles, the Americans developed the most sophisticated uses of naval gunfire for the preliminary bombardment, support for the landing and on call fire for subsequent operations. Improved fire control and better ammunition enabled the most tenacious defences to be defeated. But Isely and Crowl were correct in their comment that:

> '... the lesson gained from the experience of naval bombardment in the Pacific War must be read with care. Success depended upon deliberation, and deliberation took time. This inevitably gave the enemy ample warning of the attackers' intentions and the element of surprise was lost. Whether such tactics would be feasible in amphibious operations against a continental land mass is doubtful.'[3]

Certainly, the opportunities for a preliminary bombardment are now much more limited, especially if surprise is important, or if the aim is to achieve an unopposed landing. Even so, naval gunfire ships as part of an Advanced Force can help to develop the deception plan by engaging alternative targets to divert the enemy, to mask the main landing, and to protect the minesweeping force. Once the assault has started, the weight of naval fire can be a major factor in its success, until the ground artillery has been landed.

160   Amphibious Operations

Command and Control of Amphibious Assault Artillery Support

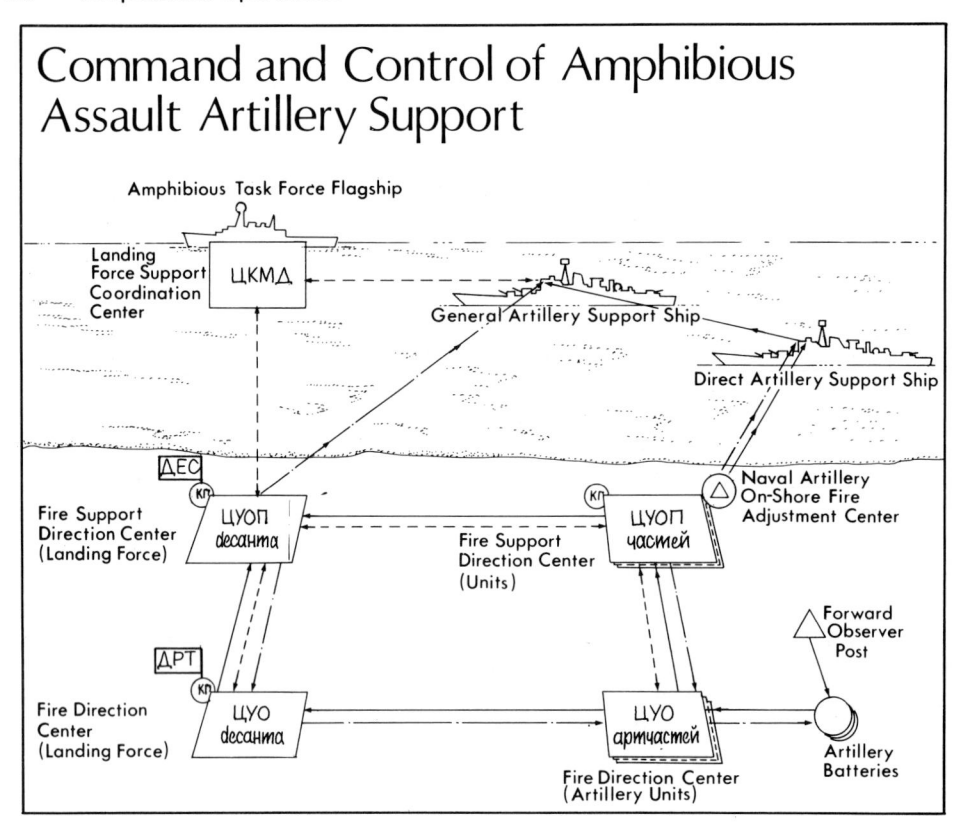

FIG. 10.3 A Soviet view of the NATO system for controlling Naval Gunfire Support

A ship could be allocated to the NGS role throughout the landing, or be detached from ASW or AD picket duties from time to time. She might anchor to obtain greater stability and accuracy if there is little maritime threat and no danger from shore artillery. Such security is rare, however, so she would normally manœuvre within a *fire support area* and remain within the danger area close to shore (some 10–14 kilometres off initially and closing in to some 5–6 kilometres once the beachhead and surrounding heights are clear) only for as long as it takes to complete a specific mission, or for a period of time during which she could support one or more units ashore as tasked through the SACC.

Modern ships have a computer which can produce the range and bearing very quickly to at least two targets simultaneously. Captain Hugh McManners RA described the scene in the operations room of HMS *Avenger*, a Type 21 frigate:

> 'The whole ship shuddered as each round crashed off into the night. The darkened room was hushed, with only the gunnery orders being audible. The green glow from the radar screen illuminated the white-hooded figures crouched over them.... The computer operator.... punches in the co-ordinates and the type of ammunition and the gun trains onto the target, holds itself on despite the heaving of the ship and the imprecision of its course, and fires itself off. When the man on the ground has sent back a correction over the radio, the operator punches it in and the gun reloads itself and fires. The real skill lies in keeping the system locked onto the land, which is

done by keeping a radar fix on a known point of land and ensuring that the known point doesn't slip. The navigator has to calculate his position very carefully, monitor it and calculate the tidal drift—as a check on the computer which takes it all into account automatically.'[4]

The essential links between the landing force and the ship are provided by the spotting teams of 148 (Meiktila) Battery in the UK/NL Amphibious Force. The battery would send a Naval Gunfire Liaison Officer to the ship to brief the ship on the land battle and the requirements of the spotters ashore. The fire would be controlled by a Naval Gunfire Forward Officer (NGFO) . . . McManners was one of them in the Falklands campaign . . . with his five man Royal Artillery and the Royal Navy spotting team.

As a moving platform—moving in three dimension—firing high muzzle velocity shells with a low trajectory, the ship is remarkably accurate using direct fire. For indirect fire, it is less precise than field artillery, partly because the low trajectory gives it a very large beaten zone at the target, and partly because of inaccuracies in the ship's positional determining system. The ship's magazines, too, have only a limited capacity and resupply is less straightforward than for a land battery. Moreover, the gun barrels cannot be elevated to give good crest clearance for indirect fire, to search out the enemy in the next valley. This is not the ideal solution when fighting in the fjords of Norway—it gives land artillery an advantage in counter battery (or anti-ship) fire. Therefore the selection of a suitable fire support area is critical, and planning is now assisted by a small portable GRID computer system called PANGS (Planning Aid for NGS) which can calculate these crest clearance problems.

PLATE 10.8 The British 4.5 inch single mounting, with a rate of fire of some twenty-four × 46 lb shells per minute, is able to deliver the equivalent fire of a field battery of 6 × 105mm guns. The shells are high explosive ground or air burst, so they have a very small anti-armour capability. (*Royal Navy. Crown copyright*)

162   Amphibious Operations

Whatever the limitations, the service provided in the Falklands satisfied the customer, the Major General (then Lieutenant Colonel) Nick Vaux wrote of 42 Commando's attack on Mount Harriet:

> '... we invoked retribution in the form of artillery and naval gunfire support. The shells burst in vicious conflagrations along the crestline, 105mm with a lurid, red flash, the 4.5 inch shells with an evil greenish glow that seemed to rise up from the stricken target. It was odd to listen to the calm, almost casual exchanges between Nigel Bedford (the NGFO) and HMS *Yarmouth*, nearly ten miles out to sea. Under his direction she could put down a devastatingly accurate weight of fire at minimum notice.'[5]

In the Falklands campaign some 9,000 rounds of 4.5 inch shells were fired, mainly on predicted engagements to harass the enemy, but also for direct support of the final attacks on the positions around Port Stanley. Not many months later, the battleship USS *New Jersey* fired her 16 inch guns during the American intervention in the Lebanon.

Faced with a major shortage of heavy gunfire support ships when the cruisers were paid off, the US Navy obtained approval in 1982 to bring the four battleships in the *Iowa* class back into commission to become the core of four new Surface Action Groups. Each ship carries *Tomahawk* land attack (TLAM) and *Harpoon* missiles, three triple 16 inch gun turrets having a range of 38,000 metres, and six twin 5-inch mountings with a range of 17,000 metres, and thus has the capability to give the Marines the heavy, long range support needed for over-the-horizon landings. Two of these ships were however scheduled for decommissioning once again under the 1990 Bush Defense Budget. This will again re-emphasise the smaller calibre guns of the USN's cruiser/destroyer force.

Such major units optimised for gunfire support are unusual, and most landing forces must depend upon frigates and destroyers, whose guns often have the primary roles of air defence and surface action, with bombardment in third place. Navies giving priority to air defence have opted for smaller calibre guns (50mm to 100mm) with a high rate of fire, while bombardment is best served by larger calibres (155mm and upwards); the 4.5-inch (114mm) used by the RN might be seen as somewhat of a compromise. A 155mm naval gun, however, as proposed by Royal Ordnance would have a range of some 30,000 metres and would enable munitions such as the US Army's Search and Destroy Armour (SADARM), APDMs and *Copperhead* to be introduced; these shells contain anti-APC or anti-tank submunitions with terminal guidance seekers (more sophisticated than, but similar to, *Merlin*). Another Army weapon which could be adapted for the Navy is the Multiple Launch Rocket System (MLRS) which could be fitted to amphibious ships or other warships.

When missiles were seen to have largely replaced the gun for air defence and surface action, there was some debate about the future need for the bombardment task. In such a climate, some measure of a nation's commitment to an amphibious capability might be assessed by its readiness to retain naval guns. The Americans have never wavered, and the Soviets, despite the proliferation of missile systems on their surface ships, included guns on the *Slava* class cruisers and the *Sovremenny* class destroyers. In contrast, the Batches 1 and 2 of the British Type 22 Frigates were equipped only with missile systems. The Falklands experience and the demands of limited actions, such as the defence of shipping against maritime

PLATE 10.9 The Soviet *Sovremenny* class has two 130mm twin turrets for Naval Gunfire Support. (*Jane's*)

PLATE 10.10 The ML *Sprite* is a small RPV which could be carried in a landrover or BV 206, requiring only a two-man operating team. It could be fitted with several different payloads including TV, Thermal Imaging, combined TV and laser target designator, NBC sensor, communications relay and ECM equipment. Launch and recovery could take place on board or ashore. It has an operating ceiling of 2,500m with a radius of 20 miles (line of sight); it may not be fully compatible with the longer range weapon systems. (*ML Aviation*)

terrorists, showed the value of the gun, and later ships (such as Type 22 Batch 3 and Type 23) have been equipped with one.

There are also developments in computers for fire control, surveillance and target acquisition. The Americans have produced equipment capable of tracking shells in flight, which reduces the need for observers to correct the fall of shot and is particularly useful for long range interdiction. There is an increasing need for real time systems for acquiring targets. Land forces are using RPVs—the British Army is being equipped with *Phoenix*—but the problem for maritime forces is the recovery of RPVs at sea, and one solution might be found in a helicopter RPV.

CLOSE AIR SUPPORT

As we have already mentioned, the USMC was at the forefront of the development of air-ground co-operation in the inter-war years, and this concept remains a cornerstone of the American doctrine, embodied in the MAGTF organisation. The air battle is central to the whole operation, and some aspects will be covered in Chapter 12 on maritime operations, but in summary, it covers winning air superiority over the AOA, and interdiction and bombardment in the preliminary and advanced force operations; with the aims of destroying enemy defences, isolating the landing area and disrupting the enemy's lines of communication. A great strength of the USMC is the ability to use the air as a force multiplier during the landings, when they can bring to bear the wide range of air assets for reconnaissance, close support of forward troops, spotting for artillery and ships' guns, and continuing the interdiction of enemy reserves and airfields.

All amphibious forces aspire to reach a similar solution. Western pilots would tend to agree with the main thrust of this description of close air support in a sea *desant* by a Soviet Air Force officer:

> '(the support) is best commenced in parallel with the approach of the first wave to the enemy shore. In this phase strike aviation units and sub units should destroy, above all, nuclear missile systems, and approaching enemy reserves and weapons which could provide a direct opposition to the *desant* units as they land or during the fight for the beachhead. In addition, the strike aviation may engage enemy ships (rocket or torpedo boats) attacking the *desant* in the landing zone.
> As the battle after the landing develops, the strike aviation goes over to *accompanying the attacking troops* with fire. At this stage its missions are mainly instigated on call from the battlefield. Strikes are put in on enemy targets which offer resistance to the attacking troops as they crop up . . .'[6]

Nor would Western pilots disagree with the writer's conclusion that

> 'Aviation has particularly difficult tasks during the battle for the landing and the initial phase of the *desant's* battle on shore. During that period there are rapid changes in the situation and not all the elements of the command and control system are functioning to the full extent. Therefore effective operations by strike aviation require, above all, a high degree of combat readiness, the application of non-stereotyped methods of action, and an accurate organisation of co-operation with the *desant* troops, the remaining branches of the airforce, and the other Arms and Services concerned with the sea *desant* landing.'

This implies a need for constant practice to perfect the art, air force doctrines usually insist upon high level central control to give great flexibility of tasking, and this tends to preclude task specialisation. Moreover, in the early stages of the Falklands operation the lack of a *Tactical Air Control Cell* (*TACC*) on board the

CVS reduced the effectiveness of the close air support by the Harrier GR3s until control was transferred to the landing force headquarters ashore. At the risk of resurrecting skeletons, a comment by Bernard Fergusson about attitudes in 1941 bears repetition:

> 'It is not unfair to say that at this stage of the history of Combined Ops the RAF was still inclined to take the view that, one bit of air being very like another bit of air, there was nothing particularly tricky in supporting an amphibious operation. This heresy did not obtain for long.'[7]

The MAGTF concept, the allocation of the considerable strength of the Marine Air elements to a relatively small ground formation, a MEB or a MEF, has met with some opposition in the past, and the USMC has had to argue vehemently to ensure that they have integral air support. The advantages of their approach are that: Marine pilots have a basic infantry training and have some understanding of the land battle; the air control systems are an integral and thoroughly practised part of the overall command system; and the ground troops have a good grasp of the use of air power in their operations. It results in an enviable quality . . . and quantity . . . of close air support.[8]

The provision of dedicated aircraft is only part of the solution, since command and control is as important as equipment. During amphibious operations the CATF controls the air battle in the AOA through the *Tactical Air Control Cell (TACC)* on board. The CLF has his own TACC which would control the air battle once

PLATE 10.11 The V/STOL *Harrier* . . . US AV8-B, or British GR-5 (shown here) . . . has a good weapon payload and will soon have an enviable night capability. It can operate from grass fields, roads, ships or prepared airstrips, so its response times are very quick and it has shown itself able consistently to meet the desired deadline of putting bombs on targets within 20 minutes of the ground commander's request; timely air support is critical. Conventional aircraft would have to loiter airborne on a *CAP* to achieve a similar solution. This affects the comparative sortie rate and the USMC has calculated that it would require 200 conventional aircraft to generate the same number of sorties as 160 *Harriers*. (8) Although the UK/NL Amphibious Force does not have quite the same relationship with a RAF *Harrier* squadron as exists in a MAGTF, co-operation has worked well on exercises and in the Falklands.
(*Royal Navy. Crown copyright*)

TABLE 10.1

USMC Aircraft

Model	Name	Role	Speed (mph)	Range (nm)	Ordnance/Payload
A-4M*	Skyhawk	Attack/CAS	645	2,055 external fuel	2 × 20mm cannons, bombs, rockets, etc.
A-6E	Intruder/	Attack/all weather/ CAS	563	2,378	bombs, rockets, gun pods, 1,400 lb armament
AV-8B	Harrier	Attack/CAS	630	680	25mm cannon, cluster bombs, Sidewinder, Maverick, rockets
F-4*	Phantom	Attack/AD Fighter	575	683	Sparrow/Sidewinder missiles, bombs, rockets
F/A-18	Hornet	Attack/AD Fighter	Mach 1.8	1,000	20mm cannon, Sparrow/ Sidewinder missiles, up to 4.2 tons iron bombs
EA-6B	Prowler	Electronic Warfare	566	955	Unarmed, carries EW and jamming equipment
OV-10D	Bronco	All weather recce, CAS Air OP Hel. escort	281 sea level	220	20mm cannon, rockets, can carry 2 litter patients, 5 paras, 3,200 lb cargo
KC-130	Hercules	Transport Refuelling	340	2,400	92 troops or 26,913 lb of freight

* Being phased out of service.

command has been transferred ashore. The TACC has modules which control all the air assets including anti-air warfare, air support and helicopters, and the USMC are soon to introduce the Advanced Tactical Air Central system with an automated planning capability. Ashore, the detailed control of air support and the assault support helicopter operations is conducted by the *Direct Air Support Cell*; it is the focal point for communications between the TACC and the ground combat elements commander, to ensure that the air and ground operations are closely integrated, and to enable the MAGTF commander to reallocate air assets to meet the developing land battle. There are, of course, a number of other agencies and individuals involved in controlling aircraft, down to the *Forward Air Controller* who directs the close air support of front line troops from the ground or the air.

ATTACK HELICOPTERS

The attack helicopter has become a vital part of amphibious operations, since its versatility, manœuvrability, speed and fire power are ideal for providing intimate support against tanks and ground troops during the landings. The USMC also uses attack helicopters as close escorts for the assault helicopters, with fixed wing aircraft providing top cover. The numbers of the Soviet *Hip*, *Hind*, *Havoc* and *Hokum* attack helicopters have multiplied in recent years and they carry anti-

PLATE 10.12 The USMC attack helicopter, the AH-1W *Sea Cobra*, which is fast replacing the earlier AH-1T version, is equipped not only with the *Hellfire* anti-tank missile and a 20mm nose gun, but also with the *Sidewinder* air-to-air missile seen here. One concern for the future is that the *Sea Cobra* has a maximum speed of 219 knots, which means that it will not be able to provide effective protection for the faster MV-22 *Osprey*. (*Marine Corps Gazette*)

helicopter as well as anti-tank weapons. The Soviet Naval Infantry do not have any of their own, but support would probably be provided by the Army or the Navy, and reports of amphibious exercises confirm that *Hips* and *Hinds* are used—on one Warsaw Pact exercise in the Baltic in 1986 two flights of East German *Hinds* neutralised an enemy fire position with missiles as the first wave landed from Soviet hovercraft. The UK/NL Landing Force has six *Lynx/TOW* anti-tank helicopters and twelve *Gazelle* utility helicopters. Neither of these types has an anti-air capability and therefore cannot protect the support helicopters in the force, or themselves, against the intimidating enemy attack helicopter threat.

ARTILLERY

It is very important to get artillery ashore early to be the main prop of the fire support systems; it reacts quickly, is accurate and is not weather dependent. There is, however, a considerable debate about the best type of artillery support for amphibious operations:

▶ On one hand, the heavy artillery, such as 155mm, can deliver a considerable weight of fire at long range, so can be used for counter battery and interdiction as well as for close support of armour and infantry. Moreover, the new 'smart' munitions are being developed for the larger calibres, and these promise a better anti-armour capability in the future. Yet the size and weight of these systems impose a considerable penalty upon the amphibious lift, and the heavy ammunition presents logistic difficulties ashore. Moreover, their lack of battlefield mobility can sometimes constrain their use, but their long range (about 30 kilometres) mitigates this to a significant extent as they can cover such a large area with fire.

▶ On the other hand, light artillery of 105mm has good battlefield mobility but cannot deliver such a weight of fire, has a shorter range (about 17 kilometres), and the scope for future development of munitions is limited (although the Americans are producing some smart munitions for this calibre).

The USMC used the smaller calibres for some years but, with the growing commitment to Europe in the 1970s, began to procure larger weapons. The 105mm howitzers are now being withdrawn from service and, by the early 1990s, the Marine Corps artillery will consist of the M198 155mm towed howitzer, and two very heavy self-propelled howitzers (53,940 lb and 62,100 lb respectively); the M109A3 155mm, and the M110A2 8-inch. The M198 weighs 15,800 lb but it can be lifted, with its prime mover, by the CH-53E *Super Stallion*. Notwithstanding the decision to rely upon the M198, the debate still rages, and one writer in the *Marine Corps Gazette* commented that it was:

> 'A fine weapon for coastal artillery but (its) weight and bulk make it a questionable artillery piece for an expeditionary force. The Marine Corps seems to realise it made a mistake here, and that it needs light, modern 105mm howitzers or more heavy mortars or both.'[9]

The UK/NL Landing Force depends upon the 105mm Light Gun, and the Dutch are to provide 120mm mortars in the near future. It would be useful to have the 155mm towed FH70 to give a heavier weight of fire, but, again, it is debatable whether such a large and cumbersome piece would be compatible with the light and mobile characteristics of the force. The answer may come from present attempts by industry in America and the UK to develop a lightweight 155mm, although there will be some technological risks in attempting to fire such a large munition from a light system.

For a small formation, a Soviet Naval Infantry brigade appears to have a large amount of artillery, with 122mm guns and 122mm howitzers, all self-propelled, and 120mm mortars, but it is still on a relatively insignificant scale compared to Soviet Army formations. The brigade would, however, expect to receive additional support from Motor Rifle Divisional and Frontal artillery in tactical hook operations.

CONCLUSION

The key to the construction of a landing force, as with all military formations, is a sound balance between infantry to win and hold ground and the provision of a wide range of fire support agencies. The successful co-ordination of the whole battle depends upon good surveillance and target acquisition, and efficient C3I. Another important factor is sustainability, and we will discuss logistics next.

11
Logistics

A prime characteristic of an amphibious capability is that the logistic support for the landing force travels with the fleet, giving a mixture of integral sustainability and operational flexibility that is essential to a strategic role. It is, however, both a strength and a weakness. A continental army would have its logistic system established long before the start of a campaign, with lines of communication in place and installations relatively well prepared and protected, allowing operations to be launched from a firm base. An amphibious force has to secure a beachhead and, even if the landing is unopposed, the enemy reaction will doubtless mean that the logistic offload and the creation of the essential infrastructure ashore may be carried out under attack.

The fundamental task of the logistic organisation is to ensure that the rations, the many natures of ammunition, including the heavy artillery shells, the bulk fuel, stores, clothing and replacement equipment are delivered to the troops in time and in the right sequence, so that the operation can continue unabated. It also has to arrange for the casualties, prisoners of war and damaged equipment and vehicles to be returned back down the chain to rear installations where they can be dealt with effectively. Its efficiency affects not only the physical capability to fight, but also, essentially, the morale of everyone in the force. The scale of the challenge is daunting; the relatively small UK/NL Landing Force has a war maintenance reserve totalling some 17,000 tons for 30 days sustainability.

Shortly after the landings at San Carlos, the inability to build up stores, ammunition and fuel ashore quickly, due to the shortage of specialist ships and movement assets, and the impact of air attacks, threatened the future of the campaign in a way that was difficult to recognise far away in London. 'We have to fight and win three victories' Lieutenant Colonel Andrew Whitehead of 45 Commando wrote in his diary; 'Against the enemy; against the appalling terrain and weather; and against our own appalling logistic inadequacies.'[1] The logistic battle, like the others, was won, but it was a close run thing. According to Christopher Donnelly, in the Second World War the Soviets also found amphibious logistics to be a challenge:

> 'Supplying transport to carry the extra supplies increased the logistic load accordingly, because the vehicles needed extra ships, maintenance, fuel and the like. The result was that, whilst a battalion assault group could be fitted into just a few ships, its support requirement doubled or even trebled the required lift capacity. This, according to the modern Soviet analysis, was never really understood in the war, particularly by the Army Front Headquarters staff, and the rear

support was consistently underestimated. There is still the danger, the same analysts are saying, that this lesson of war has clearly not yet been learnt, because it appears that the same mistake is being made today, again by senior HQ staffs who fail to appreciate the problem.'[2]

Amphibious logistics will always be a critical issue, and in this Chapter we will examine how it might be resolved in a way best to ensure success. Many of the elements of the amphibious force that we have already encountered play a part in the logistic system and they, in turn, depend upon it.

PLANNING

Logistic control is what Martin van Creveld would call a 'function orientated' system which tends to constrain the freedom of manœuvre of the CATF and the CLF, and logistics will always be in their minds when making their plans. All logisticians are frequently exhorted by the operations staffs to be *flexible* in their planning and organisation, but there is a fundamental dichotomy between this ambition and the painstaking and precise work needed to ensure a failsafe system. Once the stores juggernaut has started to move, it has a momentum which is very difficult to divert, stop or turn back. Experienced logisticians will explain that the key to the conundrum lies in very close co-operation with the operations staff from the outset; any failure to co-ordinate will be punished by dangerous delays in the logistic reaction to operational changes.

Embarkation. The best results can be achieved when the Force can be given a specific mission before it sails from the base port. Thus the operations staff can decide upon the plan in some detail and the logisticians can load the ships with the vehicles and stores in a tactical order. With less prior knowledge of the landing, the loading of the ships must be uncertain, and the availability of vehicles and stores to meet the eventual plan will be in the balance. This difficulty can sometimes be ameliorated if the Amphibious Task Force can pause for a restow, as was achieved with only partial success at Ascension Island in 1982. Furthermore:

▶ The division of the logistic support between the types of ships directly affects the flexibility of the Force, since the specialist ships provide greater scope than STUFT for quick readjustments to the plan, and they can be offloaded more rapidly. Undoubtedly, priority for space will be given to command and fighting vehicles and men, but some concessions must be made to the logistic requirements to ensure that essential resupply is not choked at a critical moment.

▶ When shipping is at a premium, there is a temptation to make use of all the available stowage space, but this reduces the tactical flexibility so that restows would be difficult as there is not enough room to reposition vehicles and equipment. In the same sense, the demand for space sometimes leads to vehicles being loaded on upper decks of the LSLs, blocking the forward helicopter platform.

Objectives. The fundamental problem is to move stores over the beach, but the CATF and CLF may well seek to secure a port or airfield among their early

PLATE 11.1   BV 202s loaded in the vehicle deck of a LPD. (*Royal Navy. Crown copyright*)

objectives as a significant bonus to the logistic plan (and for improving close air support). The capture of Cherbourg was a vital objective in the breakout phase of the Normandy landings, and the Americans always sought to build an airfield quickly on islands during the Central Pacific campaign. Both these facilities would be particularly valuable for out-of-area operations as only part of the overall British force is amphibious.

Balance. Another important range of decisions concerns the concentration of stocks during the battle:

▶ Keeping a large amount afloat gives the CATF the opportunity to redeploy the Force by sea at short notice, and this tactical flexibility is increasingly important to the concept of operations.
▶ Conversely, resupply to the front line is faster from shore installations, although the build up of large stocks holds the danger that much may have to be abandoned in a quick move.
▶ The relative proportions held in the rear installations and in the forward units must be carefully balanced. In this, the dilemma is; hold stores too far

PLATE 11.2 The RCT Landing Craft Logistic has a good seagoing capability and can carry 350 tons of stores, and has no inhibitions about beaching; it forms part of the UK/NL Amphibious Force. The SAH 2,200 hovercraft is beached in the foreground. (*Royal Marines. Crown copyright*)

forward and you may destroy the Forces' tactical mobility, and render the stores vulnerable to the enemy; hold them too far back and they may never reach the front line in time.

Beaching. When planning the disposition of the ships in the AOA, the CATF staff has to consider the logistic unloading plan, since the distance travelled by the landing craft has a considerable affect upon the time taken for a general offload. Beaching ships such as the LSLs can reduce offload times by a factor of about seven, and thus the ships would spend less time in the area of greatest danger.

Host Nation Support. Although logistics is a national responsibility in NATO; considerable help can be obtained from host nations. A level of resources, including fresh rations, labour, transport, stores and engineer services might be provided under a Memorandum of Understanding. On all operations, especially those out of area, amphibious logisticians should be prepared to supplement their integral capacity from local resources, not least to seek to replace any assets that might have been lost to enemy action.

THE LOGISTIC SUPPORT STRUCTURE

The logistic structure must be based upon a simple design; all that is needed is storage space at both ends, suitable organisations ashore and afloat, sufficient assets for movement, and people to handle the equipment. The outline of the British system, which is similar to the American, is shown at Figure 11.1. To explain some points:

▶ *The Assault*. During the first stages of the landing all resupply has to be carried out from the ships. Anticipated immediate needs, such as extra artillery ammunition, would be ready on board as *Emergency Prepacked Supplies*, preferably on the upper deck if to be delivered by helicopter, or near to the LPD's dock if by landing craft. Some may be already embarked in landing craft as a floating reserve. Reception ashore would be in the hands of:

The Amphibious Beach Unit which marks the beaching points for the landing craft and sets out stores dumps. The *Fiat Allis* lays tracking across the beach to the exit on to firm ground or roads, and the *Beach Armoured Recovery Vehicle (BARV)*, based on a *Centurion* tank chassis, recovers drowned vehicles and stranded landing craft.

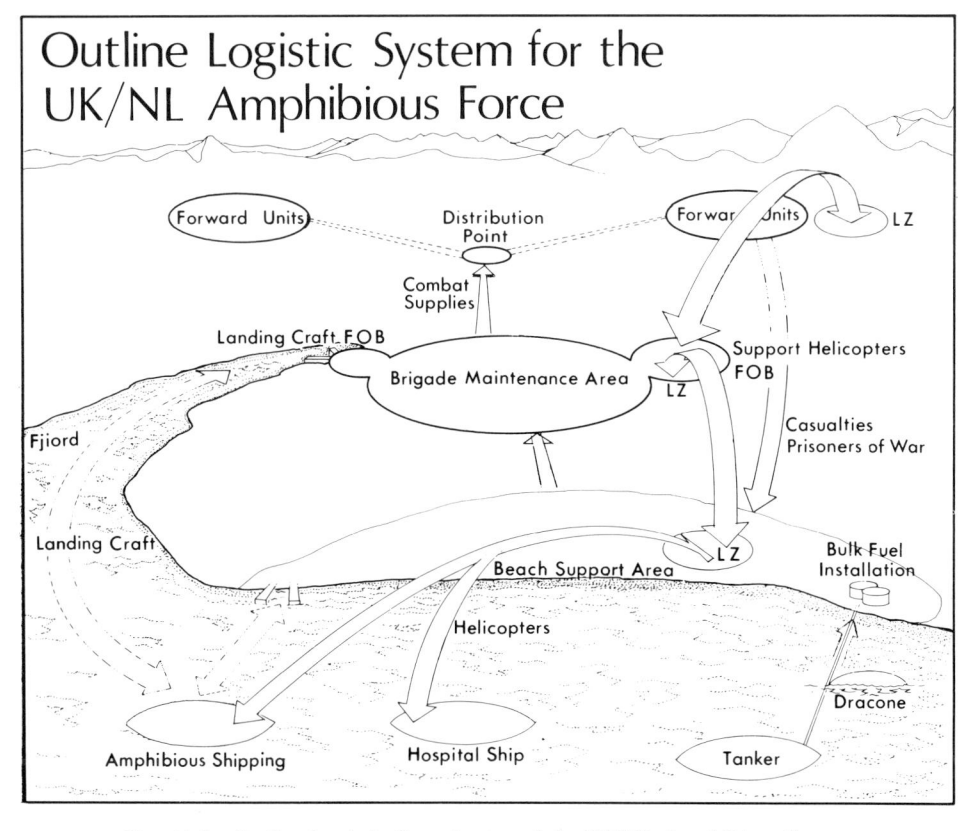

FIG. 11.1 Outline Logistic Organisation of the UK/NL Amphibious Force

174 Amphibious Operations

The Mobile Air Operations Teams which control and organise the helicopter landing zones.

▶ *First Logistic Offload.* The first logistic elements to be offloaded may be the units' first line combat supplies (ammunition, rations and fuel), or the *Advanced Logistic Group (ALG)*, depending upon the operational priorities. Under the ALG concept in the UK/NL Amphibious Force, 48 hours worth of the second line combat supplies would be carried in specialist ships for early unloading, together with other urgently needed medical and repair teams.

▶ *Beach Support Area (BSA).* Once a beachhead has been established and the fighting has moved inland, the general offload can start and the main stores base for the operation, the BSA, can be set up. This would be on or just inland from the best beach, within the anchorage and the air defence umbrella, or perhaps in a port if one has been secured. It would not only include ground dumps of stores and large *bunds* of fuel, but also such agencies as a field dressing station complete with surgical support teams, a helicopter forward operating base, a forward reinforcement holding unit and a prisoner of war cage. As the volume of logistic support builds up, the BSA will become a prime target, so it must be defended—especially against air attack.

▶ *Brigade Maintenance Area (BMA).* As operations move further inland, an intermediate logistics area, the BMA (in the USMC, the *Combat Support Service Area*), would be established behind the forward troops. This could include a second Field Dressing Station and the helicopter forward operating base might also be there. It will hold the stocks for immediate resupply to units ready on vehicles, so it is a more flexible concept than the BSA, and must move periodically to keep in contact with the forward units.

PLATE 11.3   A *Fiat Allis* laying trackway. (*Royal Marines. Crown copyright*)

LOGISTIC UNITS AND CONTROL

The success of the logistic operation depends eventually upon the men responsible for running it. The plan is drawn up, co-ordinated and controlled by the CLF staff in conjunction with the CATF staff. One officer, expert in the details of the War Maintenance Reserve and where all the stores are located in the ships, remains on board the LPD throughout the offload. The remainder of the logistics staff would move ashore with CLF's headquarters. The staffs are making increasing use of ADP to assist with the complexities of the logistic support equation.

The staffs also have to assess the best mixture of movement assets and routes to move stores forward. Helicopters are quick, but the *Sea King 4* does not carry a great load compared to a 8 tonne vehicle so, if adequate roads are available, the support helicopter might be best considered only for emergency resupply and casualty evacuation . . . the capacity of the USMC *Super Stallion* is another matter. Landing craft, the RCT *Mexeflotes* and pontoons, and local boats can set up a very effective waterborne main supply route which, in Norway, might run up a fjord direct to the BMA.

The main part of the organisation would be provided by a Service Support element; in the USMC it could be a company, a battalion or a group, depending upon the scale of the operation. The British version is the Commando Logistic Regiment RM which consists mainly of Royal Marines with some Royal Navy and Army personnel. It has four task squadrons; Medical, Transport, Ordnance, and Workshop, and RNLMC elements integrate into their respective squadrons when

PLATE 11.4 An example of the work carried out in the widely dispersed Beach Support Area; here a 4-ton vehicle is being loaded with rations. (*Royal Navy. Crown copyright*)

PLATE 11.5 The three survey ships HMS *Hydra*, *Hecla* and *Herald* were fitted out as hospital ships for the Falklands campaign, and here a *Wasp* helicopter is completing a *casevac* to HMS *Herald*. (*Royal Navy. Crown copyright*)

they are deployed. On operations the Regiment would have representatives at every stage of the system; helping to control the offload of each ship; running the *Logistic Operations Centre* which co-ordinates the details ashore; commanding and manning the BSA and the BMA; and providing the second line transport and other logistic facilities (medical, ordnance and workshop), including the mechanical handling equipments for expeditious handling of the stores in all the installations.

The amphibious ships and STUFT play a major role in sustaining the force ashore, not only in providing the sea lift, but in a number of other ways. Their sickbays, galleys and workshops can act as logistic multipliers, and hospital ships, such as the *SS Uganda* during the Falklands Islands campaign, provide an essential third line of medical support.

CONCLUSION

Logisticians the world over tend to be a gloomy lot, and make self deprecating remarks like:

'A tactician won't be impressed if, during an exercise, you tell him he can't take a hill because he's out of bullets; but try the same line on him in combat and you'll find an avid listener.'[3]

To give him his due, the same writer also said '. . . innovation is the life's blood of logistics'. Improvements to the logistic capability are being seen in better control and co-ordination, in which ADP can play an increasing role; from more capable movement assets and the introduction of 539 Assault Squadron RM; and essentially from the plans for new specialist amphibious ships.

12

The Setting—Maritime Operations

Securing local sea and air superiority is a prerequisite for the landing, but a full description of the maritime battle would clearly be beyond the scope of this book. In this chapter, therefore, we will concentrate only on some aspects of fundamental importance to amphibious operations, including the measures needed to establish the AOA and the problems encountered in fighting close to the shore.

DEFENCE AGAINST AMPHIBIOUS FORCES

The first line of defence against any amphibious operation is the enemy fleet and airforce, and Corbett's claim at the turn of the century remains a constant reminder of the threat:

> 'No expedition . . . can be guaranteed against naval interruption in the process of landing.'[1]

The scale of the opposition would depend on the nature of the conflict and the state of the war. We will take the extreme example of the North Atlantic just to illustrate the construction of a sophisticated defence. Any amphibious task force (ATF) sailing towards North Norway after fighting had broken out would face a deeply layered defence, starting in the Atlantic with torpedo or cruise missile firing *Alfa* and *Charlie* class submarines, and long range *Backfire* bombers from the Soviet Naval Airforce (SNAF). As the Force moved north, the quantity of aircraft and attack submarines would increase. It might then start to meet surface action groups and, if it ventured close to Soviet-held territory, it would be opposed by the very large offshore and inshore defence forces with small missile firing warships.

To put this in some perspective, the Forward Maritime Strategy is a complex concept for the use of the weight of NATO's and, in particular, US naval power. An ATF would be but one part of the whole and the areas of Soviet prime concern would be the defence of the submarine bastions in the Barents Sea and the Arctic Ocean, intercepting air and missile attacks direct from North America over the North Pole, preventing the Carrier battle groups from dominating the North Norwegian Sea, and seeking to interrupt the North Atlantic SLOCs. Their maritime defences might therefore have higher priorities than the defeat of an approaching amphibious force, which would be only one group of ships (albeit

178 Amphibious Operations

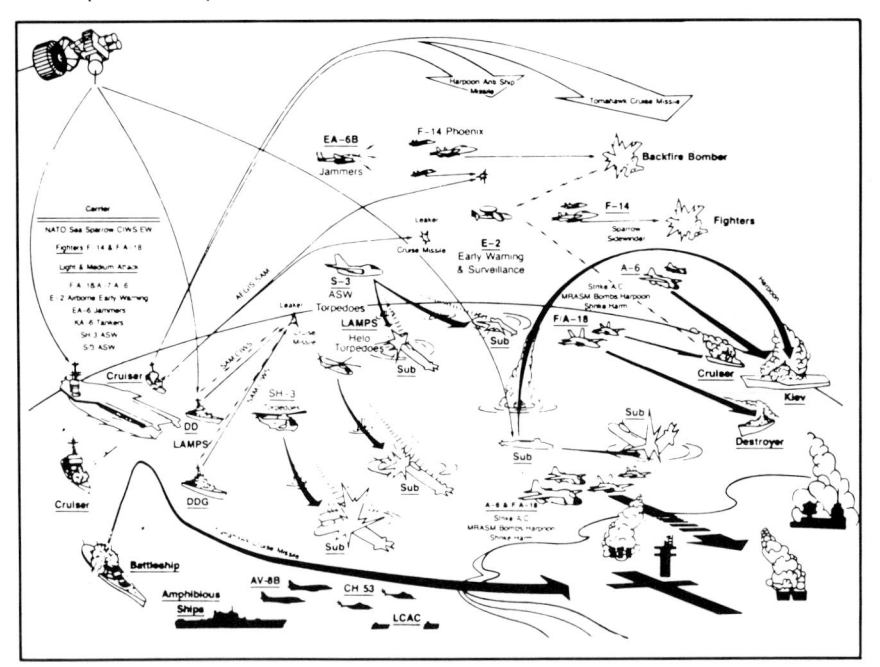

FIG. 12.1 The Complexity of Modern Naval Warfare. This illustrates how an amphibious task force might be absorbed into the overall matrix of forward maritime operations in high intensity warfare, possibly on the northern flank of NATO. Source: *The Maritime Strategy*, produced in January 1986 by the Proceedings of the US Naval Institute

fairly readily identified by intelligence sensors) in a target-rich environment; such a perspective ameliorates the dangers to an ATF, if only slightly.

In other campaigns there might not be such major opposition, and we do not wish to be tied to a specific scenario such as the North Atlantic in Transition to War or war, since these very complex cases create presentational difficulties. We will therefore concentrate upon a general approach to the conduct of the maritime campaign.

THE PASSAGE

The overall defence of the ATF on passage must be organised in depth and much will depend upon good surveillance by early warning systems, including overhead (satellite and air) and land sensors. The outer layer of the defence, range permitting, would be provided by land-based fighter aircraft. The forward elements of the naval forces would be a CVS group with a close escort of air defence frigates and, more widely spread, anti-submarine frigates and destroyers. There may also be submarines in attendance. The CVS itself would be operating *Sea Harriers* and airborne early warning and anti-submarine helicopters, and there would be support from shore based maritime patrol and anti-surface warfare aircraft. Further to the

PLATE 12.1 *Sea Harrier* operating from a CVS. (*Royal Navy. Crown copyright*)

rear, the escort for the ATF would include a balanced force of air defence and anti-submarine frigates.

An American operation would be based upon their very strong Carrier Battle groups. Elements of the USMC air wings could also be deployed forward to a friendly airfield, so their F/A-18 *Hornets* could assist the defence of the task force and, once the battle demanded it, their deep strike A-6E *Intruder* could supplement the anti-air effort by attacking enemy airfields. The seaborne element would include the carrier based F-14 *Tomcats* and F/A-18 *Hornets* of the US Navy.

A Soviet amphibious force on passage would follow the standard ground forces deployment pattern; the main force being surrounded by a protection group, preceded by reconnaissance elements, and with local air defence. Other naval forces, including air defence, surface action and anti-submarine groups would provide the outer elements of a layered defence, all protected by land-based aircraft.

AIR OPERATIONS IN NORWAY 1940

After the German invasion of Norway, the first instincts of Admiral Forbes, C-in-C Home Fleet, were to attack the enemy in Bergen on 9 April but the plan was cancelled by the Admiralty, because of concern about German air strength. Any doubts they might have had were resolved that day. The Germans had seized airfields in Denmark and in Norway, and were soon able to launch an attack on the Home Fleet; it was hardly a major engagement, but it made a great psychological impression on the C-in-C. He decided to leave responsibility for the whole of the southern area to submarines, and to operate the Fleet further north.

The decision reflected British naval air power problems between the wars. In common with the other major naval powers, Britain had continued to believe in the primacy of the battleship, but unlike in the USA and Japan there was little money to invest in supporting air power. Too much faith was put in anti-aircraft gun defence and there were no carriers deployed with the Home Fleet in the North Sea at the start of the campaign. The RAF that almost monopolised aviation investment, could have provided some support by aircraft based in the United Kingdom, but its resources were also severely limited and this was not a priority task for an air force mainly interested in strategic bombing and Home Defence, so no cover was present on 9 April. 'It is astonishing' writes Paul Kennedy, 'to discover just how much military and naval experts . . . underestimated the threat from the air to surface vessels at the outset of the war.'[3]

The Luftwaffe also played a most significant part in the ground operation. In central Norway, close air support was employed to harrass the forward defensive positions and, perhaps more telling, to interdict the rearward headquarters and base logistic areas, especially at the ports. 'Headquarters have been ceaselessly bombed' wrote General Massey who continued, 'the effect of this bombing on the conduct of operations is always serious and may be disastrous'.[4]

Following their success in Central Norway in early May, the Germans applied greater air effort against the North; again they harrassed Allied positions, headquarters and logistic bases; they attacked the fleet at sea, sinking a merchant ship redeploying the 1st Battalion Irish Guards to Bodo; and they resupplied their own forces by airdrops, reinforcing them with a parachute battalion. For some time, the Allies were able to counter this with only the limited capability from the Ark Royal. From 21 May, however, matters improved substantially when a squadron of Gladiators was flown off Furious *into the Norwegian airfield at Bardufoss. This was followed on 26 May by a squadron of Hurricanes. With their arrival some semblance of air parity was achieved and these aircraft played a significant part in the final phase in the Narvik battle.*

The evidence of the commanders in this campaign was that amphibious operations become virtually impossible without local air superiority. They wanted better air defence, both on the ground and in the air. They watched and envied the wide tactical and logistic scope of the Luftwaffe, and they sought the same capabilities for the Allies in the future. In addition, they saw for the first time the potential value of aircraft carriers for providing initial support before land based aircraft could be deployed.

ADVANCED FORCE OPERATIONS

Pre D-Day operations could include:

▶ *Supporting Operations* which would be carried out by naval, air and ground forces not under the immediate command of the CATF. They could include air raids to attack enemy positions near the beach, or diversionary attacks by nearby ground forces if the landing is to be a hook closely associated with the land battle; a normal Soviet tactic which could be equally effectively employed by Western forces.

▶ *The Advanced Force* which would usually be found from within the Amphibious Task Force organisation and would be a group of ships and elements of the landing force placed under a separate commander. Its tasks could include preliminary naval gunfire bombardments, minesweeping, beach and landing site reconnaissance and divertionary landings and raids.

The decision on the amount of preliminary activity in the AOA before the ATF arrives is a critical one for not only the CATF and the CLF, but also their superior commander, since there must be a correct balance between sound preparation and surprise. Naval precursor operations such as mine clearance, anti-submarine warfare and Special Forces reconnaissance patrols, as well as all the other advance tasks including air and naval bombardment of the objective, winning air control, and interdiction of enemy reserves and headquarters might make the delivery of the landing force easier on the day—but they could involve the surrender of the element of surprise. If one accepts, however, that modern surveillance systems will usually reveal that an amphibious task force is approaching, so that strategic surprise cannot be maintained, then a diversity of pre-D Day operations could do much to help deceive the enemy about the exact point and time of the landing. Operational and tactical surprise are essential for most operations, and are only unnecessary in rare cases when there might be no alternative landing areas or the enemy is very weak.

There does not appear to be a Soviet concept of advanced force operations, partly because of the speed at which landings are organised, although short term preliminary operations are undertaken. Mine clearance tends to be done immediately ahead of the amphibious ships as they approach the beach, which offers inadequate protection, and the concept of rather perfunctory mine clearance matches that of the ground forces in a high speed offensive. The increased use of ACVs has, however, lessened the danger from mines, and helicopters are also being used to tow mine sweeps, two practices the Soviets have in common with the USN.

RECONNAISSANCE

One inshore operation which is of great importance to amphibious warfare is the delivery (and, when necessary, recovery) of maritime special forces. Although a great amount of information about the AOA can be obtained by satellites, signal intelligence, and air reconnaissance and photography, there is still much to be gleaned by the man on the ground. This is the important role of forces such as the

PLATE 12.2   SBS operating from a submarine (*Royal Marines. Crown copyright*)

Special Boat Service (SBS), plus associated forces such as the Naval Gunfire Support Forward Observers (NGFO) of 148 (Meiktila) Amphibious Observation Battery RA and the Royal Marines Arctic and Warfare Cadre. The Americans have similar forces, the SEAL teams of the USN, the US Army Special Forces, and the USMC Force Reconnaissance Teams.

The SBS, as maritime Special Forces, are high value troops who must be tasked by commanders at the highest level, and could be used for a wide range of naval intelligence gathering and offensive operations, but some are always part of the UK/NL Amphibious Force and these would normally be allocated to the Advanced Force. Their small teams could be inserted into the area several days before the landing by submarine, surface craft, and helicopter, or by parachute drop into the sea, could make their approach by inflatable or canoe and, finally, they might swim on or below the surface to the objective. Their tasks would be the covert survey of the beaches and helicopter landing areas, obstacle clearance and the reconnaissance of enemy activity in the area. On the day of the landing, the SBS would mark the beaches and landing sites for the assault, while the prepositioned NGFOs directed the supporting fire.

Covert reconnaissance is a slow and painstaking business which makes it all the more important that there is a well thought out mission for the role of these teams in the overall intelligence plan. This could well be to confirm the final pieces of the jigsaw that the intelligence staffs are trying to fit together from the many sources at

PLATE 12.3 The Royal Marines Mountain and Arctic Warfare Cadre's main task is to train the UK/NL Landing Force in the specialist individual skills demanded by the North Norway role, but in war its mountain leaders are used as long range reconnaissance troops, and would be deployed on Advanced Force operations. (*Royal Navy. Crown copyright*)

their disposal. Suffice to say that these special operations are an increasingly sophisticated form of warfare, with good, secure and rapid communications of paramount importance.

In the Soviet case, Spetznaz... special forces... might be inserted into the landing area some days beforehand, especially for an operational level task such as an assault on the Baltic Islands launched from the Eastern Baltic. For short range hooks, the associated land forces might well send forward reconnaissance teams to the proposed objective area. Overall, however, much of reconnaissance of the beach for tactical level operations appears to be carried out by air, including the deployment of small parties by helicopter from major surface ships with the amphibious force. The clearance of obstacles on the beach and in the surf is left to assault frogmen who might be deployed by helicopter shortly before the landing, with a protection party.

THE DEFENCE OF THE AOA

Control of the AOA is vested in the CATF who would probably delegate Tactical Control for the detailed co-ordination of the air defence and anti-submarine systems. One of his main concerns is the deployment of his forces; whether to concentrate the amphibious ships relatively close to land where they can get protection from the terrain (especially in Norway where the ships can anchor close to the steep shoreline) but where they might be vulnerable to interference from enemy ground forces, or whether to disperse them at sea, with only the essential minimum close to the shore for offloading or providing support.

MARITIME OPERATIONS CLOSE TO THE SHORE

Fleets are usually designed to fight most effectively on the high seas, and their systems are often degraded when they have to operate close to land. Therefore the ATF would take advantage of any cover that is available. For example, one approach to North Norway is to sail up the Leads which run between the mainland and the host of offshore islands. An AOA based among the fjords, with the mountains rising steeply from the waterline, poses a considerable challenge to both sides, but even less demanding coastlines can require adjustments to proven techniques for combat at sea. (San Carlos was selected for the Falklands landing partly because it was 'an anchorage that would be difficult to attack by submarine or from the air and impossible to attack with air-launched *Exocet*.[2])

The main threat would be from the air, although mountains and islands would help to deter low flying fighter bombers, restrict the attack lines for enemy stand-off missiles, confuse the radar homing ones, and provide a considerable degree of security for the amphibious force. Even so, the layers of defence will need to be in place; the outer layer would remain broadly the same as for the passage. Closer in, the ships' radar and visual surveillance may well be masked by terrain, thus reducing reaction times to the minimum. They may receive help from land-based systems for local warning, and this could be an important role for the landing force. The short range *Rapier* (UK), and point defence *Javelin* (UK) and *Stinger* (USMC and NL) air defence missile systems must be landed early, not only to defend the

PLATES 12.4 and 12.5 The air defence of the AOA would depend upon short-range air defence weapons deployed both at sea... such as the *Sea Wolf* above... and ashore. The *Rapier* in the bottom picture is seen firing during trials in Norway. (*Royal Navy/Royal Marines. Crown copyright*)

186   Amphibious Operations

landing force, but also to provide the landward element of the overall matrix. The effectiveness of the ships' medium range missiles will depend upon the terrain, and it might be significantly reduced, so point defence by close in weapon systems such as *Seawolf*, *Goalkeeper*, chaff, decoys, and perhaps even the *ad hoc* arrangements for missiles and small arms on STUFT, will play a crucial role.

Torpedo firing submarines present a real danger in inshore waters as they are so hard to find, since coastal areas present particular challenges to all sonars with the fresh water from rivers creating variable conditions which need careful handling; the suspected, but well-publicized, incursions into Swedish and Norwegian waters during peacetime emphasise the nature of the threat. In war, however, these submarines may find it difficult to penetrate a combination of the natural hazards of the offshore islands and the national defensive systems often covered by the fire of sophisticated coastal forts.

A further threat from submarines and surface ships lies in their ability to launch long and medium range missiles, although firing towards the land could make it difficult to target the individual ships in the AOA. The counter to these relies upon the more distant ships, submarines and aircraft providing the outer layers of the overall defensive system.

PLATE 12.6   A sinister view of HMS *Brilliant* through the periscope of the submarine HMS *Ocelot* (*Royal Navy. Crown copyright*)

PLATE 12.7 A USN CH-53E *Super Stallion* clearing mines. (*US Navy*)

Enemy mines could cause considerable delays to the start of a landing, and could interfere with the operation after it had been launched; the classic case is the Wonsan landings in Korea in 1952 when the American landings were held up for eight days by Soviet mines laid by a makeshift North Korean minelaying force. In the shallow waters of an AOA there might be pressure, acoustic or magnetically activated ground mines.

Mining would be a significant threat in the enemy's home waters. Further afield, it would be more difficult for him; he would need good intelligence of the proposed AOA if he is to lay an effective field, or he would have to use considerable resources to cover a number of options; his capability might be large, but would not be unlimited. Submarines can carry a very limited number of mines, so their contribution would not represent a significant threat, surface vessels would find it virtually impossible to carry out offensive mining operations in alien waters, but aircraft can sow large areas in enemy waters in a relatively short time if they can penetrate the air defences—however, even then, they would probably be seen.

Clearing sufficient channels to allow reasonable movement in the AOA can be a lengthy process. It could be conducted by mine hunters, such as the British *Hunt* class MCMVs which use a very sensitive sonar to locate the mine, and then destroy it by explosive charges laid by a diver or by remote control. The USN uses the RH-53D *Sea Stallion* heavy helicopter which tows a sled with generators capable of producing the correct signature to detonate magnetic or acoustic mines. In NATO operations, much would depend upon the capabilities of the host nation, which is responsible for clearing mines in its own coastal waters.

CONCLUSION

The maritime operations; the passage, the advanced force operations, and the defence of the AOA, provide the essential framework for the landing. For much of the time that these activities are taking place, the landing force is relatively inactive and unable to affect the course of the battle. For all the planning, preparation and final training that goes on relentlessly in the amphibious ships and the STUFT, it can be a frustrating and, indeed, frightening period of waiting. No-one can have any illusions about the importance of the naval and air battle that rages about them; their part can only be successful if the amphibious task force and its escorts come through successfully to the AOA, secure it and hold it during the landing.

13

Land the Landing Force

OPERATIONAL PLANNING

We now come to the final part of the planning process and the landing itself. Operational planning might be carried out in a matter of months or weeks, depending upon the scale and nature of the task; at strategic, operational or tactical level. In an amphibious force poised at sea, or in reserve in the Norwegian Leads, however, the CATF and the CLF might be doing some hot planning.

With a clear mission from the Initiating Directive and good intelligence, the CLF will have to analyse and define a specific landing force mission and develop his concept of operations. These are not merely concerned with the act of landing, which is only a means to an end, but should encompass military objectives . . . to seize vital ground to block the enemy advance, or to destroy an enemy unit . . . to be achieved by operations ashore conducted independently, or with follow-on forces, or in conjunction with allied forces. Much depends upon the threat.

THE THREAT

The prime task of all the intelligence, electronic warfare and reconnaissance agencies is to identify the enemy, and Major General Thompson outlined his requirements as:

> 'Were there any enemy on the beaches, or near enough to react quickly, where were his main concentrations of strength, what was he doing, how alert was he and what was his morale like?'[1]

With satellite surveillance we must assume that the enemy will be aware of the amphibious threat; indeed, the very presence of allied amphibious forces draws off enemy strength elsewhere to guard the sea flank. So the coast will be under continuous surveillance but, unless the enemy has had a considerable time to prepare, few potential objectives can be expected to have coastal defences to match those of the later years of the Second World War. An American view of a worst case has been postulated[2] as a motor rifle division composed of three regiments defending about 200 kilometres of coastline. One regiment would be manning a static defensive position on the most obvious landing site, with obstacles and mines on the approaches, in the surfline, and on the beach. There would be a dense, overlapping artillery fire plan. The other two regiments would be in reserve to respond quickly to any landing with helicopters or armour, supported by air forces. There would, none the less, be opportunities to insert a landing force and, with good intelligence, these can be exploited.

CONCEPTS OF OPERATIONS

The UK/NL Amphibious Force

The concept of operations will depend upon the character and composition of the force. The UK/NL Landing Force is relatively light and reasonably mobile, so is best suited by organisation, equipment and training to operations in demanding terrain, although by no means exclusively so. It is not able to take on a strong enemy on landing, and the commanders might look for the enemy's vulnerable gaps, flanks and rear areas; headquarters, regimental artillery groups and logistic installations would be good targets. Alternatively, it could land as a covering force, or establish a base for follow-on operations or be held in reserve to counter enemy amphibious or other *desants*. There are many permutations. Not all the operations would require the whole force, since commando or even company level raids and demonstrations ... to divert attention from the main focus of attack ... could be mounted very effectively over considerable distances using landing craft and helicopters. These could be used to win intelligence, to inflict damage or to create a diversion.

The concept of an unopposed landing, however, does not imply any lack of readiness to fight, since so much depends upon how well you have reconnoitred the area, and the ability of the enemy to respond rapidly to the initial landing. No guarantee can be given that there will be no minor pockets of resistance, so the landing force must be able to suppress these from the outset. Moreover, it must be strong enough to secure a firm base against rapid counter attack and then be able to break out to complete its task.

So the tactical doctrine is wedded to the indirect approach; the ability to harness ground, the weather, night, deception and diversions to make the best use of the characteristics of the force. The availability of specialist amphibious ships is essential to this, and the addition of one or two LPH and the replacement of the LPDs will enable helicopters and landing craft to be operated in the most coherent fashion. This will give the force a better balance and flexibility, enabling it to probe for enemy weaknesses and to exploit them by landing commandos with their mortars, ATGW and supporting artillery as rapidly as possible to seize and develop successful beachheads.

US Amphibious Forces

The strength and size of the USMC amphibious MEB means that they can conduct opposed landings and thereafter engage sizeable enemy forces, especially when the power of their air wings is brought to bear. Their objective might well include the seizure of a port and airfield to permit the further enhancement by an airlanded MEB joining up with the heavy equipment from the MPS ships. The UK/NL Amphibious Force may well operate in conjunction with these much stronger forces. Joint operations could harness the different characteristics of the two forces, and we cannot but welcome the considerable fire support provided by our allies. For all the disparity in size, the present concepts of operations of the US and UK/NL forces are complementary, but some thought will need to be given to the impact of the evolving over-the-horizon concept of the US force.

Over The Horizon Assault

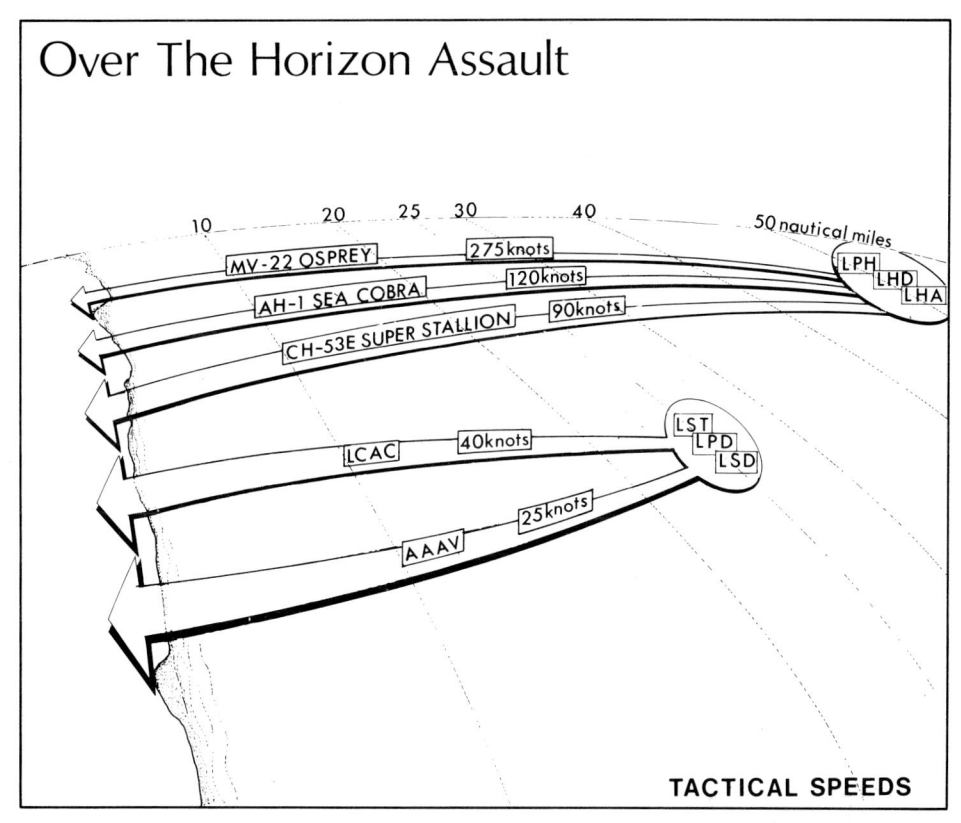

TACTICAL SPEEDS

FIG. 13.1 The Over the Horizon Concept. Amphibious staffs are used to calculating complex time and distance equations for helicopters and landing craft, but co-ordinating an assault by *Osprey* and LCAC with all the other means available in the future will pose some interesting questions

The Americans consider that existing equipment and methods make it difficult to ensure surprise; there are only a limited number of beaches which can accept landing craft, so the enemy can calculate the likely landing areas, and amphibious ships having to close the beach to launch the AAVs give too much warning to the defender and are vulnerable to mines and land artillery. With the introduction of the LCAC and the *Osprey*, assaults could be launched from beyond the range of artillery and all but the most capable anti-ship missiles . . . which must therefore be identified and neutralised. LCACs could land on 70 per cent of the world's beaches, as opposed to the 30 per cent open to landing craft. So, given good intelligence and the mobility of the amphibious ships (up to 500 nautical miles in 24 hours), the *Osprey*-borne forces could strike unexpectedly and rapidly at any point over a wide area of the littoral, and secure landing areas for the LCAC, which could deliver armoured forces ashore rapidly to counter the immediate enemy response. Understandably, many technological problems need to be resolved as this concept develops, including navigation for the LCACs, naval gunfire support, and communications between the ships and assault forces, as line-of-sight VHF and UHF

192   Amphibious Operations

radio will be ineffective at first. We can only hope that all the technological and financial difficulties being faced by the *Osprey* programme can be overcome to allow this exciting new concept to be fully developed.

One real concern is the future of the opposed assault capability. This dilemma is being openly debated in the *Marine Corps Gazette*, where one writer asked:

> 'Is it our intention to assault defended beaches? In 1984, during Congressional testimony . . . Maj Gen Glasgow said, in essence, that given an OTH capability, the Marine Corps would never again intend to assault a hostile beach. He added that we wouldn't have assaulted any in World War II if we had been offered any other choice.'[3]

The conventional view is that an opposed capability is essential; since an unopposed landing site may not be available; the force must be flexible enough to fight if the situation changes or intelligence is faulty; and the urgency of the mission may dictate an attack on a defended area. This presents a technological challenge in the design of an Advanced AAV capable of operating in conjunction with the LCAC and *Osprey*. One option is to deploy the AAV by LCAC to a Line of Departure some 4,000m from the shore, but this would slow down the landing of armour by LCAC, and so is seen only as an interim measure. The way ahead is being developed as you see in Plate 13.1.

PLATE 13.1 The USMC is planning a demonstrator programme for the Advanced AAV. Built with lightweight aluminium track and suspension systems, and a fibreglass and ceramic tile armour, it is expected to plane at about 25 knots, powered by waterjets. On land it should travel at 29 mph across country, and carry 18 marines. (*USMC*)

Land the Landing Force 193

At first blush, the introduction of the OTH concept would appear to preclude US/UK/NL interoperability, yet on closer inspection this need not be the case. Admittedly, with the USMC able to launch its first wave from a considerable distance, and to build up forces rapidly by LCAC and CH-53E, it will be difficult to meld the two forces. Matters will improve when the *Sea King* successor has been procured, which is some years ahead; if that is the EH 101 *Merlin* it would have a speed of 150 knots, greater range and (with 40 troops, too much?) capacity, but it could be launched at about the same distance as the LCAC on joint operations. (It has, indeed, been suggested as an *Osprey* substitute for the USMC.) In the meantime, tasks for the UK/NL Amphibious Force will have to be selected with care, but could include diversions, raids and flanking operations; and the lighter force could well capitalise upon the magnetic effect of the initial USMC landing in drawing off enemy from other objectives and thus offering weaknesses to be exploited.

Soviet Practice

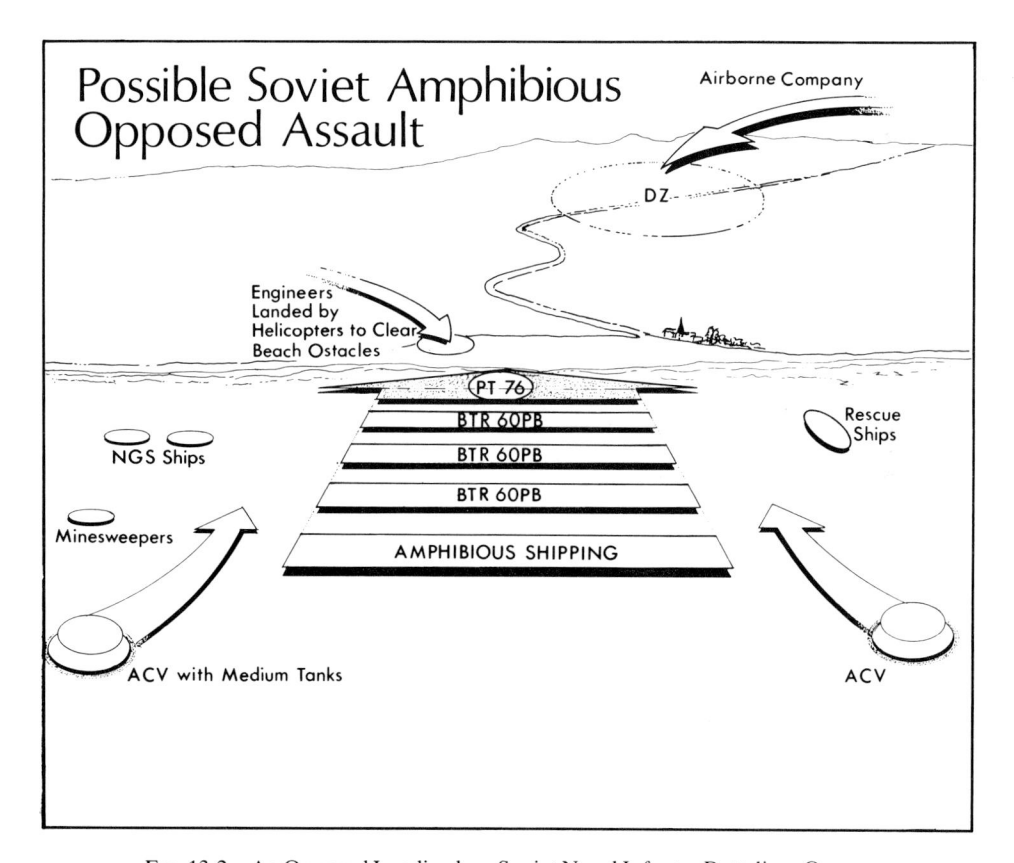

FIG. 13.2 An Opposed Landing by a Soviet Naval Infantry Battalion. On some exercises the ACVs have been used as the first wave of the assault, with amphibious ships in the second wave. The BTR-60BPs have been reported to have swum in from 3 miles out

194   Amphibious Operations

Although there are fundamental differences between Soviet and Western practice, especially at the strategic level, there are also similarities. In defence both the Soviet Naval Infantry and the UK/NL Landing Force have an anti-*desant* role. The Soviets see considerable value in landing troops behind an attacking enemy to act as a distraction or to hinder a pursuit, and they would expect NATO amphibious forces to be employed in this way to slow down the Soviet advance and enable the defenders to regroup into new positions. They would also employ amphibious landings in the advance to act as forward detachments to seize strongpoints and centres of resistance ahead of the attacking forces, with targets such as headquarters, reserves, and lines-of communication. These *desants* might well be conducted at company or battalion level and be closely co-ordinated with helicopter and airborne assaults.

The Soviets follow many of the standard operating practices as the West, although with different emphases. They are equally determined to achieve surprise, which depends upon good security of the planning and preparation of the troops and shipping, but most importantly through deception measures. In this they concentrate upon concealing the axis of main effort. There are many methods of

PLATE 13.2   The *Pomornik* is the largest of the new generation of Soviet ACVs, able to lift 100 tons of stores, a tank and 80 troops, with a speed of 50 knots. (*Jane's*)

achieving this, including the use of false reconnaissance patrols, concentrating upon areas of the secondary axis, and by leaking false orders and plans. The most important principle in all this, in Soviet eyes, is to use truth to feed falsehood by, say, the subtle use of demonstration landings at obvious points. In all this it is important to watch the enemy's reactions and to nurture his perceptions . . . or misconceptions.[4]

They also place great stress upon speed. They avoid any cross decking, or even transloading men into landing craft, and seek to land armour and mechanised infantry directly on to the beach from amphibious ships and ACVs. They would land in two waves, with the second wave prepared to draw alongside the first. They would press inland with great determination to join up with airborne or helicopter-borne *desant* forces and, ultimately, the main advance. In this search for speed, however, they have sacrificed sustainability, one area of potential weakness.

TIMINGS

Returning to the planning process; with the available intelligence and a concept of operations, the CLF can complete his plan. He and his R Group would select detailed objectives, plan diversionary and deception measures, confirm the best beaches and landing sites to achieve the mission, and plan in great detail the co-ordination of the fire support. One of the critical decisions is the timing of the assault, and the main factors in this are:

▶ *Weather*, since that will affect air, helicopter and landing craft operations.

▶ *Tide*; landing on a rising tide is preferred as landing craft could well be stranded on a falling tide

▶ *Light*. There is much debate about the effectiveness of night landings. For all the advances in infra-red and thermal imagery, the landing force can still achieve greater surprise at night, but the effectiveness of helicopters and much of the supporting fire is better by day. Logisticians may argue for a dawn landing, which allows them the rest of the day to build up supplies ashore at the fastest rate.

ORDERS FOR THE OPERATION

The overall plan for the operation will be issued by the CATF, but a crucial preliminary to the battle is the formal 'O' Group when the CLF briefs his subordinate commanders. Major General Vaux described the one before the San Carlos landing in vivid terms:

> 'Meticulous preparation co-ordination and stage management is required by the staff, as well as a compelling performance from the commander himself. For it is then that the leader briefs his subordinate commanders on how he expects them to risk their own lives, and those of their men, while carrying out his particular plan for battle. Not only must everyone understand the orders—they must also have confidence in them as well. Subsequently, of course, the whole orders procedure needs to be successfully repeated all the way down the line, from commanding officer to corporal.
>
> . . . Twenty-four hours beforehand, each unit had received a detailed operation order clarifying the role of every component of the military force that was to establish itself ashore. With this

clarification were pages of statistics listing map references, codenames, radio frequencies, supporting fire tasks, logistic priorities and timings—altogether, the document was nearly fifty pages long. We needed all twenty-four hours of that lead time to absorb, discuss and place in perspective the tapestry of the landing.

At the 'O' group, the Brigadier was able to illustrate his intentions for each unit against the detailed background of the operation order. His own orders were delivered formally and precisely, but with that personal touch for each CO which has always characterised British briefings of this kind—individual reassurance is never more important than at such moments.'[5]

COMMAND AND CONTROL OF THE LANDING

The focal point for the command and control of the landing is the Assault Operations Room (AOR) in the LPD, abutting on to the Ships Operations Room where the Naval members of the CATF staff would be controlling the shipping and fighting the maritime battle. Their effectiveness depends upon good communications, a sphere which reflects all the complexities of amphibious warfare since the systems architecture must provide the essential links between the CATF and the superior national and allied commands, and with the naval, air and land forces taking part in the immediate and associated battles. This would be an unexceptional commitment for a relatively high level headquarters, but it imposes a considerable load upon a one-star command, such as the UK/NL Amphibious Force, operating from an assault ship close to the beach.

In the AOR the COS to CLF holds sway as he co-ordinates the landing force's progress, interpreting the incoming intelligence and reading the battle ashore, always acting within his commander's concept; as ever, he works closely with the amphibious team on CATF's staff controlling the offload, and with the members of the SACC. For all their preliminary work, they are aware that their main task at this stage is the management of chaos, as the elements, the enemy and *friction* conspire to upset the best laid plans.

How does the AOR work? A useful way to give a flavour of the atmosphere is to turn to the example of the television or radio news room: in his book *The Military and The Media* Colonel Alan Hooper perceived an interesting similarity between the teamwork, professionalism, efficiency, logistical planning, flexibility and discipline demanded for military operations and for producing a news broadcast or a newspaper. Like the military commander, the News Editor makes his plan, and then it is up to the news room which receives:

'. . . a constant flow of information be it from the agency copy, telephone calls or on tape. This information is embellished by the more detailed reports provided by reporters or correspondents who either return to the office with the copy, or communicate with the office "from the field". Having received the information the (duty) editor (analogous to the COS) is constantly required to make decisions against the clock so that the various specialists in his organisation have time to produce the newspaper, the television or the radio programme.'

Hooper goes on to comment that:

'The pressure on the decision maker is common to all news media and it is probably the area of closest association with the military. The similarities in organisation may encompass other fields, such as industry, but it is the requirement to make decisions under the pressure of time, often frustrated by inadequate information, which is peculiar to the military and the news media.'[6]

The CLF's Role

Early in the landing, the CLF can usually stand back and watch his handiwork put into effect. He would have little part to play in running the mechanics of the assault and, like an army brigade commander, his intervention would be restricted to critical decisions, such as the time and place to commit reserves.

Most CLFs are keen to get ashore early to get a feel for the battle, and may well fly ashore with the R Group for a short visit to their commanding officers. The timing of the move of their headquarters depends upon the state of the battle, the build up of the beachhead, and the ability to ensure good communications; under some circumstances it might be advisable to remain embarked, and CLFs of larger formations, such as the MGRM Commando Forces on OOA operations, would be best placed afloat for some time. Major General Thompson commented after the first day of air attacks in San Carlos Sound:

> 'Command in war is complicated enough without trying to exercise it out of touch for a long time and unable to get off a ship fighting for its life. Without the amphibious ships and particularly the LPDS, with their specialized equipment, the landing could not have been done, but the day's events had convinced me, if I needed convincing after years of practice on amphibious exercises, that the whole headquarters must be got ashore as quickly as possible. This feeling was reinforced when I heard, on returning to *Fearless*, that, on orders from Northwood, *Canberra* and *Norland* were to be out of San Carlos Water as soon as possible that night and that there was talk of the LPDs leaving the anchorage each night in case of submarine attack. Whatever happened and whatever the ships did, or did not do, the Headquarters with all its equipment must get ashore so that, by the next dawn, the Brigade could be under the hand of its Commander to face whatever the day might bring.'[7]

LANDING THE HEADQUARTERS

When the time is right, therefore, the CLF will transfer his headquarters from the command ship to the beachhead. Communications are the main issue at this stage. The challenge for the landing force signals officer is to make the transition from operating on board the ship with its powerful transmitters and receivers, to establishing communications ashore with vehicle-borne or manpack, and much less powerful, sets. This is largely ensured by close liaison between Naval and Marine staffs in ship design, to ensure that interoperable equipments are fitted from the outset. It is also a matter of good operational planning, detailed resource management and careful timing; ensuring that the change of command does not take place until the landing force headquarters is properly set up on the ground with communications firmly established.

Once ashore, the headquarters has to control the land battle, and establish contact with the amphibious shipping and virtually the same range of higher command, air and naval gunfire support agencies as the CATF. This, again, calls for a much wider range of circuits than would be normally expected at this level of command, and gives the headquarters a distinctive signature of signals emissions. Electronic Warfare is an increasingly important factor on the modern battlefield, so the headquarters would be a target for enemy electronic counter measures. There are many ways to counter this threat, including the judicious use of radio silence and the ability to change locations frequently. The communicators would prefer to rely

PLATE 13.3 Part of the UK/NL Landing Force Headquarters in the Arctic clustered around one of the many small *huttes* found in North Norway, which in itself aids the camouflage. (*Royal Marines. Crown copyright*)

upon relatively static main positions, with a strong infrastructure of secure circuits giving a better chance of ensuring both reliable communications and enhanced protection. However, this does not suit the mobile nature of operations and the future will probably see increased use of portable satellite terminals and the miniaturisation of equipment.

TERMINATION

Even after the CLF and his headquarters are ashore, there is still a considerable interaction with the CATF who remains in overall command. One Commodore has commented (reflecting the spirit of the relationship more than the strict doctrine).

> 'Think of me as the Sea Brigadier; my tactical area of responsibility is behind the Brigade, and is where I continue to fight the battle in support of operations ashore'.

The Amphibious Task Force may remain in the AOA for some time, acting as a floating base for operations such as raids along the coast, and giving invaluable logistic support. When the amphibious objective has been achieved, the landing force is firmly established ashore, and the shipping is no longer required to support it, the CATF will advise his superior authority that the operation should be terminated. The superior authority may then terminate the operation, the AOA would be disestablished and the ships would sail away. The landing force would, under predetermined arrangements, come under the operational control of an appropriate land force commander ashore. A final option, of course, would be to re-embark the landing force for a new mission elsewhere, making good use of the flexibility of the amphibious capability.

14

Fighting the Land Battle

MANEUVER WARFARE

The conduct of the land battle depends upon strong leadership and the ability to co-ordinate all the elements of the landing force effectively. One term which might encapsulate the approach of the commanders is *Maneuver Warfare*, this is an American concept (hence the spelling) not specifically adopted by the British, although there is common ground, as one USMC officer has suggested:

> '... maneuver warfare is a way of thinking about battle that continually sees it as a contest of wills, not weapons. Rather than outmuscling opponents, in the tradition of the Somme, Iwo Jima, and Khe Sanh, maneuver warfare seeks to outfight opponents more in the manner of Sherman before Atlanta, the German blitzkrieg, and the British in the Falklands.'[1]

As this implies, the current emphasis in the USMC upon Maneuver Warfare seeks to change attitudes towards attrition warfare with its reliance upon immense firepower and direct infantry assaults. It is a more balanced and thoughtful approach which is based on the sound premise that success in battle depends upon the ability to win information by good reconnaissance, interpret it into sound intelligence, address the options, and then take decisive action to apply firepower and infantry strength more rapidly and accurately than the enemy. This has been reduced, or conceptualized, into the theory of Boyd's *Observation–Orientation–Decision–Action cycle* (called the *OODA Loop*). In his book *Maneuver Warfare Handbook*, William S. Lind summarises the effectiveness of the *OODA Loop* as:

> 'If one side in a conflict can consistently go through the Boyd Cycle faster than the other, it gains a tremendous advantage. By the time the slower side acts, the faster side is doing something different from what he observed, and his action is inappropriate. With each cycle, the slower party's action is inappropriate by a larger time margin.'[2]

... and so on until the enemy is rendered ineffective. Such a concept relies upon equipment that combines mobility with firepower; the good air and helicopter capabilities of the MAGTFs compensate for the relative lack of armoured fighting vehicles. The complete concept encompasses tactics which concentrate upon identifying the enemy's strong points, or *surfaces* and focusing the main effort upon his weaknesses, or *gaps*; the indirect approach is strongly endorsed. There are also considerable demands placed upon the logistic system which must be able to anticipate, rather than merely respond to, operational needs.

Does the UK/NL Landing Force operate in this way? In the Falklands operation the unopposed landing at San Carlos was certainly an example of the indirect

PLATE 14.1 Firepower... the 105mm Light Gun of the UK/NL Landing Force. (*Royal Marines. Crown copyright*)

approach, but the land campaign by 3 Commando Brigade RM has been described, in an intentional pun, as 'pedestrian' since circumstances, especially the lack of a helicopter-capable ship able to operate in the AOA and the logistic difficulties, constrained the mobility of the units who had to close with the enemy by the arduous *yomp* across the island. Once in contact, however, the emphasis was upon a form of maneuver warfare and was implemented most successfully. Despite the high quality of the Commando and Parachute units and, indeed, all the fighting men, at the time the overall fighting strength and ability to manœuvre were still limited.

Since 1982 some enhancements have been made to the UK/NL Landing Force to improve its mobility and firepower so that it could conduct the land battle in a less pedestrian fashion. More *Sea King 4's* and landing craft have been a significant help, as have both the introduction of *Lynx/TOW* helicopters, and the additional *MILAN ATGW* and 81mm Mortars. The Dutch 120mm Mortars and the *Rapier* battery will represent further steps in the right direction. Is that enough? It should remain as essentially a light infantry force with easily portable equipment, using helicopters rather than APCs for tactical mobility, and the fitness of the marines will always be an important factor in fighting over demanding terrain, which is their metier. If one looked at the strength of the USMC and was given the opportunity to select something from their inventory, the heavy artillery and intimate air support would be very tempting, but (even discounting the expense for a moment) they might well be too substantial for both the amphibious life and the concept of operations. Perhaps one would choose some of their attack helicopters for close support and for escorting the support helicopters. For the distant future, the

PLATE 14.2   . . . and Movement. It takes a CH-53E *Super Stallion* to lift the 155mm M-198 of the USMC. (*US Navy*)

PLATE 14.3 CH-46 *Sea Knight* and *Sea Cobra* on deck. (*US Navy*)

Fighting the Land Battle 203

PLATE 14.4 *Lynx/TOW. (Royal Marines. Crown copyright)*

PLATE 14.5 The Dutch 120mm Mortar. (RNLMC)

potential of smart munitions for mortars and lightweight 155mm artillery, if they are developed successfully, have considerable appeal.

DIRECTIVE CONTROL

The *Maneuver Warfare* concept also depends upon flexible command arrangements, underpinned by sound management of the supporting fire and responsive C3I based on modern, computerised, communications and information systems. The current practice of *Directive Control*, which is common to the Army and Marines on both sides of the Atlantic, provides the framework.

The aim of this method is to enable the commander in the chaos of battle to take advantage of a sudden change in circumstances, or the exercise of initiative by his subordinate, in pursuit of the overall purpose. The centrepiece is effective delegation to subordinates who must act within certain guidelines. W. S. Lind[3] has described these guidelines as two contracts between the commander and his subordinate, in which the latter must understand:

> ▶ *The Commanders Intent*; which is the commander's vision of what he wants to happen to the enemy, and the final result he seeks; it must be understood at two levels removed, so the company commander must know what is in the brigadier's mind. This is Lind's first and long term contract, in which the superior commander tells his subordinate *what* is required and leaves him great freedom of action about *how* it is to be accomplished.

> ▶ *His Mission*; what tasks does the subordinate have to do to carry out the plan? This is Lind's second and shorter term contract; the commander allocates a slice of his *Intent* which is within the scope of the subordinate, who in turn undertakes to make his actions support the mission, in return for freedom to conduct his battle.

> ▶ *His Freedom of Action*. The commander will specify certain limitations, in terms of firepower resources, timings, the need to conform to the movement of flanking formations and boundaries. Within these guidelines, however, the subordinate has the freedom to react to the changing tactical situation, judging when to obtain clearance from his commander if low-level decisions will have far reaching implications. During the battle, the commander has the ability to use his reserve in support of the subordinate, and he would usually choose to reinforce success rather than failure.

This decentralisation is not a laid back form of delegation, or worse, command without orders, but it is designed so that commanders at all levels not only accept confusion and disorder, but operate successfully within it, and at the same time are able to *generate* confusion in the enemy. In this we must emphasise the part to be played by junior officers and NCOs upon whom so much of the execution of the concept depends, fighting at the sharp end of the battle.

This approach is perhaps no more than an articulation of what many commanders have achieved in the past. But it provides a framework by which the fighting power of the excellent officers, warrant officers, NCOs and marines or soldiers in the landing force, with their supporting firepower and logistics, can be orchestrated to best effect.

LESSONS FROM DIEPPE 1942

One of the aims of Maneuver Warfare *is to shift the emphasis away from attrition warfare towards a more balanced approach. Perhaps surprisingly, some of the lessons of Dieppe and the way they were applied to the immense Normandy landings have something to say to modern advocates of* Maneuver Warfare *and to those debating the future of the opposed assault. These lessons were:*

▶ *Frontal amphibious assaults against obvious targets must be avoided. Therefore the British in Normandy landed to the flanks of known strong points where possible, to give room for manœuvre once ashore. Fergusson commented that 'Unfortunately the Americans . . . failed to profit by the lessons . . . of Dieppe . . . they poured troops ashore in the conviction that, with the help of bombardment and DD tanks, they could overwhelm the strong points by sheer weight of numbers, landing as near them as they could in order to lessen the distance to be traversed.'*[4]

▶ *The plan was too rigid. In relatively small operations such as Dieppe there is scope for flexibility, although this could not be applied to Normandy owing to its immense scale. None the less, Fergusson commented that 'Non-rigidity, so to speak, was to set in when we got our foothold ashore, and here Montgomery's insistence that every Corps Commander should be free to fight his own battle from his own beach or beaches paid off handsomely.'*[5]

▶ *The firepower was totally inadequate. This was the premier lesson at the time, since there was no heavy air bombardment, only a few destroyers and a lack of close support from landing craft. It was a lesson that had been hoisted in before Normandy and Walcheren.*

Conclusion

This century has witnessed a radical change in all forms of warfare, not least in the amphibious variety. Those who analysed Gallipoli in the 1930s produced a doctrine that remains the basis of current practice. Still today we see value in the lessons of the myriad of landings during the Second World War, although these must be kept in perspective. After some difficult years, the recognition of the place of amphibious forces in the Forward Maritime Strategy has allowed a more positive approach which makes the deterrent role more convincing, and the readiness of the forces has a realistic global, as well as NATO, dimension. The planned ship and military enhancements on both sides of the Atlantic have generated a greater confidence, and these trends have been reflected in a robust and coherent approach to developing maritime, amphibious and military concepts for managing that complex and challenging zone where sea, land and air meet.

PLATE 14.6 In all combat, the final, often deciding factors are individual skills and the fitness to fight, and nowhere more so than in the snows of arctic Norway.
(*Royal Navy. Crown copyright*)

And the future? The recent events in Central and Eastern Europe, the state of the economy and the impending demographic trough combine to make predictions about strategy, equipment and manpower extremely hazardous. In these circumstances the inherent flexibility of amphibious forces becomes more important than ever. I am confident that they will continue to provide a capability which could, when called upon, be applied with both discretion and discrimination to support crisis management in a highly uncertain world.

References

PART I

Chapter 1 · The Assault

1. Isely and Crowl, '*The US Marines and Amphibious War*', Princeton, 1951, pp. 319–20.
2. Brigadier Whitehead, Over the Beach; Amphibious Operations in the 1980s–1990s, *NATO's Sixteen Nations* (16 N) October 1986. Based on the NATO definition in *Doctrine for Amphibious Operations* ATP 8 (unclassified).
3. USMC, *Doctrine for Amphibious Operations*, LFM 01 (unclassified), para. 101.
4. Lieutenant General Smith, Amphibious Tactics in the US Navy, *Marine Corps Gazette* (MCG), June 1946.
5. Julian Thompson, *No Picnic*, London, 1985, p. 22.
6. Isely and Crowl, p. 9.

Chapter 2 · Historical Perspectives

1. G. Till, '*Maritime Strategy in the Nuclear Age*', London, 1984, pp. 224–5.
2. Kinglake, quoted in Admiral Sir Herbert Richmond, '*Amphibious Warfare in British History*', Cambridge, 1941, p. 31.
3. Quoted in Sir Michael Howard, '*The Causes of Wars*', London, 1983, p. 189.
4. Quoted in Richmond, p. 3.
5. Sir Julian Corbett, '*Some Principles of Maritime Strategy*', London, 1911.
6. M. P. A. Hankey, Submission to the Doyle Committee, July 1905, Hankey Papers, Churchill College, Cambridge.
7. '*The War Office, The Army, and The Empire: A Review of the Military situation in 1900*', p. 36 (quoted in Stokesbury, p. 196).
8. James Ladd, '*The Royal Marines 1919–1980*', London, 1980, p. 29.
9. K. J. Clifford, '*Amphibious Warfare Development in Britain and America from 1920–1940*', New York, 1983, p. 76.
10. B. Fergusson, '*The Watery Maze*', London, 1961, p. 43. (*Copyright Bernard Ferguson. Reproduced by permission of Curtis Brown Ltd London.*)
11. Richmond, p. 31. Richmond also spelt out the 'Governing Factors' as ancient truths which would have been well known by 1916.
12. For the full story, see John Laffin, '*Damn the Dardenelles*', or Alan Moorhead, *Gallipoli*.
13. J. F. C. Fuller, quoted in M. L. Bartlett, *Assault from the Sea*, Annapolis, 1983, p. 151.
14. R. R. James, quoted by Lieutenant Colonel Gillum in Gallipoli, its Influence on Amphibious Doctrine, *MCG*, November 1967.
15. J. L. Stokesbury, '*British Concepts and Practices of Amphibious Warfare, 1867–1916*', Duke University unpublished thesis, 1968, p. 185.
16. Howard, p. 206.
17. B. Bond, '*Liddell Hart: A Study of his Strategic Thought*', London, 1977, p. 71.
18. Lieutenant General H. R. S. Massey, Despatch, May 1940. *London Gazette*, 29 May 1946, para. 71.
19. Brigadier General E. L. Cole USMC, Lecture, 6 December 1923, File 5425–140, Breckinridge Library, MCCDC, Quantico, VA.
20. Ellis was a brilliant but unusually eccentric USMC officer who died during his mission to Micronesia in 1923. Bartlett, pp. 157–67.
21. Isely and Crowl, p. 28.
22. Future wars were not, according to the Chiefs of Staff, to include amphibious operations, so the ISTDC was disbanded when war was imminent.
23. Fergusson, p. 40.

24. J. Terraine, 'The RAF in World War II; Lessons for Today', *RUSI Journal*, December 1988. Quoted in Sir Maurice Dean, with a comment of his own.
25. S. G. Gorshkov, *'The Sea Power of the State'*, Moscow, 1976, p. 258.
26. Gorshkov, p. 121.
27. Howard, p. 206.
28. Churchill, *The Second World War*, Vol. IV, *'The Hinge of Fate'*, Westerham, 1951, p. 415.
29. Fergusson, p. 409.
30. Fergusson, p. 208.
31. Fergusson, p. 192.
32. Isely and Crowl, p. 582.
33. William S. Lind, *'Maneuver Warfare'*, Boulder, Colorado, 1985, p. 37.
34. Gorshkov, p. 272.
35. Christopher Donnelly *et al.*, 'Soviet Amphibious Warfare and War on the Northern Flank', Sandhurst, 1984, unpublished, p. 37.
36. Quoted in Bartlett, p. 333.

Chapter 3 · Towards a Modern Capability

1. Quoted in Bartlett, p. 337.
2. R. F. Weighley, *'The American Way of War'*, New York, 1973, p. 385.
3. A. J. Barker, *'Suez: the Seven Day War'*, London, 1964, p. 13.
4. Cmnd 1629, quoted in J. L. Moulton, 'Mobility in Amphibious Warfare', *Brassey's Annual 1962*, p. 165.
5. Moulton, p. 171.
6. Michael Carver, *'War Since 1945'*, London, 1980, p. 98.
7. *Statement on the Defence Estimates 1975*, Comd 5976, March 1975, p. 12.
8. *Statement on the Defence Estimates 1982*, Comd 8288, p. 10.
9. T. C. Linn, 'Amphibious Warfare: A Misunderstood Capability', *Armed Forces Journal International*, August 1987.
10. Till, *'The Sea in Soviet Strategy'*, London, 1989, p. 200.
11. Gorshkov, p. 276.
12. Till, *'Modern Sea Power'*, London, 1987, p. 113.
13. *House of Commons, Select Committee on Defence* (1985), p. xiii.
14. E. Grove, The Maritime Strategy and Crisis Stability, *Naval Forces*.

Chapter 4 · A Maritime Strategy for Modern Amphibious Operations

1. Corbett, p. 15.
2. Corbett, *The Successors of Drake*, London, 1900, Preface, p. vii.
3. Gorshkov, p. 214.
4. Lars B. Wallin (Ed.), *The Northern Flank in a Central European War*, Stockholm: National Defence Research Institute, 1980.
5. Captain Gretton RN, The American Maritime Strategy: European Perspectives and Implications, *RUSI Journal*, Spring 1989.
6. N. Friedman, The Maritime Strategy and the Design of the US Fleet, *Comparative Strategy*. Vol. 6, No. 4, 1987.
7. Corbett, *Maritime Strategy*, p. 36.
8. Till, *Sea Power* pp. 59–64.
9. Admiral Watkins USN, The Maritime Strategy, *US Naval Proceedings*, January 1986.
10. Gretton, op. cit.
11. Vice Admiral Stanford, in G. Till (Ed.), *The Future of British Sea Power*, London, 1984, p. 155.
12. Brigadier Ross, in Ellmann Ellingsen (Ed.), *Reinforcing the Northern Flank*, Oslo, 1988, p. 66.
13. Admiral Staveley, *Overview of British Defence Policy and the Relevance of the Northern Flank*, Kings'/MOD Seminar, May 1986.
14. Lieutenant General Pringle, Power Projection and the Role of the Royal Marines, in G. Till (Ed.), *The Future of British Sea Power*, London, 1984, p. 152.
15. J. Porter, Budget Pressures Threaten British Amphibious Fleet, *Jane's Naval Review*, 1986.
16. Sir Basil Liddell Hart, The Value of Amphibious Flexibility and Forces, *RUSI Journal*, 1960.
17. D. da Cunha, Soviet Naval Infantry and Amphibious Life in the Pacific, *Armed Forces*, October 1988.

18. John Nott, 'Our Defences All at Sea', *The Times*, 5 October 1987.
19. Corbett, p. 281.
20. Till, *Sea Power*, pp. 77–84.
21. Major J. F. Gebhardt USA, *Petsamo-Kirkenes Operations 7–30 October 1944*, Soviet Army Studies Office, Fort Leavenworth, 1988 (unpublished).
22. Dr Tomas Ries, Seminar on *The Soviet Threat to Norway* at King's College, London 4 October 1988.
23. Lieutenant Colonel Marks USMC, The USMC Expeditionary Force in NATO, 16N July 1988.
24. General Howlett, 'Allied Defence of the Northern Flank', 16N November 1988.
25. Marks, op. cit.
26. General Kelly and Major O'Donnell, The Amphibious Warfare Strategy, *Proceedings*, January 1986.
27. Lieutenant General B. E. Trainor USMC (Rtd). Defense Correspondent *The New York Times*. Interview in Washington, 4 August 1988.
28. Kelly and O'Donnell. op. cit.
29. Dr C. Gray, Maritime Strategy and the World Beyond, *Naval Forces*, No. V/88.

Chapter 5 · Limited Global Operations

1. Sir James Cable, *Gunboat Diplomacy 1919–1979*, London, 1981, p. 25.
2. Cable, *Britain's Naval Future*, London, 1983, p. 162.
3. John Keegan, Storm Warning for the Forces over Spending, *Daily Telegraph*, 27 September 1988.
4. *Statement on the Defence Estimates 1987*, p. 23.
5. Watkins, op. cit.
6. General A. M. Gray USMC, quoted in Etnyre and Patrow 'Moving Ahead, Our Corps is on the March', *Marine Corps Gazette (MCG)*, August 1988.
7. Ikle and Wohsetter, Discriminate Deterrence, *Report of the Commission on Integrated Long Term Strategy*. Washington 1988. pp. 1, 11, 14 and 66.
8. Gray, Report to Congress, *MCG*, April 1988.
9. Trainor, Marines and Third World Conflict, *MCG*, November 1988.
10. Till, *Soviet Navy*, p. 205.
11. Cable, 'Arms Control at Sea', *Navy International*, November 1988.
12. Keegan, 'Fall in, the Global Police Force' *Daily Telegraph*, 10 April 1989.

PART II: THE CONDUCT OF AMPHIBIOUS OPERATIONS

Chapter 6 · Broad Principles of Command

1. Lord Ismay, '*The Memoirs of Lord Ismay*', London, 1950, p. 120.
2. Moulton, '*A Personal View of Amphibious Operations*', unpublished.
3. Martin van Creveld, '*Command in War*', Harvard, 1985, p. 266.
4. Ismay, p. 111.
5. Piers Mackesy, 'Churchill on Narvik', *RUSI Journal*, July 1970.
6. T. K. Derry, '*Campaign in Norway*', London, 1952, p. 146.
7. J. L. Moulton, '*The Campaign in Norway 1940*', London, 1966, p. 221.
8. E. F. Ziemke, '*The German Northern Theatre of Operations 1940–1945*', Washington, 1959, p. 90.
9. *Report of the Joint committee on the Investigation of the Pearl Harbour Attack*. Released in 1946, p. 245.
10. William Pakenham *et al.*, '*Naval Command and Control*', in this series.
11. ATP-8, para. 270e.
12. *Manual of Combined Operations*, 1938, p. 21.
13. E. N. Luttwak, Letter *Armed Forces Journal*, May 1987.
14. van Creveld, p. 268.
15. Thompson, pp. 26 and 34.
16. Howlett, op. cit.
17. Whitehead, 'Are We Training for the Right War?' *Globe and Laurel*, December, 1988.
18. Colonel Krulak USMC, Letter *Armed Forces Journal*, August 1987.
19. Thompson, p. 25.

References

Chapter 7 · Planning

1. Thompson, '*No Picnic*', p. 20.
2. C. Archer (Ed.), '*The Soviet Union and Northern Waters*', London, 1988, p. 173.
3. From the report '*US Marines in Grenada 1983*', by the History and Museums Division HQ USMC, Washington, 1987.
4. F. Uhlig, Amphibious Aspects of the Grenada Episode, in Dunn and Watson (Eds), *American Intervention in Grenada*', Boulder, Colorado, 1985, p. 96.

Chapter 8 · Means of Delivery

1. Quoted in N. Polmer and P. Mersky, *Amphibious Warfare—An Illustrated History*, London, 1988, p. 57.
2. Polmer and Mersky, p. 58.
3. Until 1985 the series was called the *Landing Vehicle Tracked (LVT)*.
4. Thompson, p. 59.
5. Fergusson, p. 359.
6. J. L. Moulton, *Haste to the Battle*, London, 1963, p. 140.
7. Ross, in Ellingsen, pp. 65 and 69.

Chapter 9 · Amphibious Ships

1. C. Coker, *British Defence Policy in the 1990s*, Brassey's, 1987, pp. 157–8.
2. Colonel Brosnan USMC, An Amphibious Landing? With Civilian Ships? *Naval War College Review*, March–April 1986.

Chapter 10 · The Landing Force and its Fire Support

1. Hastings and Jenkins, p. 361.
2. Gray, Report of the Marine Corps to Congress, *MCG*, April, 1988.
3. Isely and Crowl, p. 588.
4. Captain Hugh McManners RA, *Falklands Commando*, London, 1984, p. 158.
5. Nick Vaux, *March to the South Atlantic*, London, 1986, p. 173.
6. Colonel Pilot Musial, '*The Role of Strike Aviation in Support of Sea Assault Landings*', Donnelly *et al.*, p. 184.
7. Fergusson, p. 82.
8. Lieutenant General Smith, An Assessment of Marine Aviation, *MCG*, May 1988.
9. William S. Lind, The Next Agenda: Military Reform, *MCG*, June 1988.

Chapter 11 · Logistics

1. Hastings and Jenkins, p. 266.
2. Donnelly, p. 56.
3. Colonel Smith, Team Spirit 84 Reviewed, *MCG*, August 1986.

Chapter 12 · The Setting—Maritime Operations

1. Corbett, p. 282.
2. Thompson, p. 23.
3. Kennedy, p. 303.
4. Massey, para. 66.

Chapter 13 · Land the Landing Force!

1. Thompson, p. 31.
2. Lieutenant Commander Smith USN, Over-the Horizon Operations, *Proceedings*, November 1987.

3. Lieutenant Colonel Thompson USMC, The Advanced Assault Amphibian Vehicles, *MCG*, January 1989.
4. Donnelly *et al.*, p. 59.
5. Vaux, pp. 69–70.
6. Alan Hooper, *The Military and The Media*, Exeter, 1982, p. 66.
7. Thompson, p. 67.

Chapter 14 · Fighting the Land Battle

1. Major Moore USMC, The Art of MAGTF Warfare. *MCG*, April 1989.
2. Lind, pp. 5 and 6.
3. Ibid.
4. Fergusson, p. 336.
5. Ibid.

Bibliography

This list of books is far from comprehensive, but is a cross section which would give a sound background to this subject.

Strategy

Clive Archer (Ed.), *The Soviet Union and Northern Waters*, Routledge, 1988.
Sir James Cable, *Gunboat Diplomacy 1919–1979*, London, Macmillan, 1981.
Sir Julian Corbett, *Some Principles of Maritime Strategy*, London, 1911. Brassey's new edition, 1988.
Norman Friedman, *The US Maritime Strategy*, Jane's, 1988.
S. G. Gorshkov, *The Sea Power of the State*, Pergamon Press, 1979.
Geoffrey Till (Ed.), *The Sea in Soviet Strategy*, Macmillan, 1989.
——*Maritime Strategy in the Nuclear Age*, Macmillan, 1984.
——*Britain and the Security of NATO's Northern Flank*, Macmillan, 1988.

History

Merrill L. Bartlett (Ed.), *Assault from the Sea—Essays on the History of Amphibious Warfare*, Annapolis Naval Institute Press, 1983.
K. J. Clifford, *Amphibious Warfare Development in Britain and America from 1920–1940*, Edgewood, 1983.
Bernard Fergusson, *The Watery Maze—The Story of Combined Operations*, Collins, 1961.
Sir Michael Howard, *The Causes of Wars*, in particular the chapter *The British Way in Warfare Revisited*, Unwin Hyman, 1983.
Jeter A. Isely and Philip A. Crowl, *The US Marines and Amphibious War*, Princeton University Press, 1951.
Paul M. Kennedy, *The Rise and Fall of British Naval Mastery*, Macmillan, 1974.
J. D. Ladd, *Assault from the Sea 1939–45*, David and Charles, 1976.
J. Lattice, *Damn the Dardanelles: The Story of Gallipoli*, Osprey, 1980.
L. E. H. Maund, *Assault from the Sea*, Methuen, 1949.
Alan Moorehead, *Gallipoli*, Hamish Hamilton, 1956.
J. L. Moulton, *Haste to the Battle*, Cassel, 1963. *The Campaign in Norway 1940*, Cassel, 1966.
Norman Polmar and Peter Mersky, *Amphibious Warfare—an Illustrated History*, Blandford Press, 1988.
Sir Herbert Richmond, *Amphibious Warfare in British History*, Paternoster Press, 1941.
Ronald H. Spector, *Eagle Against the Sun*, Viking, 1984.
Julian Thompson, *No Picnic*, Leo Cooper, 1985.
Nick Vaux, *March to the South Atlantic*, Buchan and Enright, 1986.

Command

William S. Lind, *Maneuver Warfare Handbook*, Westview Press, 1985.
Martin van Creveld, *Command in War*, Harvard, 1985.

Index

A-6E *Intruder* aircraft (US) 179
Aden 41
Afghanistan 46
Air Cushion Vehicle (ACV) 55–6, 128–30, 181, 195
  Pomornik class (Soviet) 129
Air Defence 160, 162
Air/Naval Gunfire Liaison Company (ANGLICO) 159
HMS *Albion* 41, 42
Amphibian tractors 3, 5, 7
Amphibious Assault Vehicle (AAV) 124–6, 142, 191, 192
Amphibious Objective Area (AOA) 106, 110, 123, 131, 137, 164, 165, 172, 181, 198, 200
  defence of 184–8
  establishment of 177
Amphibious operations 3, 9–10
  American conception of 9–12, 39–41, 43–4, 45–6, 82–3, 118, 135–6, 190–3
  British conception of 9–10, 39–43, 45–6, 135, 190
    command of 94–103
    in NATO's Maritime Strategy (*see also* NATO) 62–9, 75–8, 93
    planning of 104–12, 170–6, 189, 195
    principles of 91–103
  Soviet conception of 12, 44–5, 46–7, 85, 135, 181, 193–5
    peacetime role of 70–80
    planning of 112–15
Amphibious ships, design of 137–43
Amphibious Transport Ship (ATS) (Dutch) 145
Angola 85
Anti-Submarine Warfare (ASW) 131, 160, 181
Argentina, in Falklands War 69, 88
HMS *Ark Royal* 180
Ascension Island 170
Atlantic Conveyor 131
Auchinleck, General Claude 96
Austin Class LPD (US) 143, 145
HMS *Avenger* 160
Aviation Support Ship (ASS) 45, 112, 136, 140, 141, 145

Bacon, Francis 13
Battle of Narvik (1940) 71, 95, 104
  command at 96

Battle of the Philippine Sea (1944) 3
Beach Armoured Recovery Vehicle (BARV) 123, 175
Beach Support Area (BSA) 174, 176
Bishop, Maurice 116
Bond, Brian 21
Borneo 41
Boyd's Observation–Orientation–Decision–Action Cycle 199
Bradley, General Omar 35, 77
Brigade Maintenance Area (BMA) 174, 175, 176
Brookings Institute 43
Brunei, Limbang operation in (1962) 41
HMS *Bulwark* 41, 42, 112

C-13 Hercules 65
CH-53E *Super Stallion* helicopter (US) 132, 168, 175, 193
CVS (Light Aircraft Carrier) 82, 141, 149, 165, 178
Cable, Sir James 79, 80, 86
Cam Ranh Bay 86
Carver, Field Marshal Lord 41
Chinook helicopter 131
Churchill, Winston 14, 26, 46, 91
Clapp, Commodore 99
Combined Operations Headquarters (COHQ) 26
Command, Control and Communications (C3) 143, 168, 197–8
  Assault Operations Room (AOR) 196
  directive control in 204
Command Ship (US) 143
Connelly, Admiral 29–30
Conventional Stability Talks 86
Copenhagen (1807) 14
Corbett, Sir Julian 14, 57, 59, 177
Cork and Orrery, Lord 96
Creveld, Martin van 95, 97–8, 170
Crowl, Philip A. 159
Cuba 116

Deputy Chiefs of Staff (DCOS), Sub-Committee of 15
  The Manual of Combined Operations of 19, 23
desant 12, 31–2, 55, 67, 68, 75, 78, 132, 135, 164, 190, 194, 195

Index

Diego Garcia 49
Dieppe landing (1942) 25, 26, 28, 205
Donnelly, Christopher 169–70

East Germany, amphibious forces of 56
Eden, Anthony 38
Egypt 38–9
EH-101 *Merlin* helicopter 193
Electronic warfare (EW) 197
Ellis, Major Earl H. 22
Erie, Commodore 118
Exocet missile 184

F-14 *Tomcat* aircraft (US) 179
F/A-18 *Hornet* aircraft (US) 179
Falklands War 42, 45, 46, 62, 69, 88, 100, 123, 131, 161, 164–5, 176
   command at 98–9
   landing at San Carlos during 10, 112, 125, 141, 184, 195–6, 197, 199–200
   Mount Harriet, attack on during 162
HMS *Fearless* 42, 45, 50, 69, 143, 197
Fire Support Co-ordination Cell (FSCC) 159
Fergusson, Bernard 23, 28, 165, 205
First World War 14, 15, 22
Fisher, Admiral 14
Forbes, Admiral 180
France
   amphibious forces of 53
   Foreign Legion of 72
   role in Suez landings of (*see also* Suez) 37–8
Friedman, Norman 59

Gallipoli 13, 14–17, 19, 20, 22, 23, 91, 95, 206
Gazelle helicopter 167
Goalkeeper 186
Gorbachev, Mikhail 86
Gorshkov, Admiral Sergei 24, 31, 44–5, 46, 57, 85
Gray, Dr Colin 77
Gray, General A. M. 82–3, 153
Greece, Hellenic Marine Regiment of 53
Grenada
   People's Revolutionary Army of 117
   US invasion of 88, 116–18
Guadalcanal 3, 10, 23, 28
Guam 3, 7, 28

Hankey, Sir Maurice 46
Harpoon missile 162
Harrier aircraft 141, 165, 178
Hastings, Max 104, 153
Havoc helicopter (Soviet) 166
Helicopters 108, 112, 119, 130–3, 141, 143, 153, 166–7, 178
Herald of Free Enterprise 150
HMS *Hermes* 42, 112, 145

Heseltine, Michael 46
Higgins, Andrew 26, 120
Hind helicopter (Soviet) 166, 167
Hiroshima 34
Hokum helicopter (Soviet) 166
Hooper, Colonel Alan 196
Hormone helicopter (Soviet) 86
Howard, Sir Michael 20, 24–5, 46
Howlett, General 75

Iceland 60
Inchon, landing at 35–7, 46
Infantry landing craft 5
Intelligence 104–5, 120, 130, 189, 191, 195, 196, 199
Inter-Service Training and Development Centre (ISTDC) 23, 26, 34
HMS *Intrepid* 42, 45, 69
Iowa Class battleship (US) 162
Iran 46
Ironside, Lord 96
Isely, Jeter A. 159
Ismay, Lord 91, 96
Israel 38
Italy, landings in (1943) 26, 32, 33, 34
   San Marco Battalion Operational Group of 53
Iwo Jima 28, 112, 199

Japan 3, 22, 180
Javelin missile (UK) 184
Jenkins, Simon 104

Kennedy, Paul 180
Khrushchev, Nikita 35
Kurile Islands 77
Kuwait 41

Landing craft 120–4
Landing Craft Air Cushion (LCAC) 12, 129, 141, 142, 191, 192, 193
Landing Craft Utility (LCU) 118, 123, 130, 141, 142
Landing Craft Vehicle and Personnel (LCVP) 123, 125, 130, 142, 146
Landing Platform Dock (LPD) 41, 42, 50, 53, 85, 112, 116, 123, 136, 140, 142, 173, 175, 190, 197
   design of 143–5
Landing Platform Helicopter (LPH) 40, 41, 42, 116, 141, 149, 190
   Iwo Jima class (US) 143
Landing Ship Dock (LSD) 116
Landing Ship Logistic (LSL) 41, 50, 123, 146, 170
Landing Ship Tank (LST) 3, 4, 26, 29, 116, 120, 125

Index

Alligator class (Soviet)   44, 55, 85, 146
Ivan Rogov class (Soviet)   55, 86, 128, 145
Newport class (US)   146
Polnocny class (Soviet)   44, 56, 146
Ropucha class (Soviet)   55, 146
Layered defence   154
Lehman, John   69
Lejeune, Major General John A.   22
Liddell Hart, Sir Basil   15, 20, 65
'Limited liability' strategy   15
Lind, William S.   199, 204
Luttwak, Edward   97, 100
Lynx helicopter   167, 200

MacArthur, General Douglas   3, 10, 28, 30, 31, 36
McManners, Captain Hugh   160, 161
Mackesy, Major General   96
Madagascar   26, 91
Madden Committee (1924)   15
Marianas Islands   3
Maritime Strategy   57–69, 75–8
  future of (NATO)   87–8
  future of (Soviet)   86–7
Marshall Islands   3, 28
Massey, General   180
Mi-6 *Hook* helicopter (Soviet)   132
Mi-8 *Hip* helicopter (Soviet)   132, 166, 167
Mi-26 *Halo* helicopter (Soviet)   133–4
Midway   24
MILAN Anti-tank Guided Weapon   200
Mines   187
  clearing of   187–8
Moulton, Major General J. L.   41, 91
Mountbatten, Lord Louis   26, 46
Multiple Launch Rocket System (MLRS)   162
Mustin, Admiral   61
MV-22 *Osprey* tilt-rotor aircraft   12, 132, 191–2, 193

Nasser, Gamal Abdel   37–8
Naval Gunfire Forward Officer (NGFO)   161
Naval Gunfire Liaison Officer (NGLO)   161
Netherlands, Royal Netherlands Marine Corps (RNLMC) of   41, 175–6
  Amphibious Combat Group of   50
New Guinea   3, 31
USS *New Jersey*   162
Nicaragua   46
Nimitz, Admiral Chester   22
Normandy, landings at   26, 28, 30–1, 34, 35, 37, 91, 171, 205
North Atlantic Treaty Organisation (NATO)   41, 42, 50, 53, 93, 134, 172
  Amphibious Task Force of   177–9, 181, 184
  Baltic Approaches (BATALP) in   75
  Central Front of   44, 45, 47, 58, 59, 60, 65, 75, 77, 86, 88, 153
  CINCNORTH of   100

Commander Amphibious Task Force (CATF) of   94, 97, 98, 103, 104, 106–7, 108, 110, 112, 123, 143, 159, 165, 170, 171, 175, 181, 189, 195, 196
  role of   197–8
Commander Combined Amphibious Task Force (CCATF) of   100
Commander Landing Force (CLF) of   94, 97, 98, 103, 104, 107, 108, 123, 143, 153, 154, 159, 165, 170, 175, 181, 195, 196, 198
  exercises   100
  Forward Maritime Strategy of   58–69, 75–8, 177, 206
  Greenland/Iceland/UK (GIUK) Gap in   59
  Northern European Command of   60, 69, 86, 100
  Northern Flank of   135
  Sea Lines of Communication (SLOCs) in   58, 59, 60, 63, 75, 177
  Southern Flank of   41–2
  Striking Fleet of   61, 69, 99, 100, 143
  Supreme Allied Commander Atlantic (SACLANT) of   42, 97, 99
  Supreme Allied Commander Europe (SACEUR) of   97
North Korea   35–7
Norway   86, 121, 161, 175
  Army of   75
  invasion of (1940)   15, 19, 20, 22, 25–6, 68, 71–3, 86, 91
  air operations during   180
  role in NATO's Maritime Strategy   60–1, 63–9, 75–7, 83, 184
  Soviet operations in (1944)   73–4
Nott, John   42, 68–9
Novorossiisk   31
Nuclear deterrence   59, 77, 88

HMS *Ocean*   39
Okinawa   28, 29, 35, 47
Operation *Torch*   26
Over-the-horizon assault   12, 119, 126, 190, 192–3

Patton, General George   28
Pearl Harbor   3, 97
Poland, Sea Landing Brigade of   56
Porter, Joseph   65
Port Moresby   24
Port Stanley   10
Portugal, Corpo Fuzileros of   53
Pulan   28

Ramped Craft Lighter (RCL)   123
Ramped Support Pontoons (RSP)   123
Rapier missile (UK)   184, 200
Remotely Piloted Vehicle (RPV)   164

Index

RH-53D *Sea Stallion* helicopter (US) 188
Ries, Dr Tomas 75
Rigid Raiding Craft (RRC) 123
Roll-on-roll-off vessel 56, 142, 150

Saipan, landing at (1944) 3–8, 9, 28, 29, 123
Schlesinger, James 44
Sea Cobra helicopter 118
Sea King helicopter 131, 141, 175, 193, 200
Sea Wolf missile 186
Second World War 3, 10, 13, 23, 24, 34, 35, 44, 78, 93, 95, 123, 141, 169, 189, 192, 206
   Central Pacific campaign of 3, 6, 10, 28–31, 159, 171
   Soviet amphibious operations in 24, 31–3
Ships Taken Up From Trade (STUFT) 49, 50, 108, 123, 149–51, 170, 176, 186, 188
Sir Galahad 50
Sir Lancelot 50
Slava class destroyer (Soviet) 162
Smith, Lieutenant General Holland M. 9, 123
Solomon Islands 3, 28
South Korea 35–7
Sovremenny class destroyer (Soviet) 162
Spain, Infanteria Marina of 53
Stalbo, Admiral 44
Staveley, Admiral 63–4
Stinger missile (US) 184
Stockholm Agreement 86
Suez Canal 40, 41
   landings at (*Operation Musketeer*) 37–9
Supporting Arms Co-ordination Cell (SACC) 159, 160, 169
Sweden 75

Tactical Air Control Cell (TACC) 164–6
Tarawa 3, 28, 29
Tarawa class LHA (US) 143
RFA *Tarbatness* 42
HMS *Theseus* 39
USS *Thetis Bay* 40
Thompson, Major General J. H. A. 10, 98–9, 103, 104, 141, 189, 197
Till, Geoffrey 44–5, 59, 69, 85, 135
Tinian 3, 7, 28
Tomahawk missile 162
Trainor, General 83
Trebizond 24
Tripwire Strategy 35
Turkey, naval infantry of 53
Type 22 Frigate (UK) 162, 164
Type 23 Frigate (UK) 164

SS *Uganda* 176
United Kingdom 75
   Admiralty of 14, 15
   Air Staff of 15
   Amphibious Task Group of 10, 170
   Army of 14, 50, 59, 164
      Royal Artillery of 161
      Royal Corps of Transport of 123
   defence policy of 46, 82
   Defence Review (1974) 13, 42
   Landing Force Task Group of 10
   Royal Marines of 14, 15, 32–3, 35, 41–2, 51, 81, 136
      Arctic and Warfare cadre of 182
      Assault Squadron of 123–4, 176
      command of 95, 98, 100, 102
      Commando Logistic Regiment of 175
      at Suez 39
   Royal Air Force of 23, 39, 65, 165, 180
   Royal Navy of 13–14, 50, 59, 161, 162
   Special Boat Service (SBS) of 182
United Kingdom/Netherlands (UK/NL)
      Amphibious Force 41–2, 45, 50, 100, 105, 110, 121, 123, 128, 146, 153, 159, 169, 193, 194, 196
   148 (Meiktila) Battery of 161
   Naval Gunfire Support Forward Observers (NGFO) of 182
   Advanced Logistic Group of 174
   artillery of 168
   command of 97, 98, 99, 103, 143
   helicopter forces of 167
   mobility of 199–204
   role in NATO's Maritime Strategy 62–3, 64–5, 67–8, 75, 135, 190
   STUFT in 149, 151
United Nations 39
USA 39, 58, 116, 180
   Army of 3, 36–7
      82nd Airborne Division of 116–17
      Rangers of 116–18
      Special Forces of 182
   Commission on Integrated Long-Term Strategy 82
   Marine Corps (USMC) of 3, 4–7, 10, 28, 30, 34, 36, 43–4, 124, 132, 159
      22nd Marine Amphibious Unit 116–18
      air support for 141
      amphibious doctrine of 22–3, 93, 193
         Maneuver Warfare in 199, 204, 205
      Amphibious Readiness Group (ARG) of 47, 81
      command of 95, 97, 99, 102
      Expeditionary Force of 23
      First Division of 35–6
      Fleet Marine Force of 23
         Atlantic (FMFANT) 36, 47
         Pacific (FMF Pacific) 47
      Force Reconnaissance Teams of 182
      Marine Air–Ground Task Force of 47, 76, 102, 105, 164–6, 198
      Marine Expeditionary Brigade (MEB) of 47, 49, 50, 64, 66–7, 76, 83, 100, 135, 159, 165, 190
      Marine Expeditionary Force (MEF) of 47–9, 76–7, 99, 135, 153, 159, 165

Marine Expeditionary Unit (MEU) of 47, 83, 99
Maritime Pre-positioning Ship (MPS) of 76, 81, 150, 190
SS *Mayaguez,* rescue of by (1975) 41
Primary Control Officer of 110
structure of 47–50
STUFT in 150
training of 153
Navy of 59, 123, 137, 162, 181
  Carrier Battle Groups (CVBG) of 60, 61, 177, 179
  Fast Carrier Force of 3
  Pacific Fleet of 3
  War College of 22
  SEAL (Sea Air Land Forces) of 118, 182
Reagan administration of 45, 59
USSR 58, 61, 116, 169
  Army of 167
  Naval Infantry of 35, 44, 46, 53–6, 66, 73–4, 85–6, 114, 132, 167, 194
    airborne forces of 133–4
    artillery of 168
    STUFT in 150
    training of 153
  Navy of 31, 44, 46, 85, 167
    Airforce (SNAF) of 177

    Mediterranean Squadron of 85
    Northern Fleet of 63, 128
  Special Forces of 184

Vandergift, General 10
Vaux, Major General Nick 162, 195–6
Vertical envelopment 119, 130
Vietnam 41, 43, 44, 79, 85

Walcheren 14
  landing at (1944) 26, 32, 33, 91, 126–7, 205
Warsaw Pact 167
Wasp assault ship 136, 140, 141
Waterproofing 121–3, 137
Watkins, Admiral 60, 82
Weinberger, Caspar 82
Whitehead, Lieutenant Colonel Andrew 169
Wilmot, Chester 33–4
Wing-in-ground-effect aircraft 119, 129–30
Wonsan (Korea), landing at (1952) 187

Yak 36 *Forger* aircraft (Soviet) 86
HMS *Yarmouth* 162